D0387250

CALGARY PUBLIC LIBRARY

DEC      2010

*What I Believe*

# What I Believe

Hans Küng

Translated by John Bowden

continuum

**Continuum International Publishing Group**

The Tower Building, 11 York Road, London SE1 7NX
80 Maiden Lane, Suite 704, New York NY 10038

www.continuumbooks.com

Translated by John Bowden from the German *Was ich glaube*,
published by Piper Verlag GmbH Munich 2009

Copyright © Piper Verlag 2009

English translation copyright © John Bowden 2010

All rights reserved. No part of this publication may be reproduced or transmitted in
any form or by any means, electronic or mechanical, including photocopying,
recording or any information storage or retrieval system, without prior permission
from the publishers.

First published in English 2010

*British Library Cataloguing-in-Publication Data*
A catalogue record is available for this book from the British Library.

ISBN (hb) 9781441103161

Typeset by Kenneth Burnley, Wirral, Cheshire
Printed and bound by MPG Books Group

# Contents

# A View of the World as a Whole

'Be quite honest: just what do you personally believe?' I have been asked this question, or others like it, countless times in my long life as a theologian. I shall attempt to answer the question, not just formally and simplistically, but personally and comprehensively.

I am writing for people who are searching, who cannot cope with the faith of either Roman Catholic or Protestant traditionalists but are not content with their unbelief or doubts about faith. I am writing for those who don't want a cheap 'wellness spirituality' or short-term help in life. And I am also writing for all those who live out their faith but would like to be able to give an account of it, who not only simply 'believe' but also want to 'know', and therefore expect a view of faith which is grounded in philosophy, theology, exegesis and history and has practical consequences.

In the course of my long life, my view of faith has been clarified and extended. I have never said, written or preached anything other than what I believe. I was able to study Bible and tradition, philosophy and theology, over many years, and that has filled my life. The results are worked out in my books. One of them is even devoted to the 'Apostles' Creed', which despite its name was not completed until the fifth century. Anyone who wants to know more about its twelve very different and often disputed articles of faith (such as the virgin birth, the descent into hell and the ascension into heaven) in the light of the Bible and the present day should read that book, *Credo*, which I still stand by today. In the present book I deny nothing that I have written either there or in my *Christianity: Its Essence and History* (for example about christological dogma).

But the 'official religion' of those who associate themselves with their religious community is one thing and the quiet individual religion that they bear 'in their heart' and that only partly coincides with the 'official religion' is another. To know something of this undistorted, personal philosophy of life is psychologically a 'royal road' towards understanding the person concerned in his or her depths.

I am not one of those people who in questions of faith wear their heart on their sleeve and on every occasion communicate their convictions about faith to others, even press them on others. Tact and sensitivity are called for and required particularly in conversations about religion. In any case, as a theologian I may not replace arguments with emotion or over-hasty confessions. Therefore I often answer the question about my 'spirituality', which is so popular a term today, by saying that one can read enough about it in my books. On the other hand I didn't want to refuse the frequent request for a brief, comprehensive, generally understandable spirituality. Spirituality is far more comprehensive than faith in the religious sense, for it also embraces a whole range of spiritual activities from Orthodox mysticism and church dogmatics to esoteric and New Age currents. Thus it also diverges towards randomness.

For that reason I want to review critically the numerous spiritual elements which have matured over my life and bring them into a synthesis. 'What do I believe?' I want every word to be understood in the broadest sense.

I do not understand the 'I' subjectively. I have never felt myself to be a proud loner, even one of the elect. I have always been concerned to think in solidarity and to work with many others in my community of faith, in Christianity, in the world religions, indeed also in the secular world. I would be happy if large stretches of this book could express what is the absolute conviction of others.

So I do not interpret 'believe' in a narrow ecclesiastical sense or as an intellectualist believing. Today even conservative Catholics do not simply accept 'what the church prescribes for me to believe', to use a traditionalist formula. To believe means more than just holding certain propositions of faith to be true. Believing is what moves a person's reason, heart and hand, and it embraces thinking, willing, feeling and acting. However, since my time as a student in Rome I have suspected blind faith as much as blind love; blind faith has led many individuals and whole peoples down the road to ruin. My concern has been and is to achieve an understanding faith that, while it may have no conclusive proofs, is based on good reasons. To this degree my faith is neither rationalist nor irrational, though it is reasonable.

So 'what' I believe embraces considerably more than a creed in the traditional senses. 'What' I believe means the fundamental convictions and attitudes which have been and are important to me in my life, and which I hope can also help others to find their way in life: help towards orientation in life. They are not just psychological-pedagogical advice for 'feeling good' and 'living one's own life'. Nor, though, are they preaching from above, edifying talk: I am neither a saint nor a zealot. Rather, they are serious informative reflections on a meaningful course of life based on personal experience.

They are, if you like, meditations: the Latin *meditare* literally means 'measure out', 'measure out mentally', hence 'reflect', 'consider'. However, these are not meditations from the perspective of a monk who speaks from God's presence, but the meditations of a man of the world who seeks God. Here one can approach other dimensions of reality not only with the head but also with the heart. My spirituality is nourished by everyday experiences of the kind that many people have or can have. But it is clarified by scholarly insights collected over a long life as a theologian. It has also been affected by experiences of the world that have been my destiny, that I cannot detach from a history of struggle and suffering, a history that I have described in the two volumes of my memoirs.

Faith as a spiritual foundation for life is no longer the norm today, far less Christian faith. But more than ever, when we are being over-whelmed by a flood of information, in our often confusing times, we need not only information but also orientation: clear co-ordinates and goals. For this of course everyone needs his or her own inner compass to provide the direction for concrete decisions in the harsh reality of everyday life. I hope that this book will provide such fundamental orientation.

I have attempted to hold together and structure the abundance of questions and themes which arise by the colourful, comprehensive concept of life, as this is realized in the development of life generally, in the course of an individual life, in the story of my own life. Of course I cannot address all aspects and themes of Christian life. Many of them are discussed in the works listed at the end of the book.

I don't want readers just to take a harmless theological stroll in flat country with excursions into different provinces of life. Rather – if I may be allowed the metaphor, the image – I want them to join me in making a long, patient ascent of a mountain, with easier and more dangerous parts, unfortunately without rests at mountain huts, but always with the goal which beckons from the summit clearly before us: a view of the world as a whole. So in the first chapter I begin very simply, in an elementary and personal way; I do not fly in from heaven on a theological helicopter but begin down in the valley of everyday life with preparation: what is first of all necessary for the individual, any individual, is trust in life, fundamental trust.

*Hans Küng*
*Tübingen, November 2009*

# Chapter 1

# Trust in Life

*Fundamental trust is the cornerstone of a healthy personality: an attitude to oneself and the world going back to experiences of the first year of life.*

The German-American psychologist Erik H. Erikson,
a leading representative of the psychology of adolescence
(*Identity and the Life-Cycle*, 1959)

What is the most important spiritual basis for human life? It is a fundamental trust, a trust in life. Trust in life has its own history in every human individual. It begins as soon as a child looks on the light of the world.

## The cornerstone of a healthy personality

Of course trust in life is not simply 'there'; it needs to be learned. Erik Erikson and other developmental psychologists have investigated it empirically: the child learns to trust literally at its mother's breast. Acquiring fundamental trust is vitally important for the healthy physical and psychological development of the small child. If a child is already damaged at the time of weaning – by psychological illnesses, by the withdrawal of the person to whom it relates or by emotional deficiencies in uninterested or overtaxed carers (the 'hospitalism' already investigated at an early stage by René Spitz) – a fundamental trust cannot come into being. For Erik Erikson, the first stage in the development of the infant (roughly the first year) is almost identical with the stage of basic trust.

Further researches have shown that the mother (or her surrogate) forms the basis of trust for all the infant's discovery of the world. One doesn't have to have five younger sisters and a younger brother as I did to observe precisely how a child, once it is capable of crawling its way towards discovery of the world and contact with other people, time and

1

again seeks eye-contact with its mother and begins to cry as soon as it loses it. And in the second year, while the child is now capable of moving out of sight of its mother, it constantly returns to its mother and shows anxiety when they are separated.

In opening itself to its mother in this way, the child – slowly detaching itself from its mother – becomes open to other people, to things, to the world. New researches reinforce how important the early time is for a strong self. The more uncertain a child is in its bond with its mother, the more it is blocked in building up relations with other people, since it is totally occupied in building up at least a reliable bond with its mother. And conversely, from trust in the mother (or her surrogate) there forms in a complex process – I shall not enter here into the place of the father and much else – that initially naïve and unquestioning fundamental trust of the child which makes a secure position in life possible for it, but which is constantly put to the test. What has been my experience?

## Trust in life put to the test

I am one of the countless people who, on the basis of a relationship to mother, father and others in my surroundings that, although intact, has by no means been without problems, have gained a strong trust in life. But my trust has also been time and again put to the test by life itself. From the beginning we human beings learn not only through upbringing but through our own experience and often also through personal suffering. The old proverb 'The burnt child fears the fire' is not a chance observation.

I still recall what is perhaps my earliest personal experience: as a 3- or 4-year-old I put my left index finger in a bread-cutting machine to get out a little bit of bread, while at the same time turning the handle with my right hand. The top of my finger and the nail dropped into the machine. Acting swiftly, an excellent doctor was able to put the top back on my finger with the help of skin from my father's leg, so that today you can hardly notice any difference.

I shall always remember the first dead person I saw: I was 6 years old at the time. My grandmother was killed in a tragic car accident, with my grandfather at the wheel. There she lay, pale, at rest and beautiful; only a small red spot of blood on her forehead bore witness to her fate. They told me that she was now 'in heaven'. But these and many other experiences did not leave me with any psychological trauma, nor could they shake my trust in life.

So on the basis of many personal experiences – despite my great respect for psychotherapy – I have my reservations when faced with those psychoanalysts who want to discover a trauma from early childhood in all too many later problems. Of course I know that already at an early stage and from then onwards more and more severe crises of trust can come: through failure in school, education and personal relations, through a hopeless future, unemployment, betrayed friendship and the first great disappointment in love, and finally through failure in a job, loss of health, the often intolerable burden of existence.

So sooner or later, by encountering crises the unquestioning, unconditional, arbitrary trust of the child, who is at first fully dependent on its mother, must become a matured, responsible fundamental trust: the well-considered, critical trust of the adult who has become independent in the unfathomable, almost incomprehensible reality of the world and human beings. Authentic self-confidence is the presupposition for a strong and compassionate personality. And sooner or later one arrives at a deliberate fundamental decision about one's attitude to life, to one's fellow human beings, to the world, to reality. Without a mature fundamental trust, a trust in life, one can hardly survive the crises of life.

## An apparently sure philosophical basis

Two decades before I first read a remark by Erik Erikson – as a theological student in a papal college in Rome run by the Jesuits – I grappled with the question of a secure foundation and a secure basis of knowledge: six semesters of philosophy with a history of philosophy, including excellent introductions to the thought of Kant and Hegel. I concluded my study of philosophy with a licentiate thesis on Jean-Paul Sartre's existentialism as humanism, which was in fashion in the 1950s.

In Rome I learned something that I hold firmly to even now: Latin clarity, terminological precision, intrinsically coherent argument and strict discipline in work. So after three years I was firmly convinced that I had acquired a totally certain scholarly basis for my career which I could explain rationally at any time.

I still remember clearly, after my licentiate work in philosophy, walking with a Swiss friend from the German College to the Pincio, Rome's biggest park. We thought it great that we had worked out for ourselves a clear and utterly rational philosophical foundation for theology: a natural basis of evident principles of being and conclusions derived with methodological strictness. On this natural basis of reason and philosophy we now needed only to build up the supernatural superstructure of faith and theology with the same thoroughness. Then we would be equipped for life: for dealing with ourselves and others, for our work, our understanding of the world, our use of time. So we thought. But this two-storey scheme of reason and faith proved deceptive. I began to have more and more doubts. Was this neo-scholastic *philosophia perennis* a viable and certain basis?

## What I doubt

I never really got rid of an ultimate doubt, which at first I didn't take very seriously. Now doubts are part of faith. There are silly or superficial doubts that can easily be removed with information. But there are intelligent doubts that go deeper and become established in us. So even in my days in Rome it became clear to me that I couldn't be as gentle and 'balanced' as our model fellow-student and prefect who later was to become a very narrow-minded bishop of a great German diocese.

At an intellectual level all this seemed crystal clear to me, but at the existential level there remained a suppressed uncertainty. It kept forcing itself on me even during my first semester of theology and made me doubt that everything was ultimately illuminating, calculable and provable. Is it really so clear, so obvious, that my life has a meaning? Why am I as I am? I have weaknesses and faults that I cannot simply wish away. Why must I accept myself as I now am, with my positive and negative sides? It seemed difficult to accept myself on the basis of rational arguments.

And what do I really want? What is the meaning of my freedom? Why isn't it simply orientated on the good? What drives me? Why is guilt possible? And doesn't the possibility of failing, going astray, incurring guilt rebound on the one who willed human beings to be this way, so that I am relieved of this burden? It seemed impossible to affirm my highly ambivalent freedom on the basis of a rational insight.

In the face of such questions and tribulations, and of methodical searching of my conscience, the allegedly evident principles of being put forward in Greek Thomistic metaphysics were of little use to me, namely that being is being and not not-being. But isn't being really not not-being? Every entity has as such identity, truth and goodness. But isn't the entity often contradictory, untrue, not good? What about the evil in the world?

In the age of nihilism and existentialism one could also dispute the classic principle of being – with reference to the ambiguity, transitoriness, fallenness, lostness, even nothingness of human existence. Didn't Jean-Paul Sartre, whose existentialism understands itself as humanism, describe human beings as '*trou d'être*', a 'hole in being', which has to design itself freely? And didn't Nietzsche urgently formulate the 'suspicion' that engenders mistrust of all that is and should be good and true, and especially of any metaphysics?

## Crises in life

I have always experienced myself as a human being who is in many respects contradictory and divided, with strengths and weaknesses, a long way from the perfection I desire. I see myself in no way as an ideal person, but as a human being with his heights and depths, day sides and night sides, with all that C. G. Jung calls the 'shadow' of the person, what human beings are all too eager to foist off, repress, suppress instead of working through. And don't many people in their hearts want to be someone else? Just a little more intelligent, rich, beautiful? Often we accept the world more easily than ourselves, as we are or have been made by others: 'But the simple is always the most difficult,' I read in Jung. 'In reality simplicity is the highest art, and so accepting oneself is the embodiment of the moral problem and the core of a whole world-view.'

I don't advocate a pessimism about life which *a priori* supposes that every action will be a failure; there are also successes in life, progresses, gifts, happiness. But even successful people are hardly spared crises that put everything in question. Such crises can affect people even in their youth, or even more in mid-life, in a fatal illness which is possible at any time, or in a professional fiasco, or in a depression in retirement and old age. If someone has achieved all that he could and at any rate cannot achieve more, what then . . . ?

What I felt in my student years I saw aptly described a decade later by a Catholic theologian in Tübingen who was teaching there a good decade before and likewise outside a theological faculty. It was Romano Guardini who, in 'The Acceptance of Oneself', published in 1960, the year I was called to Tübingen, wrote:

> The task can become very difficult. There is the rebellion against having to be oneself: why should I? Do I want it? . . . There is the feeling that it is no longer worth being oneself: What do I get out of it? I'm bored with myself. I'm against myself. I no longer expect anything of myself . . . There is the feeling

that one has been deceived. One is imprisoned in oneself: I'm only so much and want to be more . . . I have only this gift and want greater, more shining gifts. I always have to do the same thing. I keep coming up against the boundaries I've mentioned. I always make the same mistake, experience the same failure . . . All this can lead to an endless monotony, a fearful surfeit.

But how can I arrive at a positive fundamental attitude to this questionable ambivalent reality of the world and myself without lapsing into irrationality? That is now my big question.

## Putting off a decision about life

There are people who carry around with themselves for years an existential doubt about their human existence that they are unable or unwilling to get rid of. I am one of those people. In this connection I remember Martin Walser, with Günter Grass my contemporary and one of the most eloquent writers of the present time. I had just one short and friendly conversation with him, in the interval of a Bayreuth performance. I asked him whether it wasn't time to tackle the question of religion in a novel. His answer was that in fact he carried this question around with him unresolved, but that the time had not yet come. Now we are both 80. And Martin Walser writes in his most recent novel of the 74-year-old Goethe who in the vigorous passion of old age burned with love for a young woman and failed to the point of ridicule. Does this reflect Walser himself? Has he finally given Goethe's question 'What do you think about religion?' the answer, 'I've put it on ice'?

My fundamental question at the time was not about religion but about my attitude to life generally. How can I arrive at a constructive attitude to life which embraces the whole of human experience, behaviour, action, if I am oppressed by just how questionable the reality of the world and myself, their value and dignity, actually is? How can I gain a firm standpoint and make my life a success?

Evidently this fundamental question is about my own standpoint, which is free and therefore responsibly chosen. I am neither totally pre-programmed by my heredity or my unconscious nor totally conditioned by my environment. I am, within limits, free. Despite all the exaggerated arguments of neurophysiologists, I am neither an animal nor a robot. Within the limits of what is innate and what is determined by my environment, I am free in terms of self-determination and responsibility for myself. Granted, I cannot demonstrate this freedom of choice and decision theoretically. But at any time I want to I can experience it practically: at a particular moment I can keep silent – no, I want to speak, or would it be better to keep silent? So I could also do otherwise. Now I'm doing something different. This is an experience not only of doing but also of not doing, unfortunately not just of success but sometimes also of failure.

Even in the small everyday questions of life I can make decisions in one way or another, but I can also do that in fundamental questions, indeed in the question of my basic attitude to life. I can also evade that question, postpone it, suppress it, can live by the day, can avoid certain consequences. Psychologically there are many possibilities, but from a philosophical point of view there is the fundamental alternative of a positive or a negative option. And I have experienced that it helps to consider carefully these two possible attitudes to life that dramatically force themselves on us in any life crisis.

A deep-seated mistrust of life is possible. I can say a more or less conscious *No* to any meaning in my life, to reality generally. There is the nihilistic alternative, whether reflected on philosophically as assent to the absence of any meaning, or experienced pragmatically in the sense of 'it makes no difference' (to avoid more trivial words). Time and again those choosing it find sufficient that is negative to conclude that life is absurd, broken, empty, worthless and meaningless. Such deeply mistrustful people cannot be satisfied by anything. They also spread around themselves an atmosphere of dissatisfaction, complaint and cynicism.

But a fundamental trust in life is also possible. Despite all the meaninglessness I can say a deliberate *Yes* to the meaning of my life, I can say *Yes* to reality generally despite all the questionability, adversity, nothingness. Of course this is a risk in view of the obvious possibility of disappointment, in the face of failure that happens time and again. Of course I want my life to succeed; despite all my weaknesses and mistakes I want to have sorted myself out, to be content about myself. I don't want a failed but a successful life. What will help me here?

## Not a very helpful theology

So even as a student I wanted a clear answer to the question: Why should I say a fundamental *Yes* to my life? My teachers in Rome helped me to pose the problem, but I had to find the solution for myself. I remember very clearly how I perplexed my first spiritual director with this question. He referred me to – God. But questions about my own standpoint, about the meaning of my life, my freedom and reality in general seemed to me to be more fundamental, more urgent than the question of God, which logically should be considered only in second place.

He parried with the knock-down argument that such insistence was ultimately rebellion against God. What was I to say? I said farewell, quiet and unsatisfied. How should I believe in God when I could not even accept myself? I was told that I had to 'believe'. But on the other hand, one learned at the Pontifical Gregorian University, 'faith' applies only to the 'upper' levels of the distinctive truths of the Christian revelation (Trinity, Incarnation . . .). Belief is not to be looked for at the 'lower' natural level of reason. There *ratio*, knowledge, alone must prevail: evident insights and rational arguments.

In my last years in Rome I had another experience. Protestant theology, too, which I came to know with admiration through Karl Barth's monumental dogmatics, has no answers here. In this fundamental question should I rely *a priori* on God's word? Simply read the Bible? But what about the billions of non-Christians who do not read the Bible because they cannot read it or do not want to read it or because they cannot read at all?

Many Protestant Christians also ask this question seriously: can all these non-Christians find a firm standpoint in their lives, attain a trust in life? Isn't belief in the Christian God a presupposition for any *Yes* to life and any ethic built on it? These are vital questions on which Protestant theology too is still working.

## The fate of 'unbelievers'

While at the Pontifical University I was nobly studying treatise upon treatise of neo-scholastic theology, worthy theses which forty years later in essentials found their way into the Roman 'World Catechism'. I was becoming increasingly fascinated with the problem of a reasonable basis for human salvation and the 'salvation of unbelievers'. *De salute infidelium* was the title of a seminar that offered me much material from the Christian tradition. But it ultimately left me unsatisfied; it showed no convincing solution to the salvation of non-Christians and how they could find firm ground to stand on. There are indeed still Christians today who call for a hell – as a warning to be responsible. This hell is of course exclusively for the others, those 'outside', *extra ecclesiam*, those of other faiths or unbelievers.

The world religions were for me just one aspect of the problem of 'unbelief'. As early as 1955 I travelled for the first time to North Africa, with its Muslim stamp, and a few years later all round the world. I met countless people with the most varied skin colour, culture and religion. Are all excluded from salvation, indeed destined for hell? After all, the Bible says 'God wills that all shall be saved' (2 Timothy 2.4). The other aspect of the problem of 'unbelievers' is for me the growing number of non-Christians in the middle of Europe, in my closest surroundings, at the university. It seems to me to be unacceptable to suppose that the adherents of other religions, and even more atheists and agnostics, cannot achieve any firm standpoint in their lives, any trust in life, in other words that belief in the Christian God should be the presupposition for any *Yes* to reality and any ethic.

We heard much of atheism and agnosticism in the lectures in Rome, but in a very abstract form. Even modern philosophy was spoken of detached from the lives of those who practised it. As if in one place an intellectual system had given birth to another and this in turn to a third! Didn't existential questions, indeed lives, stand behind the pioneer thinkers of 'secular modernity'?

However, for me the question of a conscious rational foundation of human existence was still unresolved. A key experience – again, however, a negative one – proved for me to be a long conversation in 1953, on my second and last home leave during my seven years in Rome. At that time I was doing practical pastoral work for several weeks in Moabit, a suburb of Berlin, in the church of St Laurence. There I spoke among others with a young artist who had roughly the same difficulties with the meaning of life as I did. But with all my philosophical and now theological training I nevertheless proved incapable of giving a convincing answer to my con-versation partner. Even excursions into aesthetics were of little use. Again the question: how to gain a secure standpoint? My decision at the end was firm: no longer to evade or suppress the question but to take the offensive against it.

## A spiritual experience

In the German College there was a 'spiritual director' sworn to strict con-fidentiality: the 'spiritual'. I had the good fortune here to come upon an extraordinary man, Wilhelm Klein, an experienced and widely-travelled Jesuit with a thorough philosophical and theological training, utterly shaped by Hegel. He died in 1998 at the age of 102. He remarked that the Gregorian theses on reason and revelation were 'as clear as water', but were also 'only water' – one of his typical *bons mots*. I sought out this *homo spiritualis* after my return from the north.

Of course I again received the answer that I expected, to which I had long been allergic and which I had firmly resolved to attack with arguments that would finally force a resolution to the conflict: you must believe! Believe? Believe? That's not an answer. I want to know! But suddenly, in the middle of this conversation, an insight flashed into my mind. I am reluctant to speak of an illumination, but it was a spiritual experience. At any rate this intuitive knowledge did not come simply from my conversation partner nor through my own conceptual efforts. Perhaps from outside, from above?

'Believe?' Evidently this fundamental question is not about believing in the traditional Catholic sense of the intellectual acceptance of supernatural truths of faith, usually in the form of dogmas. However, it is also not about believing in the Protestant sense of the justifying acceptance of God's grace in Christ. My personal insight perhaps had something to do with this, but it was simpler, more elementary, more fundamental. The deliberately rational grounding of human existence is concerned with the questions that both Christians and non-Christians put 'before' any reading of the Bible itself: how can I gain a secure standpoint? How can I accept my own self with all its shadow sides? How do I accept my own freedom that is also open to evil? How can I affirm meaning in my life despite all the meaninglessness? How can I say *Yes* to the reality of the world and humankind as it is in its enigmatic and contradictory nature?

What suddenly happened to me? In this existential question an elementary wager was required of me, a wager of trust! What a challenge: venture a *Yes*! Instead of a bottomless mistrust in the garb of nihilism or cynicism, risk a fundamental trust in this life, in this reality. Instead of mistrusting life, venture to trust life: a fundamental trust in yourself, in others, in the world, in the whole of questionable reality.

In Dag Hammarskjöld, the then General Secretary of the United Nations, many years later I found the idea expressed like this (dated Pentecost 1961, four months before his death on a peace mission on the frontiers of the Congo):

> I don't know Who – or what – put the question, I don't know when it was put. I don't even remember answering. But at some moment I did answer Yes to Someone – or Something – and from that hour I was certain that existence is meaningful and that, therefore, my life, in self-surrender, had a goal.
>
> (*Markings*, 1964, p. 169)

## No fear of deep waters

This strange experience filled me with unbounded joy. In the act of saying *Yes*, venturing fundamental trust, risking trust in life: in that way and only in that way I can go on living my life, that is, adopt a positive fundamental attitude; in that way I can continue and preserve my upright stance.

That means that I now deliberately made my own that fundamental trust which I got as a child, which I maintained in puberty and adolescence, and never gave up as a student. And the unbounded joy which I experienced was similar to the joy I experienced as a child while swimming, when for the first time I had the experience that the water really supported bodies, even mine, that I entrusted myself to the water, that all alone – without support or any aids – I could trust myself to the water. No theory, no observation from the bank, no dry swimming course conveyed this to me. I had to venture it myself, and I did: the now well-considered trust in life of an adult, mature person.

However, this was a quite critical trust in life. At that time it was already clear to me that this trust in life had nothing to do with excessive trustfulness or cheap optimism. The reality of the world and myself, often so sorry a reality, didn't change. All that changed was my fundamental attitude to it. It had by no means become a 'whole' world, but as before remained stamped by contradictoriness and threatened by chaos and absurdity. Nor had my self in any way lost its shadow side. It remained impenetrable, fallible, threatened with guilt, mortal. My freedom was still capable of anything, as was that of my fellow human beings.

But I can understand that many people, even if they can swim, have an almost insuperable fear of deep water: perhaps they might go under. Parents who give swimming lessons to children under five are warned by experts against carelessness, since little children still do not know how to estimate dangers. I must confess that in my younger years I too felt a slight unease when under a lowering sky I swam mother naked far out into my native lake and became aware that it was almost ninety metres deep and that no one could come to my help here. If one does not want to go under when swimming in the open air, one must try not to stop, but keep moving, incessantly, unwearyingly, to reach a shore again. And if one gets into a mist one must ensure that as soon as possible one makes out the trees on the shore as landmarks.

Life in the world is no well-protected swimming pool where one can feel ground under one's feet at any time and take a rest. Life has its abysses and in politics and business is often more like a shark tank. Those who strive to lead a well-protected life, secure on all sides, will sooner or later be confronted with the experience that their life always remains insecure, always has highs and lows, opportunities and dangers. It is important not to be rash on the heights or despondent in the depths. People do well to form a realistic picture of themselves and to refrain from idealizing images of themselves which demand too much.

But isn't it unreasonable if I rely on the water without evidence, although supported by many examples? No, I experience the rationality when actually swimming. Nor is my trust in life in any way irrational, in any way closed to examination. Certainly my fundamentally positive standpoint, my attitude to life and reality generally, which in principle is anti-nihilistic and conservative, cannot be demonstrated as it were from outside, 'objectively'. It cannot first be demonstrated as evident or rational, something that could then be the foundation of my fundamental trust. There is no such presupposed 'Archimedean point' of thought. And even so critical a thinker as the Austro-British philosopher and theorist of science Karl Popper cannot avoid at least presupposing the rationality of reason as the basis of his 'critical rationalism', as he expressly says (*Revolution or Reform*, ET 1976): a 'belief in reason'.

Rationalist philosophers may regard such a trust in reason as irrational; Popper himself speaks of an 'irrational decision'. But in so doing they make the irrational basis of their rationalism evident. I myself would in no way describe this relying on the self, this fundamental trust in reason, as irrational. For the trust in reason cannot be proved *a priori* but is experienced in the trusting: in the use of reason, in the opening up of oneself to reality, in saying *Yes*. The fundamental trust in reality, like other fundamental experiences such as love or hope, cannot be proved in advance by an argument, or even in retrospect. It is neither a premise of my decision nor its consequence. Rather, this fundamental trust can be experienced in living out my decision, indeed in the act of trust itself, as completely meaningful, as rational.

A nihilistic *No*, a cynical primal mistrust, cannot be shaken by any arguments, however rational. But it gets entangled in always greater contradictions. Friedrich Nietzsche's work, life and mental breakdown have shown that in a moving way. By contrast a fundamental *Yes* can maintain itself consistently in the practice of life, despite all difficulties and obstacles. I have experienced that. One can live through all tribulations and disappointments by constantly standing firm and then taking new steps. This is a primal trust which in the face of all the attacks of frustration and despair becomes a lasting hope. In this way one can practise the virtue of *perseverantia*, of holding fast, of persistence, of endurance.

## Trust in life and religious faith

Can one also call fundamental trust 'faith'? My answer is that one can, but shouldn't. There have been philosophers such as the highly respected Karl Jaspers who spoke of a 'philosophical faith', but without clearly distinguishing between faith and fundamental trust. Conversely, others have all too quickly seen fundamental trust theologically and mystically as 'primal trust' (thus the Basle psychiatrist Balthasar Staehlin), but sometimes also polemically in an anti-Enlightenment way.

To clarify: since my student years I have felt it important to distinguish between fundamental trust and belief in the sense of a religious belief or belief in God. In no way did I want to interpret people theologically, in a different way from the way in which they interpret themselves. I did not want, like other theologians, to make Nietzsche a believer in God, and atheists and agnostics hidden, 'implicit' or, as the theologian Karl Rahner put it, 'anonymous' Christians. It became clear to me at an early stage that Jews and Muslims especially would regard this way of theologically making them 'anonymous' as an attempt at a Christian takeover.

Here the relationship between fundamental trust and belief in God can be very complex. According to my experience – and this is confirmed by Erik Erikson – one can distinguish between three groups of people:

- There are people whose trust in life is based on a religious faith. They are religiously motivated in their lives to extraordinary sacrifice, but are also capable of tolerating setbacks and holding fast in crises: convinced and convincing believers.
- There are also people who describe themselves as believers but have no trust in life, in human beings, in themselves. They find themselves in a precarious situation. With their hands they so to speak reach out to the clouds in heaven, but on this earth they find no real foundation. They are alien to the world, religious enthusiasts with no feet on the ground, who have nothing under their feet.
- Finally there are people who have a trust in life, without at the same time possessing a religious faith. It cannot be disputed that with their feet on the ground in some circumstances they can go through life as well as or sometimes even better than specific believers. They draw

their fundamental trust from human relations, from productive work, from a humane ethic, from scientific or political activity.

From this I would conclude that atheists or agnostics too can lead an authentically human, humane and in this sense moral life from their fundamental trust. Nihilism does not necessary follow from atheism. At this point I must contradict Dostoievsky. Even if God did not exist, not everything is allowed.

## Trust also as a basis of science, politics and business

The insight grew in me that fundamental trust determines not only the first stage of human development but all through life remains the cornerstone of the psychologically healthy personality, to which fundamental mistrust forms the lifelong counterpart. For everywhere – to take up the keywords of the psychoanalyst and psychotherapist Horst Eberhard Richter – it is a matter of 'standing fast' and resisting instead of 'fleeing' and evading. Fundamental trust is the foundation of a sense of identity, but it has to be maintained in endlessly new ways through all social and psychological conflicts. Thus fundamental trust remains a lifelong task, has to be given one again and again.

However, fundamental trust is important not only for individual but also for collective life. Thirty years ago I wrote in *Does God Exist?* a long chapter on 'fundamental trust' without finding much interest from the guild of theologians and philosophers. I also wrote about fundamental trust as the basis of ethics and science. Later it became increasingly clear to me how trust has incalculable importance for the whole life of society, even for global politics and global economics.

It did not need the global economic crisis of 2008/9 for people to feel keenly what a lack of trust can mean; thus they can also assess fundamental trust in its social dimension. The core of the crisis is the mistrust between the big banks with its fatal consequences for business all over the world, for house owners and countless private customers. More than ever we can recognize the fundamental importance of trust for business dealings world-wide; indeed as a consequence of the economic crisis people are suddenly talking of trust as the most important currency in viable financial markets, of disappointment in that 'trust in the system' which is so necessary.

I do not exaggerate in any way when I describe trust as the basis of human social life. In business today there is more trust between superiors and employees, between colleagues and partners. But controls cannot in any way replace trust, and professional competence cannot replace characteristic strengths, or efficiency replace character. What are called for are powers of leadership that relay trust; only they can bind together and motivate in hard times, strengthen the trust of employees in a business and provide orientation for present and future. In the face of an increasing lack of trust, not least in the financial sphere, advisers, representatives, buyers and analysts must concern themselves anew with lost trust and cultivate truthfulness, courage and moderation. Here a reasonable trust, particularly in the financial world, includes a degree of scepticism and requires a radical assessment of risks. So trust never replaces one's own power of judgement, nor can it make the regulation by the state or international regulation of the financial markets superfluous.

In all this it is tremendously important always to remain aware that neither a state nor a church authority, neither a statesman nor a pope, has the right to unconditional and consequently uncritical trust. I can illustrate this from a little story: 'You must have trust in me,' Pope Paul VI told me as a young Council theologian on 2 December 1965, at the end of the Second Vatican Council, in a private audience: *Deve avere fiducia in me.* Can one say no in such circumstances? I replied: 'I have trust in you, your holiness, *ma non in tutti quelli che sono intorno a Lei* – but not in all those around you.' This was a directness unusual in a curial milieu, which made the Pope gently shrug his shoulders. Had he asked for my help in a serious reform of the Curia in the spirit of the Council, I would certainly not have refused him my trust. But the absolutist Roman system, which he evidently did not want to give up, in agreement with the hard core of the Curia, did not deserve and does not deserve such trust.

And now, almost fifty years later, I can recognize in retrospect what is important for any spirituality today: in all trust in life, wisdom about life is also required – the applied power of judgement, a balance between trust and justified reservations, in the individual case also between scepticism and mistrust. To refuse trust in a particular situation can be decisive for a career. On the other hand I was time and again to give an opportunity to people, to things, in trust, in the hope that the strength would be given me to endure setbacks and hold my head high. It will be worth thinking more about a way of life, the meaning of life and a model of life. But first let's talk about joy in life.

# Chapter 2

# Joy in Life

*I never lie down at night without reflecting that – young as I am – I may not live to see another day. Yet no one of all my acquaintances could say that in company I am morose and disgruntled. For this blessing every day I thank my Creator and wish with all my heart that each one of my fellow-creatures could enjoy it.*

Wolfgang Amadeus Mozart to his father on 4 April 1787
(four years before his death)

Trust in life is good, joy in life is better. One can say that if one is thinking of true joy and not of *Schadenfreude*, which according to the proverb is said to be the finest joy. *Schadenfreude* has even entered the English language as a loanword, because the expression 'malicious pleasure' does not necessarily include harm (*Schade*).

Some people have been asking what has got into sober Londoners: in 2009 more than 800 buses propagated the message 'There's probably no God.' However, this campaign is immediately understandable once we realize that it is a reaction to a warning by fundamentalist believers, who previously on the same buses had threatened all non-believers with eternal damnation in hell fire. In this way the joy in the life of non-believers is spoilt – probably not without *Schadenfreude* – by the threat of an unpleasant end. So the confessing atheists have added to their denial of God the cheerful sentence, 'Now stop worrying and enjoy your life.'

This atheist campaign, which is said also to have spread to other countries, is financially supported by the protagonist of a 'new atheism', the evolutionary biologist Richard Dawkins. After serious works in his professional sphere he had published a book with the title *The God Delusion* in 2006. With this light-hearted, one-sided and smugly unenlightened criticism of religion he would certainly have come under the judgement of that philosopher who at the end of the nineteenth century was the first solemnly to proclaim the 'death of God', Friedrich Nietzsche. At the same time Nietzsche mocked 'our lords the scientist and physiologist' who 'lack passion in these things, the suffering in them' (*The Antichrist*, no.8). They could not appreciate what it means to have lost God. They greet the cry of the 'madman, "I'm looking for God! I'm looking for God," with a great laugh'.

## 'Joyful science'

Nietzsche's parable of the 'madman' occurs in his book *Die fröhliche Wissenschaft* (III, no.125). [The title is notoriously difficult to translate; two common renderings, 'The Gay Science' and 'The Joyful Wisdom', are each unsatisfactory in their own way. The German really means 'The Science of Being Joyful'.] 'Joyful science' means that Provençal *gaya scienza* of the singer, knight, free spirit with which there is a dance beyond morality (with 'songs of Prince Free-as-a-Bird'). For Nietzsche this is the decisive step to an inner and outer 'healing', to new joy in life, joy in life without God!

In 2009, when I was giving a lecture in the Swiss Engadine valley, 2000 metres above sea level, as I looked down from my hotel to the Silsersee I remembered that in 1882 Nietzsche wrote his work here in a new state of elation; for his health had markedly improved on his first stay in Sils-Maria. How could I ever forget the parable of the 'madman' that from the start produces three powerful images of God? The madman exclaims: 'How were we able to drink up the sea? Who gave us the sponge to wipe away the entire horizon? What did we do when we unchained the earth from its sun? Whither is it moving now? Whither are we moving now?' Then comes a cascade of questions about the consequences of the death of God: 'Away from all suns? Are we not perpetually falling? Backwards, sideways, forwards, in all directions? Is there any up and down left? Are we not straying as if through an infinite nothing? Do we not feel the breath of empty space? Has it not become colder? Is not more and more night coming all the time? Must not lanterns be lit in the morning? Do we not hear anything yet of the noise of the gravediggers who are burying God? Do we not smell anything yet of God's decomposition? – Gods too decompose. God is dead. God remains dead. And we have killed him.'

Nevertheless, with his 'gay science' Nietzsche wants to make clear that for the future of humankind the death of God means a new kind of light and happiness, of relief, cheerfulness, encouragement, dawn. Now the horizon is free again. Our ships can sail to meet with any danger, any venture of knowledge is allowed again; the sea is open again, and perhaps there has never yet been such an open sea.

So is there more joy in life without God? The further consequences of the death of God prove to be more than the shock and darkening which then show themselves in Nietzsche's personal fate. At the end of his life, shortly before his breakdown in 1889, he calls back God, who to him is pain and happiness in one:

> No!
> Come back!
> With all your afflictions
> All my tears gush forth
> To you they stream
> And the last flames of my heart
> Glow for you.
> Oh, come back
> My unknown god! My pain!
> My ultimate happiness! . . .
>                    (Dionysus Dithyrambs,
>                         Ariadne's lament)

Happiness – the eternal longing of human beings. Happiness – the great spell. Happiness – the true magical formula?

## Is the main thing for me to be happy?

'With a little bit of luck' – to quote a famous refrain from *My Fair Lady*, still my favourite musical – and cheerfulness, undoubtedly I will get through life more easily than with constant if cultural pessimism. Today shouldn't we perhaps cultivate more 'Anglo-Saxon optimism' rather than 'German *Angst*' (the apparently typical German word *Angst* has also been taken over into English)? But both are generalizing slogans. For the United States and British media too know as their Our Father, 'Give us today our daily fiasco'. Conversely, German feature writers time and again disseminate cultural contentment. However, it has always impressed me that the programme of the first American Constitution of 1787 already contains the justified pursuit of happiness alongside the right to life and freedom. And it was not a German but an English philosopher, the social reformer Jeremy Bentham, who as early as 1789 built his influential system of morality and law on the principle of the 'greatest happiness of the greatest number'. Here English makes a clear distinction between the good fortune of fulfilment ('happiness, *beatitudo*') and the good fortune of chance ('luck, *fortuna*'). Can perhaps a happy life arise from fortunate chances?

I attach much importance to the happiness of the moment: if, for, example one morning the landscape before me lies snow-white in the sunshine, or if someone has said a good word to me or shown a friendly gesture, or I have been able to give someone joy. Here is a little happiness in the everyday. But no one can give duration to the great happiness of momentary peak experiences: the sound of music, the overwhelming experience of nature, the ecstasy of love. 'Stay a while, you are so beautiful'; Goethe's Faust already wanted this of the 'moment'. It takes a lot to be happy and little to be unhappy: *Bonum ex integra causa, malum ex quodlibet defectu* – good arises only from a perfect cause, but evil from any lack, as I already learned as a student in Rome. And the neurobiology of happiness teaches me that very different information in my brain can produce endomorphines, happiness hormones, which make one euphoric, and evoke feelings of happiness. But at the same time it warns me that custom produces dullness and our biological system of happiness is not set up for the long term.

So I am sceptical about attempts to compel happiness artificially. Too often the human longing for happiness is led astray politically. Too often it is exploited commercially. Nor can happiness be induced by advertising. Those who cannot control their senses will find no happiness in life. Drug consumption – and almost everything these days counts as a drug – certainly produces momentary feelings of happiness, but in the long run reinforces sadness. There are no drugs for a happy life and lasting joy in life.

Happiness cannot be increased at random even with income. To have millions is satisfying, but it does not make one automatically happier. Greed, always wanting to have more – as the global economic crisis shows – leads to speculation and personal catastrophes, to losses of billions and mass unhappiness.

What is decisive for happiness in life is not the financial situation but intellectual attitude and activity. In fact there is something like a – relatively – happy life: happiness understood not as elation but as a basic mood, which lasts even through unhappy situations, accepting life as it is without being content with everything. Time and again I admire people in wheelchairs who often seem to me to be happier than many healthy people. I admire parents who radiate courage and joy in life despite their handicapped child. I admire those brave women and men (Christians and others) whom I was able to get to know in the slums of Nairobi, San Salvador and Chicago in selfless service of the poorest of this world.

Happy are all those people who despite all their everyday troubles are clear about themselves, are content with the life they live and have not lost the cheerfulness of their hearts. The slogan of our society, fixated as it is on experience – 'the main thing is for me to be happy'– is certainly not my axiom for life. Hedonistic enjoyment of life is all too often disappointing, and even the most refined enjoyers of life sooner or later get in a situation where the 'fun' ceases and all satisfaction is at an end. Lasting joy in life is not expressed in the statement 'I am happy' but in the statement 'I am in harmony with myself, sorted out, satisfied'. This does not exclude highs and lows.

## Happy co-existence

'What was the best day of your life? What was your greatest joy?' These are interview questions that I normally don't answer. Too much depends on the perspective, the circumstances, even the time of life. I have experienced many days of joy. But abiding everyday joys are as important to me as days of joy that are fleeting.

On my 80th birthday a correspondent told me what had pleased her most about her visit to me: 'How you can enjoy so many things that I haven't yet enjoyed.' With the best will in the world I cannot now remember what I was enjoying then. But I am certain that it had to do with my conversation partner herself: how she gave herself and what she told me. In fact I have always been able to enjoy many things. Mostly, beyond doubt, the people, the men and women, with whom I live and without whom I could not live and work at all. I have mentioned some of them by name in the two volumes of my memoirs (and in the little book *Women in Christianity*) and I hope to give them more appreciation in the third volume.

I lead a generally enjoyable social life. I am not a born hermit. Of course I cannot meet everyone with the same friendliness. One likes some people, does not like others and yet others leave one indifferent. But I have always experienced how good for me is the friendliness shown to me by complete strangers, how encouraging is the goodwill and gratitude expressed in letters. Just as a small child needs a mother or similar person to relate to, to gain trust in itself and in the strange world, so too grown

men and women need others to show and keep their trust in an environment which is not always friendly. A trusting, open education aimed at self-respect and tolerance can be important for the whole of one's life.
To put it more clearly: in order to find myself in reality I need a 'you'. Not just an it, not just another thing, a not-I, but rather another I which is capable of freedom, help, goodness and understanding and who in conversation becomes an intimate friend, one who accepts trust and shows trust. As I explained earlier, that applies to a successful business life and efficient politics, to the activity of authorities, organizations and institutions, and applies even more to the whole personal sphere. Without trust there can be no friendship, love, partnership, marriage or even psychotherapy. The disappearance of trust that can be observed so often today not only in politicians and journalists but also in managers, doctors and priests – often caused by moral failure and individual guilt – has serious effects. In the face of an accumulation of breaches of trust critical verdicts are justified, but not generalizing pre-judgements and prior condemnations.

The way in which people of different origins, nations or religions can live together happily in Europe in particular is time and again disturbed and destroyed by sweeping negative judgements that are handed on and propagated by certain media. These relations have happily survived between Catholics and Protestants. But just as so many people once held the view 'Don't trust a Jew', so today we hear – equally unacceptably – 'Don't trust a Muslim'. And some Jews and Muslims think the same of Christians. In India some Hindus think in the same way about Muslims or in Sri Lanka nationalist Buddhists about Tamils, and always vice versa. Disparaging labels are attached to 'unbelievers' by 'believers' of different provenance: atheists, sceptics and doubters of all kinds, and again also vice versa, not to mention the notorious political generalizations such as 'the' Germans, 'the' Swiss, 'the' Americans, 'the' Chinese. My experience is the opposite: in all nations, religions and cultures I have met men and women who could be trusted and with whom I could work in trust.

## You can't trust everyone

Of course one cannot *a priori* trust everyone. Certainly I am normally prepared to give a certain benefit of trust to people who meet me. But sometimes there are those who give serious occasion for mistrust. And in addition there is an unpleasant genre of people who can also be found in politics, business, culture and the academic world even if they do not always appear to be so. At best they believe in themselves and otherwise literally in nothing (Latin *nihil*). They do not recognize any values, norms, trust, ideals and are therefore not unjustly called 'nihilists', following Turgenev's novel *Fathers and Sons* (1862) and Friedrich Nietzsche.

I have grappled intensively with fundamental nihilism, whether or not this is reflected in philosophy, and my views can be read in my book *Does God Exist?* Friedrich Nietzsche saw more clearly than others this particular type of person emerging for our time. For him the horizon of meaning has been swept away, he no longer knows any supreme values, binding norms or reliable pointers. And there is nothing anyone can do about it. I remain convinced that there is no rational argument which can compel someone who asserts that this life is ultimately meaningless, that the world is ruled by chance, by a blind destiny, by chaos, absurdity and illusion, in short that everything is ultimately nothingness, to rethink. Such a person cannot be refuted theoretically. After all it could be that this human life is ultimately meaningless, worthless, nothing, joyless. In other words, human beings have the choice.

However, in political elections in our democratic societies hardly any politician or person in public life would dare to profess as loudly, openly and solemnly as Nietzsche's Zarathustra a fundamental nihilism of values and norms. Far more widespread today is a trivial, practical nihilism: in fact to live as if 'nothing' counted, as if 'anything goes', as long as life is fun. This is a superficial 'joyful science' or mode of life.

Personal discrediting or defamation is not at all to my liking. But one does not need to be a self-righteous moralizer to prefer to keep a distance from the advocates of such an attitude, particularly when they understand themselves as cynics (from the Greek *kynikos* = doglike, shameless). They do not just use the acceptable methods of irony, satire and sarcasm, as for instance in political cabaret or good comedy, but in a malicious way they deliberately expose – particularly in the power struggles of politics, business or publicity – those who think otherwise to a mocking, devastating, indeed annihilating criticism, and in so doing dispense with all truths, values and norms. Malice is related to cynicism in being a stylistic means of systematic disparagement and defamation, above all in journalism.

Nihilism, cynicism and malice are destructive attitudes to life that can destroy the real joy in life in those who adopt them and in others. There are unpleasant examples of the kind of person – here I am also thinking of earlier experiences in faculty meetings – the presence or absence of whom changes the whole atmosphere of a gathering. One would like such temperamentally grumpy contemporaries who make life difficult for their fellow human beings and themselves to be given rather more genuine joy in life.

## Joy in nature

'You enjoy many things.' For me that especially includes joy in nature. I have got this from my mother; I can still hear her voice in my ears: 'Look, how beautiful it is . . .' It can be quite simple things. I cannot talk with plants, as some people claim to do ('rubbish!' a botanist acquaintance said to me). But I can delight in a single rose in my study, and how many species of roses there are, differing in colour, forms of petals, and so on! And I watch with amazement how the marvellous rose-red Japanese ornamental cherry quickly buds, blossoms and fades in front of my window.

Yes, there are thousands upon thousands of things in nature in which human beings can delight – if they want to. For there are people, even educated people, who get no enjoyment from nature. They lack a deeper sensitivity to nature, just as others lack a deeper sensitivity to music or art. There are literary scholars who completely live in the world of their book no matter where they are. Or scientists who look at the whole world only through their physical, chemical or biological spectacles – with no sense of its beauty and splendour. Or people who live only in their business world and yet others whose whole life turns only on fashion, cosmetics and health. Nature is at best a marginal phenomenon in their existence. They fail to note all the things that happen in nature and what inestimable enrichment escapes them in their lives.

I have often lived in big cities where many people can at most afford house plants, and I have missed nature there very much. Like the sun, nature is a power of life for bodily and spiritual well-being. Since my youth I have worked as often as possible in the fresh air. I can well understand people who, if they have no garden, develop a balcony culture, and I understand those who fall in love with a particular patch of earth or a landscape. Every day I enjoy the impressive panorama that I always see before me in Tübingen, always different depending on the weather, the time of year and the time of day: the unbuilt-on green Österberg in the middle of the city and in the background the Swabian Alb. Similarly, in my Swiss homeland I have a view of the Alps and in front of them between gentle hills the Sempachersee, which responds to the slightest breath of wind and reflects the sky with changing surface and modes.

All of us have our own experiences of nature if we look for them, including great ones that embed themselves deep in the memory. All my life I will remember how when skiing for the first time on a marvellous winter day on the Weissfluhjoch at Davos I was overwhelmed by the panorama of the countless sunlit, snow-covered peaks of the Alps. And I was similarly gripped when for the first time from the Pacific Île des Pins I dived deep and long with oxygen equipment and swam through the coral reef with its gorges in unreal blue-green light, all the fish and other creatures with their bizarre forms around me. I know that many people can forget the passing of time when snorkelling over a reef.

But please, for all the joy in nature, let there be no false nature enthusiasm. In some circumstances the same landscape can make me afraid. When the ocean heaves or the hot wind thunders through the high Alps; when the snowstorm whistles icily in one's face or the mist swallows one up completely while skiing downhill, or the oxygen runs out when one is swimming underwater, then nature shows its other, threatening, indeed sometimes terrifying face. Nature can show itself as much an enemy as a friend to human beings. For centuries nature, from the mountains to the sea, has been felt to be hostile.

But when speaking of nature we think not only of landscape and vegetation but also particularly of animals.

## And the animals?

There are theologians today who think that animals have virtually nothing to do with our faith. It is enough for them to reflect on them very briefly in their theology of creation. Albert Schweitzer once remarked: 'Just as the housewife who has scrubbed the parlour makes sure that the door is shut so that the dog does not get in and disrupt the work she has done by his pawmarks, so European thinkers take care that no animals run around in their ethics' (*Culture and Ethics*, 1971).

But times have changed. Here I am thinking not only of the excellent programmes we see on television about wild animals. Professor Bernhard Grizmek, who won an Oscar for his film 'Serengeti must not die' and is the figurehead of the international animal protection movement, is unforgettable. There are two developments above all which have given the animal protection movement, founded in the nineteenth century, a wide influence:

- The theory of evolution, now confirmed by microbiology. This has worked out the kinship of human beings with animals, especially the higher primates. Human genes differ from those of chimpanzees in only one per cent of the elements in the chain of the hereditary substance DNA.
- The principle of sustainability. This requires us to deal sparingly also with flora and fauna and at the same time to think beyond the moment towards future generations. Today increasing note is being taken of it also in business.

Some people do not like any animals. I love animals, but – for reasons of time and space – will not allow myself any domestic animals apart from the occasional ants, wasps and spiders. However, I know a lot of people to whom a dog or a cat gives joy despite all the inconveniences. Is the dog man's best friend? Animals can be companions for life, especially for people who are lonely. And why shouldn't human beings attribute personal properties to animals – dependence, loyalty, feelings of sympathy, joy and suffering? They are confirmed by more recent research: highly-developed animals can in fact show feelings in the same way as human beings do. And experienced teachers point out that domestic animals that have to be looked after and cared for bring some advantages for the development of children.

I delight above all in the birds that fly around and chirp in our neighbourhood, which is rich in trees. The bird reserve by my lake at home is a paradise for birds. And when swimming, time and again I keep noticing all the different water birds, from the swan to the great crested grebe.

Animal lovers have sometimes asked me whether perhaps birds, but also cats and dogs, go into a kind of 'eternal' paradise, an 'animal heaven'. I dare not answer Yes, and on the contrary have reservations at the erection of more and more animal cemeteries at a time when for reasons of space people argue for cremation instead of burial. I also have reservations when people play off the allegedly uncorrupted, natural animal against the allegedly utterly false and selfish human being. Are animals really better than human beings? At any rate animals are not human beings.

On the other hand animals are also not simply commodities or goods that human beings can dispose of as they please. They are by no means 'soulless automata', as at the beginning of modern times the rationalist philosopher René Descartes, who split off the rationally thinking subject from an objective nature, concluded – a view which has resulted in the industrialized mass rearing of animals that is all planned in terms of the abattoir and makes animals machines of production and providers of raw materials.

Contrary to what even Immanuel Kant thought, human beings have responsibilities towards animals. This prohibits them from tormenting animals. But in my view there is no basis for an extension of the commandment against killing to the animal world and a general limitation of humanity to a purely vegetarian diet, even if that could be a practical option. Nevertheless, wherever possible and necessary animals deserve protection and care from human beings. Children should learn not to torment animals, and especially should not mistreat the domestic animals entrusted to us. In an age of animal protection we also look quite differently from before at the well-being of domestic animals or working animals and try to give them appropriate living space, care, food and transport. And if an animal has to be killed, that must be done as quickly and painlessly as possible. However, the circumstances in which we keep animals is still far from satisfactory.

The 'limits to growth' and the threat to the basis of human life today require not only knowledge of nature and the natural sciences, but also the protection and preservation of nature. The saying from Genesis 1.28 ('Fill the earth and subdue it'), which is much quoted and in modern times often misused, is not to be understood as complete exploitation by modern science and technology but to be implemented in the spirit of the cultivation of the original garden of Eden. Human beings must co-operate with nature.

In principle the eco-social market economy requires a balance between economy and ecology. Ecological knowledge, which in our generation has been enormously expanded and popularized, is not enough. It must give rise to ecological responsibility, a responsible way of dealing with resources and technologies, local, national and global, all supported by an ethic of 'reverence for life' formulated first by Albert Schweitzer and acknowledged in the Declaration toward a Global Ethic of the 1993 Chicago Parliament of the World's Religions. The Declaration stresses our special responsibility for the planet earth and the cosmos, for air, water and land.

## Not nature mysticism, but a bond with nature

For all my joy in nature I cannot be a nature mystic. That means that for me the experience of nature does not replace the experience of God. I observe, regard, respect, wonder at nature, but I do not believe in nature. I do not make nature God, I am not an all-divinizer, a pan-theist.

Convinced by modern science, I remain constantly aware that the whole of nature stands under the cruel laws of evolution: the 'survival of the fittest' applies from molecules to predators. Darwin's essential insights have been confirmed by microbiology. However, the social Darwinism which does not go back to Darwin himself and which seeks to justify life-threatening predator capitalism has not. 'Eat and be eaten' reminds me of the ironical statement that my teacher in Rome often applied to social life: *'Pisces maiores manducant pisces minores* – the big fish eat the little fish.' This is a law of nature and human history that is difficult to reconcile with pleasant human co-existence, but also with a divine 'intelligent design'.

Unfortunately there is no perfect world of peace between animal and animal, man and beast. We do not live in the kingdom of God of the end time, for which in the Bible the prophet Isaiah already longed (11.6), where the wolf lies down with the lamb and the wild cat with the kid, where calf, young lion and cow are side by side and a little child looks after them.

So I have no illusions. Always and everywhere living beings can survive only if they harm, even destroy other living beings. We human beings for our part can do no more and no less than limit the damage as far as possible. We cannot simply turn back time. As soon as we want cheap eggs or chickens, we promote modern mass animal rearing.

There is at present a passionate argument as to whether and how animal experiments are morally permissible but this should not degenerate into – as some abroad would say – a typically German fight of faith by ideological extremists. In my view no reasonable animal protector is calling for the abolition of animal experiments that are relevant and tragically necessary, an abolition which would mean that ground-breaking research into the neurosciences went abroad. But on the other hand hardly any rational neuroscientist defends the retention of animal experiments that, for example, readily inflict torture on higher developed animals such as rhesus monkeys. Research into Alzheimer's in Germany almost completely dispenses with experiments with apes in favour of research with flies, worms, fish and mice.

So we should be able to achieve a sensible ethical balance that with the ultimate aim of healing and diminishing human suffering minimizes the suffering of animals and where possible avoids it. In experimental research into serious illnesses of the brain it should comfort us that animals do not experience death, if it is not cruelly protracted, as human beings do. Moreover, more recent animal research confirms that animals live completely in the present; only human beings have an authentic self-consciousness, consciousness of time, consciousness of history, consciousness of an end. Only human beings think about death. Only they have a language with complex sentence structures, the capacity for strategies through which they weigh up alternative courses of action, and the capacity for self-reflection – all presuppositions for abstract thought and directed states of mind such as love and hatred, convictions and wishes, fears and hopes. Charles Darwin already called only human beings 'moral beings'. Animals are exclusively guided by instincts and cannot of course assume any responsibility. According to our present state of knowledge, in the whole cosmos only the human being is a subject in law that in claiming rights can also assume responsibilities. But the cosmos in which human beings live harbours a mystery.

## Cosmic religion

Despite all my objections to a nature mysticism I can get something from Albert Einstein's 'cosmic religion' which 'corresponds to no anthropomorphic concept of God':

> What a deep faith in the rationality of the structure of the universe and what a longing for understanding of the tiniest reflection of the reason revealed in this world must have been alive in Kepler and Newton for them to be able to disentangle the mechanism of the heavens in the lonely work of man-years.
> (*Religion and Science*, 1930)

In other words, I can come to believe in the rationality of the structure of the universe, desire to understand it. 'Only those who have devoted their lives to similar ends', Einstein continues, 'have a living idea of what inspired these men and gave them the strength to remain true to their goal despite countless failures. It is the cosmic religion which gives them such strength.' I may add how impressed I am, wherever I get a glimpse into experimental science, at how much strength, patience and endurance are needed, often for years, to arrive at an important result with worms, fish or flies.

However, we now take seriously something with which Einstein still had difficulties because of pantheistic tendencies: that order ('cosmos') and necessity are only one side of the universe. The other is disorder ('chaos'), the vagueness, indeterminacy, chance that shows itself in the whole development of the cosmos, and especially in quantum mechanics, and that Einstein therefore rejected.

Anyone who has acquired a little knowledge about the fantastic progress of the natural sciences in the two centuries since Kant can only marvel. But the very progress in the natural sciences has also shown their cognitive limits, in the macrocosm and in the microcosm. These limits need to be thought about, but they should not disturb our joy in life. Quite the opposite.

With the same reverence as that with which Immanuel Kant, philosopher and natural scientist, regarded the starry sky above him, often before I go to bed I look at the endless breadth of the night sky, clear with stars or more often with different cloud formations. What tranquillity and grandeur the starry heavens radiate, as long as they are not outshone by human lights! And so I reflect again on the great questions that the cosmos puts to human beings, in what the philosopher Hegel calls a 'devotion of thought'. I know that if space travellers ever succeeded in finding a way to the middle of the Milky Way above me and back again to our earth, they would find a humanity that in the meantime would have grown about 60,000 years older. But what is that when set against the 13.7 billion years which astrophysics calculates has elapsed since the Big Bang at the beginning?

In view of the silence of the unimaginably great spaces I do not feel the terror that at the beginning of modern science the mathematician, physicist and philosopher Blaise Pascal expressed. Nor do I feel it in the face of the equally tremendous abysses of an infinitely small micro world. Here elementary particle physics has established unbelievably tiny processes: in the order of magnitude of a billionth of a centimetre (1 billion = 1 million million) and time-spans down to a trillionth of a second (1 trillion = 1 million billion).

So I do not feel terror but rather an unquenchable desire to know, a 'longing for understanding' as Einstein put it. What is our reality? What is real, reality, if even words like 'part' or 'spatial extension' have largely lost their significance for sub-atomic particles, if the mode of reality of core-building blocks – protons, neutrons and even more quarks – remains completely unexplained for physicists?

It is small comfort for a theologian that even physicists sit on islands of knowledge and have only a very limited picture of the cosmos. They admit that in spite of all their success in research still only 4 per cent of the universe is known, namely ordinary visible matter, the stars, planets and moons. So for physicists, despite costly investigations of the universe and into the depths of the earth, all the rest, 96 per cent, remains literally in the dark. Therefore they speak quite appropriately of 'dark matter' and 'dark energy', completely unknown entities.

What we know is a drop. What we do not know is an ocean. The founder of modern physics, Isaac Newton, is held to have said this and it will probably be true for a long time. In the nearer or more distant future scientists will certainly shed some light on this darkness; they will make it very much clearer what reality lies behind the images, ciphers, comparisons they have to use, all their concepts, models and mathematical formulas. But, I ask myself, will the physicists, natural scientists generally, then perhaps raise more clearly those issues which seem to arise at the point where their knowledge comes up against limits which it cannot go beyond?

## Approach to an impenetrable mystery

'Do you believe in the theory of evolution?', I am asked, particularly by fundamentalist Bible believers in the United States. Many want the biblical story of creation, rightly understood, to have at least the same status as the theory of evolution in schools. I reply: 'I do not believe in the theory of evolution since for me it is scientifically proven.' On the basis of an impressive wealth of physico-chemical, palaeontological, embryological and morphological material I know, despite all the gaps in our knowledge that still exist, that humankind is the product of a billion years of slow development. In our time this is sensationally confirmed by molecular biology, according to which all living organisms on our planet contain two forms of a particular molecule (DNA and RNA), which fix the blueprint for all living beings.

But I also know that the theory of evolution does not solve all the questions which nature puts to us. I have discussed fundamental questions of the natural sciences with many physicists, chemists and biologists. The more reflective among them do not limit themselves to their own field of work and special area. In view of the unimaginable size of our universe, the complexity of the evolutionary world and the unforeseeable development of life, even intellectual life, on our planet, they also know feelings of amazement, reverence, joy. And they do not close themselves to the great questions of human life, which seem to transcend their science. Even if one does not share Blaise Pascal's terror at immeasurable space, one should reflect on his insight into '*la grandeur et misère de l'homme*', the human being – nothing in the face of the universe and everything in the face of the nothingness. 'Infinitely removed from understanding the outermost limits, the goal of all things and their origin are insuperably hidden from him, in an impenetrable mystery . . .' (*Pensées* 84).

'*Un secret impénétrable*' – really an impenetrable mystery? In fact natural science since Pascal and Descartes has displayed a fantastic history of success over more than three hundred years, but has not produced any convincing answers to the fundamental questions of the whence and why, the what and whither of the process of development analysed by it since the Big Bang of 13.7 billion years ago. With the great majority of physicists, I am convinced that the events at the point of time t = 0 are in principle hidden from physics, and even empirical methods with growing breadth and refinement (e.g. at the European nuclear research centre CERN in Geneva) will not help us to understand what was before this point in time. Far less can the speculations about earlier or other universes made through computers help further here, since they are not backed by any empirical evidence.

The great mystery of science that is manifestly 'impenetrable' for science is: why is there something and not nothing? This is, according to the brilliant mathematician, philosopher and ecumenist Leibniz, the basic question of philosophy. If we spell it out in the light of our present knowledge – where do the space and time, energy and matter given first with the Big Bang come from? To put it more forcefully: where do the universal natural constants already given before the Big Bang come from: the charge of the electron e which is always the same, Planck's quantum of efficiency, the Boltzmann constant k, the velocity of light c . . . ?

In the face of the cosmos and the questions resulting from research into it, it seems to me that above all intellectual modesty is advisable. While the ongoing thrust of research and knowledge may be asserted, there is need for a realistic insight into the limitations of knowledge and the finitude of all that is human. What is the human being in this universe? These who take themselves too seriously in science, business or politics and overplay the great questions of life would do well to reflect on their 'place in the cosmos'. And those who in the private and public sphere only circle round themselves, instead of troubling themselves with the greater whole, should reflect a little on their finitude and transitoriness, as this is expressed not least in the constant cosmic circling of all the inhabitants of earth – happily not perceived by us. At around 1000 kilometres an hour we are circling on our own axis. But at the same time our globe is circling the sun at more than 100,000 kilometres an hour. And yet again our whole stellar system is circling at 800,000 kilometres an hour around the centre of the Milky Way, a circling which causes no giddiness – unless someone is constantly rotating around himself. Which in the long run destroys the joy of life.

## Joy in life to the end

Have I perhaps become too serious? But this chapter is meant to be less an exercise in happiness, wit and cheerfulness than a serious reflection on what gives me delight, what can be the foundation for joy in life. I have been concerned more with sources of joy in life than with their forms of expression. These are obvious: what would our lives be like without the humour which relieves so many sufferings of soul and body, masters difficult situations and gilds our everyday life? And what would life be without the laughter which according to the serious philosopher Kant is one of the three things, together with hope and sleep, which heaven has given human beings to counteract the wearinesses of life. I shall be discussing much in due course in connection with the meaning of life and the ground of life. As I have said, I shall move on step by step, and later discuss particularly the question of God carefully and thoroughly. But now I want to address a last threat to life.

Often as I look up at the night sky in amazement, wonder and reflection, one thing I do not find there: comfort. No star shines on anyone who has lost a beloved person, anyone who has been betrayed by a friend or partner, anyone who has lost their job. And even more, faced with the approach of death one cannot expect any comfort or encouragement from the pitch-dark heaven.

So can joy in life as a basic mood be maintained to the end when one thinks of human transitoriness and mortality? Isn't a fundamental pessimism about life ultimately more appropriate for human beings? I shall not give an over-hasty idea here but only a provisional one: joy in life can be sustained better if one keeps one's sense of transitoriness and death, which is possible at any time, in front of one than if one suppresses it. Of course I don't mean by that an angst-ridden constant staring at death and certainly not hell and the devil. What I mean rather is a cheerful relaxation that takes into account that one's human life will come to an end sooner or later – and for me, I trust, this will not be an ending but a consummation. That is why I have put at the head of this chapter a remark by Wolfgang Amadeus Mozart, who, as he wrote to his father, never went to bed without thinking that perhaps he would not see another day, but was by no means morose or sad in dealings with his fellow human beings.

I discussed years ago with the sceptical Mozart biographer Wolfgang Hildesheimer, perhaps the most sensitive German writer on music of our time, what Mozart calls a deep innermost 'happiness'. Understandably a pessimistic person on account of his fate as a Jewish emigrant, Hildesheimer wanted to see in the Mozart of the last months a joyless man, despairing of human beings and God, who because of his manifest professional, financial and health difficulties had 'given up'. But here Hildesheimer overlooked the fact that to his very last day Mozart worked indefatigably. He passed over Mozart's last and probably most important symphony, in shining C major, the Jupiter symphony, and also the conclusion of other great compositions in the year of his death: dances, the joyful *Magic Flute*, the coronation opera *The Clemency of Titus*, the clarinet concerto and his very last, unfinished work, the *Requiem*, which he had been rehearsing on his sickbed the day before his unexpected death.

It was no 'speculative self-soothing' (as Hildesheimer puts it) when Mozart wrote in a letter to his father four years before his own death: 'As death – when we consider it closely – is the true goal of our existence, I have formed during the last few years such close relations with this true, best friend of man, that his image is not only not terrifying for me, but is indeed very soothing and consoling! And I thank my God for graciously granting the opportunity (you know what I mean) of learning that death is the key which unlocks the door to our true happiness.'

So joy in life until the end of our lives is – in principle – possible. The conditions for that need to be considered. At around the same time as Mozart the young genius of romanticism, the writer Novalis (Friedrich von Hardenberg), for whom the 'blue flower' was the image of finitude and infinity, dream and reality, wrote in his novel *Heinrich von Ofterdingen*, which remained unfinished (he died the next year at 29): 'Where then are we going?' And the answer is: 'Always home.' Always home? Where, one asks, are human beings at home? And what is their way there, their way through life? That is another question.

# Chapter 3

# Way of Life

*Our different religious and cultural traditions must not prevent our common involvement in opposing all forms of inhumanity and working for greater humaneness. The principles expressed in this Global Ethic can be affirmed by all persons with ethical convictions, whether religiously grounded or not.*

Declaration toward a Global Ethic of the Parliament
of the World's Religions, Chicago, 4 September 1993, ch.1

We have looked at trust in life and joy in life. Now we turn to the way of life, but where are the waymarks?

By the lake in my Swiss homeland I have often asked myself: how do these flocks of birds – of starlings, gulls, grey geese – operate? They do not follow any commanders, no authority co-ordinates their movement, the individual bird evidently has no idea of an overall strategy. Yet the whole flock moves in a determined order and in often bold patterns. It even performs evasive manoeuvres when a bird of prey invades the group. More recent researches into birds have investigated the phenomenon and speak – as do researches into ants or fish – of a 'swarm intelligence'. The individual creature does not understand the whole, it simply fits itself into the group or colony, but instinctively it finds the way – with the help of particular techniques such as cries or scents.

With human beings it is different. Every individual has to find and take responsibility for his or her own way through life. Indeed the human race as such had to seek and find its own way in the midst of the animal world over tens of thousands of years.

## Humankind's way of life

Nowhere have I reflected so intensely on the origins of humankind as in Africa, on the borders of Zambia and Zimbabwe where the Zambesi thunders hundreds of metres into the depths through the Victoria Falls. There at the end of the 1990s we filmed for the first part of the television series 'World Religions on the Way', to quote the subtitle of the series 'Tracing the Way'. North of there begins the famous Rift Valley, that gigantic African–Syrian trench. From the discovery of prehistoric tools and skeletons we have learnt that from that place man as he is today, *homo sapiens*, began to make his way over the globe.

The human being was markedly a late developer. In the evolution of the cosmos – over 13.7 billion years in all probability – *homo sapiens* first developed 200,000 years ago in tropical-subtropical, warm Africa, rich in wild life. I have never found it difficult to accept that in terms of their development human beings have much in common with their closest relations, the anthropoid apes: from the number of chromosomes, through the positioning of the teeth and the development of the brain, to their social behaviour and certain preliminary stages of an idea of the self.

But the special position of human beings over and against animals has likewise interested me. They are marked by their upright walk (with a rump held vertical) – in our days a symbol for the ethical attitude of human beings. Then of course they have self-awareness – which has likewise become an ethical concept – as a presupposition for a complex syntactical language. Only human beings gifted with language, as I have said, have the capacity for strategic and abstract thinking and for self-reflection, have directed states of mind such as love and hatred, hopes and fears, convictions and wishes. All this was the basis for a higher cultural development of humankind and above all for a humane ethic.

This double structure of human beings has shaped my faith, my spirituality. I am never only mind or only impulse. In the light of my evolution I am always both an intellectual being and a being which is driven. My 'spirituality' also includes my 'corporeality'. Therefore human beings are not superior to animals 'spiritually', nor can human beings and animals be put on the same level biologistically. So I do not count myself among those believers who think that they can smash scientifically proven facts with a Bible in their hands. But I also feel little sympathy for those scientists, in principle hostile to nature, who with reference to their scientific results and constantly borrowing from the well-known history of the scandal and criminality of Christianity and other religions support an allegedly scientific atheism – intended for naïve readers. I take scientific arguments and criticism of religion seriously, and I ignore criticism that is not serious.

## Learning to behave in a human way

I learned from socio-biologists that beyond doubt human beings, who come from the animal kingdom, initially had above all an egoistic orientation; indeed, in the early phases of becoming human they needed this to survive. However, that genes already are 'egotistic' and new species arise purely by chance, as Richard Dawkins has worked out, is only one side of the structure of evolution. More recent gene research shows that new species and organisms arise not only through selection but also through co-operation, creativity and communication, and only in this way could evolution keep differentiating.

It is even more beyond doubt that in the case of higher animals there is a genetically predisposed co-operative behaviour, above all among relations who carry similar genes, in other words a kind of 'reciprocal altruism': 'As you to me, so I to you' – something in expectation of something in return, as can be observed particularly in the anthropoid apes. Thus a rudimentary ethical behaviour is already rooted in the biological nature of human beings. This fact is emphasized by the long-time director of the Max Planck Institute, the Tübingen evolutionary biologist Alfred Gierer, from whom I have learned much:

> Our basic genetic equipment also includes the capacities of empathy, of putting oneself in the situation and the thoughts of others. It is on this and similar aptitudes of social behaviour that the very great capacity of our species 'man' rests, which is a decisive precondition of chances of life and survival.
>
> (*Was ist der Mensch? In vieler Hinsicht sich selbst ein Rätsel . . .* ,
> Berlin 2008, pp. 103–5)

At the same time social researchers confirm me in the view that a biological-mechanistic interpretation is not enough to explain the origin of human ethical values and criteria. For in the case of human beings, and only human beings, with the capacity for languages developed a unique capacity for co-operation, and this had to be learned socially. With the evolution of strategic thought the capacity for empathy also developed – into a fellow feeling with others in their fears, expectations, hopes, indeed above all in the family group, into unselfishness. This became fundamental for human social behaviour. Thus human beings from primaeval times slowly had to learn to behave in a humane way. It follows from this that human beings are the only living beings that at an early stage could establish social and cultural norms and develop them further.

## An ethic for survival

After the session in Africa, filming for 'Tracing the Way' led us to the heart of Australia, to the gigantic monolith Uluru, the sacred mountain of the primal inhabitants. I have not forgotten the profound gaze of many of these people, at rest with themselves, looking into hidden depths; it is as if they still have a knowledge that we 'civilized' people have long since lost. It was therefore important for me to show that these 'Aborigines' (Latin *ab origine* = from the beginning) in particular are not what people call primitive 'nature peoples', but possess their own culture, a 'tribal culture'. Happily, in 2009 in a political U-turn, Australia adopted the declaration on the rights of indigenous people passed by the UN General Assembly in 2007: a right to self-determination for the original inhabitants, not so much to make their own laws but primarily to be able to determine their own lives and cultural survival. Presumably under President Obama the United States, and then Canada and New Zealand, will follow.

I have often come upon the question: do the primal inhabitants really have 'culture'? They have not developed a script, a science or a complex technology. But, cultural anthropologists have explained to me, their thinking is quite logical, plausible, indeed stamped with a passion for ordering things and for human relations. And beyond doubt the primal inhabitants also have an elementary ethic which has helped and still helps them to make a life for themselves and survive, and to the present day is fundamental to a human togetherness.

That helped me better to understand a kind of basic principle of anthropological evolution; right from the early days of humanity, when basic needs were felt, orientations for human behaviour imposed themselves: particular conventions and customs, that is ethical criteria, rules, norms, directives. These were put to the test throughout humankind in the course of millennia. They had so to speak to find their way into the sequence of generations.

Of course in the early tribal cultures – and even today – these values and criteria are unwritten norms, not formulated as propositions. They were handed down through a family, clan and tribal ethic in stories, parables, comparisons and customs. But it was not by chance that similar norms developed in the most varied regions of the earth, since they concentrated on the most important areas of life. First of all on the protection of life – the prohibition against killing people, except in certain circumstances such as settling conflicts and punishing violence.

Therefore it was no coincidence that Albert Schweitzer put 'reverence for life' at the centre of his ethics. But from the start they were also concerned with the protection of property, with the protection of honour and with the regulation of relations between the sexes. These four perspectives of a primal ethic became important for me when I was working out what the different cultures had in common.

Of course there were long periods of familiarization and testing before the universal recognition of such practical norms came about. After the period of hunters and gatherers, who probably totalled only a few million in all, a higher cultural development took place. The extension of agriculture around 10,000 years ago brought a marked increase in population and at the same time a differentiation of cultures that finally led to the high cultures and high religions. Now the norms were also formulated as propositions and written down. In some cultures they were put under the will of God or – an example is the Ten Commandments of the Hebrew Bible – under the authority of the one God.

Over all the centuries such commandments have been handed on from generation to generation. I keep hearing one particular objection today: these commandments are constantly being broken. My answer is, 'Of course, but what would the world look like without them?' An ethic always goes against the empirical facts; it does not mean a state of *is*, but a state of *ought*. However, the question seems important to me. In today's situation, how may one create new respect and persistence for ethical norms – as pointers to human good?

## Pointers that fail?

No human being comes into the world an adult. Every newborn human child has to learn for itself on the way to adulthood what the human race had to learn on the long way to becoming human. I was able to experience this myself in my own family and outside it. Indeed how to be human needs to be learned by every human being, of course not in the style of a Robinson Crusoe alone on an island, but in the midst of human society.

For many centuries numerous customs and usages were socially taken for granted, and were safeguarded by religious and patriarchal authority. For a long time in Europe the elementary norms of being human were communicated by family, school and church, despite all their deficiencies and one-sidedness. But in a modern Europe that was secularizing itself they increasingly ceased to be taken for granted and generally binding.

Now in individual cultures there are also periods of forgetting and ignoring these norms; there are times or areas of moral neglect. Institutionalized religion, which itself has fallen behind and is in crisis, usually shares the responsibility for this.

Aren't religions often pointers that fail? In Europe and America in such cases people quickly think of allegedly unenlightened Islam. It would be more natural for us to think of the fundamentalist currents in Protestantism and especially in an unenlightened Roman magisterium. There have also been more hopeful times. How enjoyable it was for me in 1963 to give lectures right across America on the renewal and opening up of the Catholic Church to the wider Christian and secular world – backed by the truly ecumenical Pope John XXIII and the young Catholic President John F. Kennedy.

At that time the Catholic Church had reached a high degree of credibility with the Second Vatican Council (1962–5) and as a theologian I could refer to it directly as an authority on moral orientations. But how sorry things became in the post-conciliar restoration that soon set in, which brought with it a fatal decline in the credibility of the church. For millions of Catholics Pope Paul VI's 1968 encyclical *Humanae vitae*, which condemns any form of contraception as a grievous sin, was the parting of the ways. This 'pill encyclical' provoked my 'Inquiry' into the papal magisterium with the book *Infallible?* (1970; ET 1971). But instead of responding to the critical 'inquiry' in a positive way, the church government attempted to silence this questioning Catholic theologian, discrediting me within the church by withdrawing the church's licence to teach and liquidating me academically. As is well known, in both cases the action was ineffective.

The sexual morality demanded by the Pope, the stumbling block at that time, is today accepted only by an increasingly small minority of Catholics, and this despite solemn confirmation by the popes who followed, despite all papal journeys, speeches and documents. Papal authority, infallibility, inerrancy was permanently shaken, as was confirmed by the incomprehensible mistakes made by Benedict XVI over the Protestant churches, the Muslims and Jews, the Indios and also the millions in Africa infected with AIDS.

Why must I note this? Because since then for the great majority of Catholics the gulf between 'What I believe' and 'What the church prescribes for belief' (thus the formulation of the Catechism) is widening, in both moral and dogmatic questions. The Protestant churches, which usually protest too weakly against the unbiblical and unecumenical authoritarianism in Rome, evidently cannot compete with this loss of credibility for Christianity.

Now the question of humankind's course into the future imposes itself all the more urgently. After all the ideological errors and inhumanities of the twentieth century are there pointers, points of orientation, signposts for this? That is a fundamental moral question.

## Where do we find orientation?

My own life has become a great adventure of the spirit with constant new challenges as a result of all the experiences and conflicts described in my memoirs. With the support of many people, after the great conflict with Rome in 1979/80 I succeeded in working out my thoughts about a dialogue of religions and a common ethic based on fundamental trust, the foundation for which I had already laid. In dialogue with scholars from Judaism, Christianity and Islam, from Hinduism, Buddhism and Chinese religions, but also with the secular ideologies, I deepened them and shaped them. So finally in 1990, a decade after the conflict with Rome, I was able to present the Global Ethic project. During these years 'What I believe' underwent an extraordinary enrichment, deepening and differentiation.

In past decades – despite all the immense progress in medicine and pharmacy, not to mention space travel and the Internet – the way of humankind has not become easier. In all the regions of the world many people are now asking: under what basic conditions can we as human beings survive on a habitable earth; can we shape our individual and social life in a more human way? A new kind of responsibility has accrued to us through this unprecedented scientific-technological progress – for those among whom we live and our environment but also, if the way of humankind is not to end in the abyss of a nuclear war or an environmental catastrophe, for our posterity. Hans Jonas already developed that in his book 'The Principle of Responsibility'.

In the meantime the long and all too one-sidedly praised globalization of the markets, technology and the media also gives us a globalization of problems, from the financial markets and new plagues (AIDS, bird flu, swine flu) to criminality, drugs and terrorism. And the global economic crisis which broke in on us in 2008 – by no means unpredictable – confirmed in me the insight that if globalization is not to have inhuman effects it also calls for a globalization of ethics. In view of the problems of global politics, global economics and global financial systems there is need for a global ethic that can be supported by the world religions, and also by non-believers, humanists, secularists. Here I passionately oppose the foolish tendency to produce a division of world society into secular and religious society. Today's world needs both secularity and religion. But there is one thing above all that it does not need: fanaticism – and the fanatical secularists are as wrong as the fanatical religious fundamentalists.

Of course I know that today ethical problems have to be reflected on in the context of the post-modern individualization and pluralization of secular society that are taking place at the same time. Far be it from me to see these processes, as many churchmen do, only under the negative sign of decay and 'de-Christianization'. After all, they have given us an infinite amount of individual freedom, though they have also reinforced the lack of orientation.

Psychology and psychotherapy can help a great deal in this crisis of orientation. I made a sympathetic investigation of Sigmund Freud thirty years ago and was even awarded a prize by the American Psychiatric Association for it. But the problems of ethics were for a long time simply hidden by some psychiatrists under the rubric of the repressive 'superego', as though the conscience was only a control authority developed by the wrong kind of education, indeed a neurotic illness. On the other hand those theologians who for all moral questions of human beings referred only to the freedom of the conscience and subjective justice behaved in just as one-sided a way. Freedom of conscience certainly cannot be a subjective arbitrariness. That raises a question both for education and for leading one's life: by what measures is the conscience to be directed (and can the conscience itself be shaped)? On what co-ordinates am I to orientate myself with my inner compass – particularly in view of the boundless ocean of information on the Internet?

Unprecedented technological progress has indeed not made the question of the moral progress of humankind superfluous, as has often been expected, but has raised it again, in view of the growing problems from the technology of the gene to the atom. We are all increasingly having the experience today that human beings are coping with everything possible and not just themselves. So more and more people are asking: Where does ethical orientation come from? How should I establish it? More precisely, where in all the many possible choices in present-day pluralism is one to find one's way in life and maintain it?

The questions become more acute when we remember that we live in an open society, i.e. in a society that is open to the future and thus happily also open to the truth. But in a democratic society in which there is a free interplay of intellectual and social forces, is a minimum agreement on fundamental values, norms and attitudes to be reached? This is already necessary for a humane co-existence within our families and school classes, but also in our businesses and large societies right down to the functioning of a democratic state. If most people happily reject a totally subjective arbitrariness and lawlessness, where then do the criteria, priorities, ideals, where do the signposts of our life come from?

Hardly anyone today wants to defend publicly and in principle an immoralistic 'beyond good and evil', because that would tolerate such crimes as the abuse of children, indeed babies, which increasingly takes place with the help of the Internet. But haven't certain moral criteria that were formerly taken for granted fallen out of use? I recently confronted a gathering of highly-gifted students with the provocative statement that they were probably the first generation in which even children and young people transgress the age-old prohibition of killing: children murder children, pupils murder teachers, children murder parents. We are often experiencing a trivialization of violence; the threshold of violence has become lower, particularly in schools. But violence against the self is also increasing, as in excessive drinking to the point of unconsciousness, and this at an increasingly earlier age.

Of course one may not express such criticism without self-criticism, remembering a remark of Karl Valentin: 'Children do not let themselves be educated; in any case they do what we do.' It is easy for the younger generation to point to defective examples in their parents' generation. If for adults the elbows become the most important part of the body, one need not be surprised at similar modes of behaviour among young people. All the big lies of some war-crazy politicians and the great frauds of certain managers, all the crimes of violence and meaningless wars, also work as negative examples.

However, we can no longer get ready-made ethical solutions from heaven or from a fundamentalist reading of the Bible for the countless unavoidable decisions required in individual and political life today – as moral theologians still did in the early modern period, for example in the question of whether interest was permissible. On the other hand we can also no longer – like the peoples of the twentieth century in questions of contraception or artificial fertilization – deduce solutions from an allegedly unchangeable universal human nature, the 'natural' law. Rather, today we must time and again seek new differentiated solutions 'on earth' for all the complicated problems and conflicts, and often work them out in the interplay of various specialists.

At any rate today a rational ethic can no longer presuppose a system of rigid, unchangeable norms handed down by one's forebears to be received passively. Rather, ethics today must deliberately start from an often impenetrable situation and a dynamic complex reality. And a way must be found which takes account both of the historical development of moral norms and their cultural differentiation. For norms without a concrete situation are hollow, but situations without norms are blind. In the face of a 'permissive society' in which all seems relative, where nothing is true and everything is to be allowed and anyone may do anything, the public discussion of human rights and fundamental values, of political and social, public and private morality, shows me that there is undeniably a need for reliable criteria, binding norms, abiding values, i.e. an ethical orientation which is not, as often traditional morality was, repressive, oppressive, but liberating, indeed life-affirming.

## An ethic for everyone

On 10 March 1989, a year of revolution in Europe, I gave a lecture at the University of Chicago, 'No World Peace without Religious Peace', and proposed putting the question of a common fundamental ethic of the religions on the agenda of the Parliament of the World's Religions planned for four years later to mark the centenary of the first Parliament of the World's Religions held on the occasion of the World Exposition in Chicago in 1893. My book *Projekt Weltethos* (1990) appeared as early as 1991 simultaneously in London and New York under the title *Global Responsibility: In Search of a New World Ethic*. At that time the word globalization was not on everyone's lips. On 27 February 1992 the Executive Director of the Council of the Parliament of the World's Religions came especially to Tübingen to persuade me to produce the draft of a declaration on a global ethic for the Parliament.

For me this was a tremendous challenge. I had the advantage that two decades earlier I had thought through the fundamental ethical problems as described above; otherwise I would have failed in this intellectually highly demanding task, which required me to change my plans for the next semester. I have never laboured for so many hours, days and months over so few pages of text. For me and all those who helped me this was a long process involving inter-religious consultations and many discussions and improvements. Finally, our work was presented to the delegates of the Parliament and published on 4 September 1993 as 'Initial Declaration toward a Global Ethic'. The considerations which guided me in the composition of this Declaration might be interesting. I had thoroughly studied the criticism of Nietzsche and others of the morality of Christianity, indeed religion generally, as a morality hostile to life. Therefore I wanted deliberately to develop a life-affirming ethic and not replace, but supplement, negative moral judgements by positive ethical imperatives throughout.

However, it would have been crazy of me to plan to reinvent the wheel of ethics. Rather, I wanted to call to mind the elementary ethical norms as they occur in the thousand-year-old spiritual heritage of humankind and as I had researched them. These norms were not to be fetters and chains that unnecessarily restrict or even stifle human life. Rather, they were to be helps and supports, waymarks, for maintaining direction on the ways of life, to enable people to be constantly rediscovering and realizing virtues, attitudes, a meaning in life. And this not just for religious people but for all people. Therefore the Declaration of the Parliament of the World's Religions explicitly states: 'We trust that our often millennia-old religious and ethical traditions provide an ethic which is convincing and practical for all women and men of good will, religious and non-religious' (Global Ethic Declaration, ch.I).

Of course, in working out the Declaration I saw myself confronted with thousands of questions, above all: what should apply for all human beings and each individual? Are there irrevocable criteria that even the leading forces in politics, business, science and the religions should observe? Can there really be a fundamental norm for human beings without exception?

A first thing was and is certain for me: we live in a world with a diversity of religions and cultures. One cannot appeal to one religion against all others. And secondly, we no longer live in the Middle Ages or the time of the Reformation. In view of the millions of non-religious people in the modern world, as a religious person one can no longer refer simply to religion for a common ethic. That brings up the main problem: on the presupposition of the plurality of religions and ideologies, can there be a fundamental norm, a fundamental criterion which is to apply to all men and women today?

## Humanity the basic criterion

On 17 December 2008 I received the Otto Hahn peace medal in Berlin. After the war the Nobel prize-winner Otto Hahn, who discovered the splitting of the atom (1938), had devoted himself resolutely to peace and opposed the equipping of the German army with nuclear weapons. The prize was awarded to me by the Mayor, Klaus Wowereit, particularly – and of course this delighted me – for 'exemplary commitment to humanity, tolerance and dialogue between the great world religions above all in the framework of the Global Ethic project'.

This was the occasion for me in my ceremonial speech to a predominantly secular public to correct the misunderstanding that a global ethic can be grounded only in the world religions, and to sketch out a philosophical basis for which I had already laid the foundation thirty years previously in my book *Does God Exist?* From there I could call for an alliance of believers and non-believers in the Global Ethic project.

Particularly in respect of humanity, I could therefore already formulate as a fundamental norm of an autonomous humane morality the following elementary distinction between good and evil:

- 'Good' is not simply, as traditionalists and integralists think, what applies always and everywhere: the 'good old', the tradition, has often proved itself to be misanthropic.
- But 'good' is also not simply, as revolutionaries and pseudo-revolutionaries always think, the new: the 'crazy new', the revolution, has often proved all too rarely to be philanthropic.
- No, put in a totally elementary way, good is what – whether old or new – helps human beings to be truly human.

How often I have been asked, especially after incomprehensible crimes or scandals: Why can human beings created by God be so evil? This is a question that one can also put easily to oneself on particular occasions. The most elementary answer is that human beings, who come from the animal kingdom, had to learn to control their drives rationally, drives towards food, sex and self-preservation, which correspond to the instinctive modes of behaviour in animals and relate to their fellow human beings. And even today all human beings from childhood onwards have not just to develop a fundamental trust. They must also learn to control, shape, sublimate, spiritualize their motivations, needs and interests – including those that are strongly shaped by higher spiritual stirrings.

Only in this way can young people shape their lives in a truly humane way. And this is a lifelong process which is not always successful and which with every individual is marked by setbacks and errors.

From that perspective 'evil' is what violates, harms and hinders humanity. Evil is especially what makes human beings sink to an inhuman level, so that they behave like evil animals, as beasts, bestially. Against this, over thousands of years criteria of the human have developed which we find in all the great traditions of humankind, both in religious people and in philosophers. What unites Immanuel Kant, Henry Dunant, Rosa Luxemburg, Thomas Mann, Albert Schweitzer, Hannah Arendt, Martin Luther King, Nelson Mandela and the man who from the beginning supported me more than anyone else in the Global Ethic project – the great musician Yehudi Menuhin? They were all advocates of humanity, advocates of true humanity, and the travelling exhibition of the Global Ethic Foundation presents them as such in image and word. As early as the 1980s Walter Jens and I had recognized the Nobel prize-winners for literature Heinrich Böll, Hermann Hesse and Thomas Mann in three double lectures as 'advocates of humanity'.

So humanity is the first fundamental principle of a common ethic of humankind, a global ethic, as that Declaration toward a Global Ethic of the 1993 Parliament of the World's Religions in Chicago defines and explains: 'Every human being must be treated humanely.' Is that perhaps a tautology or a commonplace? By no means, as one immediately notices if one reads the Declaration further and discovers how it spells out this principle of humanity: 'Every human being – whether man or woman, white or coloured, young or old, rich or poor – must be treated humanely and not inhumanely, indeed bestially.' As notorious representatives of inhumanity one need only mention Stalin, Hitler, Mao or Pol Pot.

Looked at in this way 'humanity', like 'art' or 'history', needs no more precise definition to be practised. 'Humanity' does not mean a particular image of human beings. Such images are always conceived from a specific perspective – Christian, Jewish or Muslim, socialist or liberal, biological or economic . . . images of human beings are often in conflict with one another. But 'humanity' here means a fundamental ethical state and standard that is expected of all human beings independently of their particular images.

This brings me to an extremely hopeful aspect of the idea of the Global Ethic that can also perform a mediating function in present-day discussion about ethical education and religious education. It would certainly delight many others as well as me if our church leaders finally understood that they can bring Christian values to bear effectively only in connection with universal human values and not in opposition to them. Instead of a strategy of confrontation and polarization a strategy of solidarity and understanding is needed. I dedicated my book *Christianity: Its Essence and History* (1994; ET 1995) in gratitude to four Christian personalities from the different churches who embodied this attitude in an exemplary way: Pope John XXIII, the Ecumenical Patriarch Athenagoras, the Archbishop of Canterbury Michael Ramsey and the first General Secretary of the World Council of Churches, Willem Visser't Hooft.

## A humanistic ethic and world religions meet

For all the immense differences, humanist ethics and the ethics of the world religions meet precisely at the point of an elementary humanity. Confucius, the Buddha, Moses, Jesus of Nazareth and – Muslims attach the utmost importance to this – the Prophet Muhammad are also, each in his own way, advocates of humanity. For me personally it has seemed clear since my six years as a pupil at the state humanist grammar school in Lucerne that I understand myself both as a Christian and as a humanist. I laid the foundations for this and illuminated it in every respect in my book *On Being a Christian* (1974; ET 1977).

The 'Declaration toward a Global Ethic' of the Parliament of the World's Religions is also a humanistic document, which even the non-religious can accept. Programmatically it states 'that every human being must be treated humanely! This means that every human being without distinction of age, sex, race, skin colour, physical or mental ability, language, religion, political view, or national or social origin possesses an inalienable and untouchable dignity, and everyone, the individual as well as the state, is therefore obliged to honour this dignity and protect it.' Human rights and human responsibilities have their foundation here.

So it is not a matter of an exaggerated individualistic ethic. The principle of humanity applies to the human individual, the individual being and his or her actions, but at the same time also to human institutions and structures. These are to serve human beings and to promote being human, the humanization of human society, not do it harm, but to work for the well-being of the whole.

The basic demand for humanity is defined more closely by the age-old Golden Rule, the principle of reciprocity, mutuality. It is proverbial and has been familiar to me since my youth: Do not do to another what you would not want to be done to you. But its fundamental and universal importance for human society first dawned on me in connection with a global ethic. It already appears five hundred years before Christ with the Chinese Confucius: 'What you do not want yourself, do not do to others.' It goes on to appear in similar formulations in all the great religions and ethical traditions of humankind. It has found a so-to-speak secular form in Immanuel Kant's imperative: 'Act in such a way that you use the humanity, both in your person and in the person of any others, always also as an end, and never merely as a means' (*Foundation of the Metaphysics of Morality*, BA 66f.). Or as the 'English Hippocrates', the doctor Thomas Sydenham, clearly formulated the Golden Rule in the seventeenth century for medical practice: 'No one has been treated by me otherwise than I would want to be treated if I had this illness.'

This Golden Rule of mutuality is the second fundamental principle of a common ethic of humankind. On every occasion I have also said to representatives of politics, business, culture and sport: this Golden Rule should apply not just between individuals but also between social and ethnic groups, nations and religions. But, I am often asked: how are these fundamental principles of an ethic of humanity, a global ethic, to be expressed in the form of concrete criteria?

## Pointers towards more humanity

In preparing the 'Declaration toward a Global Ethic' I long reflected on this and also discussed it in the framework of an interdisciplinary and inter-religious colloquium in the summer semester of 1992 at the University of Tübingen with other scholars: from what standpoint should one order the rest of the vast ethical material for this Declaration? One possibility would be to follow the classical virtues, the cardinal virtues of wisdom, boldness, moderation and justice, which are often *changed* for the theological virtues of faith, hope and love. But this seemed too individualistic. Another possibility was to follow particular problem fields such as sexual and bioethics, business, medicine and state ethics. But these are far too complex for global perspectives.

For me a lively conversation at supper following my seminar with scholars from the Hindu, Buddhist, Chinese, Muslim and Christian traditions resulted in the decision for a third possibility that I had already long considered. My brief questioning of the table produced a fundamental empirical consensus: there are four ethical imperatives which occur not only in the Ten Commandments of the Hebrew Bible, confirmed in the

New Testament and the Qur'an, but also in Patanjalil, the founder of Yoga, in the Buddhist canon and in the Chinese tradition: 'Do not murder, do not steal, do not lie, do not misuse sexuality.' The early history showed me that this agreement is no coincidence. All over this planet, as I have already emphasized, at a very early existential stage people were interested in protecting their life, their property, their honour, their sexual relations. The primal ethic lies at the heart of a global ethic.

It encourages me today that the Global Ethic Declaration of 1993 has not only not lost any of its topicality but on the contrary has gained tremendously in significance since the global financial and economic crisis which broke out in 2008/9 (and which I had demonstrably feared for more than ten years). For alongside the failure of the markets and the failure of the institutions comes a manifest failure of ethics. And so the crisis brings with it talk of a return of morality, of the need for an ethic in business, in politics, science and especially in scandal-ridden sport.

But it is not enough for philosophers to speak only of the categorical imperative and theologians only abstractly of the conscience, whereas politicians, business leaders, scientists and sports officials speak quite generally of the need for trust, a sense of responsibility and conscientiousness. We must speak concretely, boldly and clearly of ethical values and standards with a definite content. Of course we should not get bogged down in detailed discussions of ethics but reflect on those age-old norms of humanity which in our time were programmatically ignored by Fascism and Nazism, by state socialism and then by turbocapitalism and neo-imperialism. We urgently need an ethical foundation without which in the long term a society will not hold together, an ethical framework without which no new world order and no new global financial architecture can function.

Thus a culture of humanity must be promoted under four perspectives. I shall sketch out quite briefly what is spelt out at length in the 'Declaration toward a Global Ethic' (see www.weltethos.org on the Internet). Every individual and every institution has a fourfold responsibility:

- Commitment to a culture of non-violence and a respect for all life: respect life. According to an age-old directive: 'Do not kill' – do not torture, torment, violate.
- Commitment to a culture of solidarity and a just economic order: act justly and fairly. According to an age-old directive: 'Do not steal' – do not exploit, bribe, corrupt.

- Commitment to a culture of tolerance and a life in truthfulness: speak and act truthfully. According to an age-old directive: 'Do not lie' – do not deceive, forge, manipulate.
- Commitment to a culture of equal rights and partnership between men and women: respect and love one another. According to an age-old formulation: 'Do not commit immorality, do not abuse sexuality' – do not cheat, humiliate, dishonour.

These guidelines of the 'Declaration toward a Global Ethic' of the World Religions recurs with identical content but in UN language in the proposal by the InterAction Council of former heads of state and governments under the presidency of the former Chancellor Helmut Schmidt for a 1997 Universal Declaration of Human Responsibilities (see www.interactioncouncil.org on the Internet).

But to avoid any misunderstandings: ethical imperatives are not laws that some body must first decide on. They are given *a priori* and are aimed at voluntary commitment. But they could and should be confirmed by a body of world society.

Of course all these directives also apply to me personally. But at the end of this chapter the question arises: are they enough for me to go on my way with? Obviously not.

## Going my way

In particular my seven years of strict pre-conciliar Roman education have taught me not to allow myself to be intimidated even by church authorities and always to go my own way in life in critical solidarity with my church. I was and am grateful in all controversies to know that there are loyal companions at my side near and far. 'Going my way' – in my student days in Rome this was the title of a film starring the most popular American entertainer of the time, Bing Crosby. In it he played a young non-conformist curate who cheerfully and resolutely went his way against the resistance of his conservative pastor.

But my conflicts have not been resolved as harmlessly as they were in that film. Even with much trust and joy in life, even with tried values and norms of life, it is by no means easy to find one's own way, to meet the decisions which arise time and again and to keep saying, 'Be who you are.' Don't let yourself be governed by others, define your own role. Don't go round in circles, don't be egocentric. Don't yield. Go forward. 'Avanti, Savoia!' (the slogan of the Italian freedom fighters in the nineteenth century) was written for me by the great Karl Barth in his own hand on a personal card accompanying his momentous letter on my dissertation on 'Justification'.

For the younger generation today some decisions – choice of job, partner, place to live – are apparently easier to make. Personal free space has grown and in the media age information of all kinds is much easier to get. On the other hand, the abundance of information by no means diminishes the lack of orientation, but rather sharpens it. We are not lacking in knowledge of what is at our disposal, but in orientation.

However, many decisions in life can be implemented only in the face of resistance. You bang your head against the wall usually at the cost of your head. But the turncoat is hardly an upright character. I have attempted wherever possible to find a way between dogmatic stubbornness and assimilative weakness that combines constancy with a capacity to adapt.

There are critical situations that require of people a difficult, momentous decision in life. People used to speak of 'Hercules at the crossroads': according to the ancient saga the young hero retreated into a lonely area to consider what course he should take. Two very different female forms met him, first 'Vice', who showed him prospects of all the pleasures and delights of the world. Then 'Virtue', who held a more modest way in prospect on which he could become a master in all that is good and great. Both women spoke to him at length and showed their advantages – and the weaknesses of their rival. Hercules had the choice between the easy way of enjoying life and the laborious way of virtue. He chose virtue as his way.

Many people today, particularly young people, often face an even more fundamental choice. Not only between 'vice' and 'virtue' but also between the meaning and the meaninglessness of life. And with meaning comes the question: what is the meaning of life, my life? The next chapter is devoted to this.

# Chapter 4

# Meaning in Life

*We can, if we understand our cause (which must be presupposed here), compel the individual or at least help him to give an account of the ultimate meaning of his own actions. That does not seem to me to be so very little, even for purely personal life.*

The sociologist and economist Max Weber, 'Wissenschaft als Beruf',
lecture to students of Munich University in winter 1918/19
(*Gesammelte Aufsätze zur Wissenschaftslehre*, p. 608)

We are on the way of life with trust in life and joy in life – but what is the meaning of life?

It is not always simple, even for theologians, to go one's way. I will never forget driving back from Munich to Tübingen in my VW on 3 May 1962, lonely and depressed as I was. 'It would be best if you ran into a tree,' I thought to myself. 'What more can you expect from theology if even the theologian who could have understood you the best doesn't understand?' I was 34 years old and for two years – contrary to my original career plan – had been Professor of Fundamental Theology in the University of Tübingen. I had developed my inaugural lecture on the theology of the Second Vatican Council, which was to begin in October 1962, into a book on the 'structures of the church'. However, this was fundamentally different from traditional Catholic dogmatics because of its thorough biblical foundation and exact historical treatment throughout of the history of the churches, councils and papacy. With this book before us in manuscript form, I had just had a vigorous dispute about the Vatican I (1870) definition of primacy and infallibility with the leading German Catholic theologian, the Jesuit Karl Rahner, whom I revered. I was dependent on his positive verdict both for publication by the Catholic Herder Verlag and for the church's permission to print (*imprimatur*) that I needed. In the first volume of my memoirs, *My Struggle for Freedom*, I have described in detail how the dispute turned out and was finally settled so that the book could meet its deadline and appear before the beginning of the Council. In those dark hours I had no inkling that things were to get even worse for me, and in some respects for Rahner, after the Council. The question of the meaning of my theological career, indeed of my life generally, posed itself to me there with far greater urgency than in my student days.

## What are we on earth for?

It can break in on any person at any time: the question of meaning. So wouldn't it be better deliberately to orientate oneself in life before meeting a great crisis? At any rate, isn't that better than theoretically working one's way through the more or less brilliant and sometimes tedious discussions of philosophers and men of letters of the concepts 'life, meaning, meaning of life'?

Of course I don't think it completely meaningless to discuss the question disputed since the Middle Ages of whether our concepts are only names (*nomina*) for individual phenomena in reality, as the 'nominalist' tendency asserted, or whether our universal concepts are grounded in the real world, as the intellectual trend of 'realists' assumed. Put in today's terms: does the meaning lie in the things themselves or only in our heads, our thoughts? Do things have an inherent, indwelling meaning, or do we construct this meaning ourselves and attribute our linguistic fictions to things? One can reflect and speculate a great deal on whether there are several meanings or only one meaning, a meaning for specific spheres of reality or phases of life or a meaning for the whole of human life, the whole of reality. I shall come back to some of this.

But rather than going on at length about the theoretical meaning of the question of meaning, it seems to me more important that we should be clear that for centuries human beings in general did not raise the question of the meaning of life in this way at all. Both for the people of the Hebrew Bible and those of the New Testament and still even of the Middle Ages the question of the meaning of life was irrelevant. Why? Because they began from the assumption that this question has been answered once and for all. It was certain that the meaning of life was God and the keeping of his commandments. And the faith of the individual was supported by the whole community of believers. So why seek the special meaning of the individual human life?

To that degree this is a typically modern question. The first person to formulate the question of the meaning of life as the first question of his catechism was that jurist, humanist and theologian, preacher, writer and church leader who made Protestantism significant for the world through his piety, his clear theological synthesis and his sense of the organization and international relations of the church, the Franco-Swiss Reformer Jean Calvin, who is usually viewed in Germany in negative terms. Whereas Martin Luther concentrated on the problems of law and gospel, Calvin began his Geneva Catechism of 1542 with the fundamental question: 'What is the main purpose of human life – *la principale fin de la vie humaine?*' He gave the succinct answer: '*C'est de connaître Dieu* – to know God.' As to the second question, Why? – 'Because he has created us and put us in the world to be glorified in us.' So the glory of God is the meaning and purpose of human life.

The Catholic Catechism first took up the question in the seventeenth century. And the standard answer, which has remained in my memory since my childhood days, is: 'What are we on earth for? To know God, to love him, to serve him and one day to come to heaven (or attain eternal life).'

Only the Dutch Catechism of 1948 mentions happiness on earth: 'to be happy here and in the world to come'. And only after the Second Vatican Council did the *New Catechism: Proclamation of Faith for Adults*, which appeared in the Netherlands in 1966, spread quickly all over the world to be promptly persecuted by the Roman Inquisition, treat the question of the meaning of life in all its dimensions. Only here is there a mention of a longing for happiness in things great and small, of a longing to be good, but also of our 'wounding through illness, disappointment, guilt and need'. But I don't want to anticipate by covering up the question of meaning with the question of God. I want to raise it directly in today's secular context.

## The question of meaning in science and business

After the Reformation and the end of the Wars of Religion the Enlightenment began to have its effect. I shall go into that later. Here are just some key words. In the seventeenth century it had begun in England with the 'Freethinkers', who wanted to be free of religious dogmas, and in the eighteenth century in France took a turn towards atheism with the '*libres penseurs*' and the encyclopaedists, on the one hand among the middle class under the influence of materialist natural science and on the other among the working class under the influence of Karl Marx and dialectical materialism.

The sociologist Max Weber, one of the great thinkers of the early twentieth century, stated in his impressive lecture on 'science as a profession' to students of Munich University in the difficult winter semester of 1918/19:

> It is the destiny of our time with its distinctive rationalization and intellectualization, above all demystification of the world, that in particular the ultimate and most sublime values have retreated from the public eye, either into the realm of mystical life behind the world or into the brotherliness of direct relations of individuals to one another.
>
> (*Wissenschaftslehre*, Tübingen ³1968, p. 612)

So it is not surprising that people in our 'demystified' world find difficulty with all the philosophies and theologies, world-views and religions that offer themselves as authorities that give meaning. Many are made uncertain because in this situation their own religious (or non-religious) standpoint seems to be radically relativized. In such a situation, Max Weber thinks, the professor should not make himself a prophet, demagogue and messiah who imposes or forces a standpoint on his hearers. Rather, 'in intellectual honesty' he should be concerned to help his hearers to 'clarity'. He should 'compel the individual, or at least help him, to give an account of himself about the ultimate meaning of his own action' in order to decide between 'the last possible standpoints in life' (pp.607f.).

As we saw, a basic decision on life already takes place in fundamental trust or mistrust, in yes or no to the meaning and value of reality generally. But in the sciences too, contrary to what Max Weber assumed at the time, it is not just a matter of 'value-free objectivity', which the university teacher has to observe everywhere. Even in the natural sciences and in economics, interests play a large role; even there the question of meaning must be raised time and again. The global economic crisis shows us the danger of an economy and technology without meaning. Economists, bank managers, analysts and rating agencies, journalists and philosophers have disseminated a faith in the precise 'scientific' predictability of the economy and the possibility of steering it completely untroubled by the irrational factors, the dangers and the side-effects at work everywhere. But it has now been proved that no mathematical extrapolations and economic-sociological models can predict economic developments with certainty, indeed that all calculations rest on certain assumptions that in fact are usually excessively optimistic and credulous about progress.

In the United States, too, the voices critical of such science are growing. The Victorian historian Thomas Carlyle had already called economics 'the dismal science', and the phrase was taken up in 2008 by the Harvard economist Stephen Marglin in a book with the subtitle 'How Thinking like an Economist Undermines Community'. That may be an exaggeration, if it is meant to refer to all economic thinking. But in Europe the global economic crisis is spurring on those economists who do not share the American credulity in mathematics and who think less in numbers and statistics and therefore more in 'orders', in values and overall social connections. For them the meaning of the market economy is a balance between individual market freedom and social justice; it is a free order that does justice to men and women, an ethically founded ecological-social market economy.

So the question of the meaning of individual social life must be seen in connection with the meaning of society, nature and humankind. But now, after these reflections on the question of meaning in science and economics, I want to turn to the same question of meaning in the individual human life, my life.

## The individual's question of meaning

My life has not been harmonious, without friction and free of conflict. No life avoids crises. The word 'crisis' comes from the Greek *krinein* (= separate, distinguish), and means the point at which a difficult development comes to a head. Like other key words that are important to me, such as trust and civil courage, remarkably the key word 'crisis' has been neglected for a long time in theological dictionaries and handbooks. It is particularly significant for our situation, where one can speak of an accumulation, a piling up, of crises, indeed a fundamental crisis.

Any one of us can encounter a crisis in our lives, a crisis of sickness, a crisis of faith, a real life crisis. We all have to cope with this as best we can. There is risk in every decision in life. Like the development of the economy, the development of a human life cannot be calculated in advance and taken in hand. At any rate one should factor in the risk as far as possible and alongside the 'best case scenario' always take into consideration the 'worst case scenario'.

In some circumstances decisions in life can be reversed: one can study economics instead of theology or vice versa. One can also look for a completely new field of activity. But most of the decisions in life are irreversible: 'Make your bed and lie on it.' One has trained for this profession and not that. It makes little sense to be gloomy all through life about a wrong choice of profession (I'm thinking of a successful painter and decorator, who saw himself called to be an artist, or a lawyer, or a priest). If one seriously cannot and does not want to change the decision, one does better to stand by the choice made and attempt to make the best of it.

We all keep facing decisions about religion. I know some people brought up without religion who stay without religion and others who set out in search of religion because they have none. I know those who grew up in different religions or confessions and persisted in their childhood faith and others who were concerned to have an enlightened faith. I know of many Catholics who parted company with their church (again particularly in most recent times) but also quite a few who despite dissatisfaction with the church hierarchy are involved in a community, and I know of those – Catholics, Protestants or Orthodox – who have changed their faith community. It is praiseworthy that in today's secular society no church authority can compel people to believe. Everyone can choose freely and in crises of faith can make a new choice or even choose no religion at all.

And we must maintain that one can also have a supportive ethic for life without religion. But whether the ethic has a religious foundation or is purely human, looking back on my own life I can confirm sociological investigations that assert that ethically orientated people find it easier to arrive at a happy stocktaking of life than so-called hedonists. What is true here is that enjoyment of life and real meaning in life are two different things.

## Loss of meaning

I can understand that people in particularly distressful situations can question everything: What is it all for? What gives my life a direction, a meaning? However, these are questions which one tunes out in everyday activities, where simply to get by is a full-time occupation.

No one and nothing can compel someone to ask about a meaning in life. One can simply close oneself to this question. Thus for example the professor of education Hartmut von Hentig (born 1925), whom I esteem highly, explained to me that he does not know the purpose of his life and does not need to: 'My life is its own end,' he once remarked (*Christ in der Gegenwart* 36, 1999).

With all due respect, isn't this too shallow an answer? Should I tell all the countless people who have encountered a crisis of meaning which they cannot get over and who despair of life that they should see their purpose in life itself? That sort of thing is of course easier to say when as a professor, looking back on a long life, one may think that in all the successes and failures one 'has had a good life', and in some respects I could also say that of myself. And of course no power in the world can 'prescribe' such meaning. But what about the distress of those who have not had a good life and those who are also thinking of a good death? Doesn't one have to reflect more deeply over this, particularly if with Hentig one can see in the various tasks more the 'means of life' than the 'purpose of life'?

How does one look for a deeper meaning, a meaning in life, when a crisis of meaning is felt world-wide? Unfortunately, I have often found that in society, in parties and in groups, in newspapers and magazines, people prefer to joke about such questions; the attitude is cool, distanced, ironic . . . But I have also experienced that if a question is put to me explicitly or someone comes up against a limit situation, answers to such questions can prove highly emotional: Yes, what is it all about? Why, what is it all for? I don't know and probably can't know.

Of course there are also cynics today, even among young people, who quickly come up with statements such as: everything in politics, economics and society is corrupt. But sometimes I want to retort: Really? Really everything? Or does this reality look as it does to you only because you yourself look at it like that? Don't I see a loving relationship or a business relationship in one way when it's going well and in another when it's in crisis? And don't people experience a business failure or a divorce differently if they are themselves concerned and not reading about it with amusement in the tabloids?

Be this as it may, I think it advisable that the question of the meaning of our lives should have been raised before we suffer an existential shock, some stroke of fate that we can hardly be spared in the long run, a loss of meaning which can easily result in depression, aggression or addiction.

I have in view the loss of meaning for those many people whose whole religious or political system of meaning, whose 'world-view', has collapsed for some reason. I am thinking of the loss of meaning for a long-serving employee of a firm or a bank official who has suddenly been made redundant and now proves to be completely superfluous. But I am also thinking of businessmen who in the global economic crisis have to lose firms built up over decades, or house owners who have to give up their homes. I am thinking of the loss of meaning for people in mid-life when all that is attainable has been attained and the many things not achieved (dream job, dream property, dream partner) have become unachievable. I am thinking of the loss of meaning for husbands or wives who have lost their irreplaceable partner or their most deeply beloved child, or those paralysed by a traffic accident or unexpectedly struck with cancer. I am thinking of the loss of meaning for countless older people whose senses and organs are becoming noticeably weaker and who fear dementia in old age. And I am thinking of young people who want to know what kind of purpose their lives have in the present time of crisis and struggle to interpret and make sense of the world.

But I don't want to go on speaking of negative cases that oppress and depress us. Rather, without undue dramatization, I want quietly to offer reflections on the various possibilities which individuals today have or use to give meaning or new meaning to their lives. Perhaps a deeper connection will appear in our lives, a connection which is there, but which may have been hidden by more superficial matters.

## Working to live

So what is the meaning of life? Anyone who like me was born in 1928, the year before the great stock market crash, and grew up in the time of Nazism, Communism and the Second World War, knows that for many of the older generation answering this question for a long time presented few difficulties. Those who have to toil for survival – and such people today form the majority in many countries of Asia or Africa – have an immediate meaning in life in their short-term goals of getting food, clothing, somewhere to live. They don't normally suffer crises of meaning.

In the period after the Second World War, work understandably stood right at the centre of human life, first for survival, then increasingly for a better life. In this working society leisure time took second place. Work brought not only security in life and a rising standard of living. Work was the basis for a new ethic, an ethic of achievement and success. Indeed work guaranteed virtually a new meaning in life: 'I want to achieve something for myself and my family', a step up the social ladder and prosperity.

For me personally little has changed in this respect. Or should there be a meaning in life without work? A meaning in life by doing nothing, a meaning in life through leisure, contentment, living life to the full or through renouncing achievements as far as possible, through resignation and fatalism, through dropping out or protesting? The temptation to drop out may sometimes even seem appealing to managers and politicians, indeed scholars, when too much pressure is put on them. But I don't necessarily find the way to myself like this; rather I find my own shallowness, not the meaning of my life. So is there meaning in work?

I am regarded as an indefatigable worker. And in fact I am one of those lucky ones who can say that their work is their hobby. But really it isn't a hobby for me, far less a job, but rather a calling. I know that I am in the service of great tasks that demand all my strength. I work even in the 'holidays'. That means that I read, study, write and am content with that – especially when I can do it, say, interspersed with swimming and listening to classical music, in the beautiful landscape and fresh air of my homeland.

But I am not a 'workaholic' who sees nothing but his work. I am not a 'working animal' that does its work mechanically, impulsively, meaninglessly, even for the sake of the money. No, I am utterly involved in the cause, but I am always completely myself. I work passionately but not doggedly. I know that I am one with those around me, who often work as intensely as I do. But of course for me, too, a question arises as I grow older.

## Living to work?

I am getting older, everyone is getting older. The meaning of life can change, not precisely with the seasons, but with the time of life. I was at the Second Vatican Council (1962–5) with Karl Rahner and Joseph Ratzinger. Despite all my personal admiration for him, Ratzinger and I are still fundamentally separated in our assessment of the cultural revolution of the 1968ers and their demands for emancipation, enlightenment, reform, transparency and tolerance. The student revolts of 1968 from Berkeley, California and Ann Arbor, Michigan through Paris and Frankfurt to Berlin and Tübingen constantly shook the revived society of work and achievement, indeed the whole 'sound world' of normal citizens, religious and secular. For it was no longer work, no longer achievement, income, career, social prestige that stood in the centre of interest of the then rising younger generation, the students and their sympathizers in the media and political parties, but rather utopia, social critique and action, hostility to convention, lack of compulsion, autonomy and self-realization. These were the new slogans in which I discovered – unlike Joseph Ratzinger – much that was true and good, despite all my criticism.

Here evidently a new attitude to life was emerging. It was now no longer about sheer survival and also no longer about middle-class better living, but time and again about a new experience. 'Work, work' – is this really the meaning of life? At least the question seemed to me to be justified. A counterpoint was due: meaning in life doesn't come only through work. Human life is more than work. Work is an important element but not the basis of life. Our human activity embraces not only work but all our personal and family events, all social, political and cultural action; it embraces not only business, *negotium*, but also *otium*, leisure. This is not to be identified with idleness, inertia, laziness; leisure embraces relaxation, free time, play, sport, music, rest.

I also had to tell myself that the controversies in theology, church and society sometimes made the utmost demands on me – often engaged as I was in 'single combat'. But if in all the work I no longer found rest, if I made work, even gainful work, an end in itself, if I became chronically stretched or over-stretched, if I went from deadline to deadline and yet stood still, if hyperactivity led to an unpleasant feeling, despondency, a feeling of exhaustion, finally a burn-out – then I would be experiencing in modern form what Paul and Luther called 'the curse of the law'. And countless people do sigh under the 'law of work'. They suffer from the pressure to achieve, to get on, the pressure to succeed, to work. So it is understandable that the question arises: is there no liberation from this compulsion?

## Experiencing life

In the last decades of the twentieth century there developed in the secularized countries what sociologists such as Gerhard Schulze have analysed as an 'experience society'. This is a society in which it is no longer work but the continually new experience, the event, that stands at the centre. Here experience has become an end in itself, even in the form of religious 'happenings' (*Die Erlebnisgesellschaft: Kultursoziologie der Gegenwart*, 1992).

I am no exception to this. There is so much that we do not need but would love to have. From a new wardrobe to a new car, the value of the experience is often more important than the actual value. The meaning of life is not so much work as the search for the beautiful experience and, as people today say, the 'aestheticizing' of everyday life. Everything is to be more pleasing, more beautiful, more enjoyable. And 'what gives pleasure must be allowed!'

Like many of my contemporaries I find it problematical that in our society, as well as work, experience has become a dominating sphere of daily life. What is on offer is becoming more and more sophisticated, and we, the purchasers, are more and more demanding. We have become used to having new things all the time. Today's grandiose advertising industry, with a turnover of billions, shows us happy, mostly young faces every day. But everyone – despite their longing to remain young and the achievements of the cosmetic and fitness industry – is growing older and will eventually be old. Today's orientation on experience should not become leisure-time stress; pleasure in life should not result in frustration in life.

I have nothing against experiences. My memoirs indicate that I have had untold numbers of experiences, pleasant and unpleasant, and my life has been rich in encounters with people from different regions of the world and different ways of life, extraordinary events and travels, success and joys, and sometimes, too, in suffering and defeats.

For all my experience I have not become a playboy, a 'bon vivant' or a hedonist. These types are concerned only with pleasure and sensual enjoyment and achieve no lasting happiness. So I ask myself whether 'Experience your life!' is really the meaning of life. Of course many people endure very boring work on the assembly line or in the office simply to be able to afford better experiences. And I have often noticed that so many conversations, even in so-called 'exalted circles', are focused on leisure time, football, health, television, holidays, travel, etc. That's all very well, but is it enough to make people more content? What demonstrates better than the present-day society of abundance that even today no abundance in the world is capable of satisfying the human hunger for experience?

## A fulfilled life?

Research into satisfaction has given me two important answers to the question why human beings can be satisfied only temporarily. First, a good experience, of whatever kind, can be planned only to a certain extent; it cannot be created. I have also experienced that. However well something is planned it can end in disappointment, and the second visit to the same holiday destination is no longer the great experience it was the first time.

And secondly, new and better offers keep overtrumping the earlier ones. They make the old ones boring and so prompt new experiences. If this were not the case, our economy, which is built on tempting offers, wouldn't function at all. So even if we experience a moment of fulfilment, we soon come up with the question, 'What next?'

It is indeed a paradox: the more people get accustomed to the quest for satisfaction, the less it presents itself. It was not I, as a theologian, it was the sociologist Gerhard Schulze, whom I have already mentioned, who remarked in reference to our experience society: 'Weekends and holidays, but also partner relationships, professions and other areas of life come under a pressure of expectation which produces disappointment. The more unconditionally experiences are made *the* meaning of life, the greater the anxiety about missing out on experiences . . .'

This is also my conviction: like work, indefatigably arduous work, so too experiences, constantly new experiences, are not enough in the long run to guarantee fulfilment in the long term to normal human life in present-day living conditions. But behind all the work and experience lies the existential question: live for what?

We men and woman are paradoxically pensioned off earlier and earlier, but at the same time remain capable of work and also satisfaction longer, and now even more seek a fulfilled life. Voluntary work calls for time, work, energy, but gives joy and satisfaction and also keeps us from tiring of life in the old age that many of us now reach. All work and experience in a job, leisure and retirement ultimately have a meaning only if human life itself has a meaning. For me the central point is therefore: how does human life as such gain for me an abiding meaning which can support me through the various phases and ages of life? Are there still abiding values in life?

## Fulfilling oneself?

No one can any longer overlook the fact that much of what used to give meaning to work and experience is in crisis, because not only is the economic-financial basis in danger, but also the value basis of our society has been eroded. Of course much is only a change of values and not a loss of values. But since some previous systems of meaning and authority in church and society have largely lost their power, it must be said that morality, which used to teach children the difference between good and evil, human and inhuman, has often become quite random. For example, the Ten Commandments have largely been forgotten. Children, treated as partners, can become little tyrants. We adults give a bad example with our attitude of 'anything goes'. In politics the naked will to power is all too often praised as a positive characteristic of politicians. In the financial and real economy, greed for profit, megalomania and corruption are spreading to an unprecedented degree. In some media a decadent exhibitionism is being propagated and sexual perversion is regarded as a completely normal form of entertainment.

I don't want to bewail the situation, or become bitter in my moralizing. But I am not the only one who says that especially with the younger generation, in such a situation it has become harder to argue for a truly good life and to call for closer ties and a long-term commitment and responsibility. Good advice does not come cheap, nor does the advice of many psychologists and psychotherapists who are also in search of meaning.

Their advice is often along these lines: in view of all the scientific, political and religious relativizations and revolutions and in view of the vacuum of meaning which is becoming more evident, you must find the meaning in yourself: 'Work on yourself, exhaust your potential, develop your own goals, your morality, discover your meaning in life. Define what you think is meaningful and determine the principles by which you want to live . . .'

So should I too advise, 'Fulfil yourself'? Is this the meaning of our life? I ask in turn: Does self-fulfilment really give an ultimate meaning in life, which provides a direction to life? Does it give what is important, in particular to psychologists and psychotherapists: personal identity and integrity, a feeling of coherence and stability, to enable one to survive serious crises?

## Isn't too much asked of the self?

I am certainly the last person to say anything against self-fulfilment. For all too long in the Christian tradition self-fulfilment has been denounced as an addiction to the self. Instead self-surrender, asceticism for the sake of asceticism and creeping to the cross have been required. I have always criticized these tendencies and have also emphasized that trust in life and trust in the self are the cornerstones of a healthy personality.

So I regard it as a special dispensation that through a stable family life and a humane homeland, a good education and training, I have developed a strong self-awareness of the kind that is now being expressly called for in the education of children. Without inner strength, psychological stability and the strength to resist (resilience) I wouldn't have been able to survive unscathed all the struggles for 'disputed truth', during which I was hurt many times. Often the arguments that I presented were interpreted by my opponents as arrogance, my well-founded 'inquiries' as presumption, my critical positions as a heightened ego and my healthy self-confidence as a lack of humility. I have been given many proud warnings to be humble.

But humility has nothing to do with moral cowardice or servility. Humility doesn't mean immediately getting on one's knees if objections come from above. Humility is personal modesty, but not remorse and self-surrender. Humility presupposes courage, and courage means not being afraid even of public conflicts or of often unavoidable hurts to oneself and others. I am convinced that not only the state but also the church needs people with self-respect and a healthy culture of disputes. It is well known that the apostle Paul and some of the saints in the course of church history were not squeamish when they attacked abuses and defended themselves against their superiors, even against Peter. Their haloes were added afterwards. They too showed envy and a failure to understand, but they never lost their self-confidence.

However, I have to concede that I often find it difficult to lie down in the face of the situations and abuses in the church and theology. Some of my sharp words may have proved polarizing. Some of my witty points perhaps seemed malicious. But I have always avoided personal defamation. Even if people have denied me a Catholic disposition, put my faith in Christ in doubt, I have never given like for like. I could compile an attractive little dictionary of taunts if I wanted to list all the coarse, crude, insulting names and attributes which have been pinned on me verbally, in letters or publicly – often by very pious people who promised to pray for me. So it is pointless to ask me to be more gracious and sensitive to church dignitaries who often over-react.

Being self-confident does not mean being egocentric; we all have our defects and need to remain inwardly modest, allowing ourselves to be questioned and then listening to justified criticism. But we should also fight, though not for ourselves alone. My effort was also to support others, those who have no voice or find no hearing. And I have committed myself to a great cause, which for me was and is the renewal of the Catholic Church, reunion of the separated Christian churches and finally dialogue between the religions and civilizations on the basis of a common ethic of humankind. So in this sense there is also self-fulfilment.

But psychologists and psychotherapists have recently warned against a 'trap of self-fulfilment'. Some marriages fail, some human relations break up. And when does this trap snap shut? The moment when self-realization is detached from self-responsibility, shared responsibility, responsibility for the world. Here I am thinking not only of certain war-loving politicians, avaricious managers, power-hungry trade union functionaries, scholars in search of glory, unscrupulous physicians and hypocritical clerics. I am thinking of our quite ordinary everyday life and an egotistic self-fulfilment wrongly understood, which can manifest itself in each and every one of us in the most different forms and shapes.

Self-determination, self-experience, self-discovery, self-development, self-fulfilment are utterly to be affirmed – as long as they do not lead to narcissism, pre-occupation with the self and lack of consideration. Often it is the little things that get on our nerves today. I am not the only one who gets annoyed about inconsiderate people in public who in buses, trains, planes, on streets and in squares cause disturbances with their mobile telephones, their shouting and crude behaviour, often just to show off, taking liberties for themselves which deny others their freedom. Psychiatrists report that there are increasingly blind parents who interpret the bad behaviour of their children as an expression of above-average intelligence.

But in order to lead a successful life don't children need an ethical education alongside their psychological training for successful self-fulfilment, an education that today would have to build on the principle of humanity and the Golden Rule of mutuality, on reverence for life, solidarity, truthfulness and partnership? It seems to me that only on such an ethical foundation will even the basic rules of positive education really function; the parents need to state clear rules, set limits and act consistently.

But it is also the case with adults that self-assertion sometimes calls for overcoming the self. An inner spiritual void – which is possible even in a dedicated group or clique – can be filled only through values in life and meaning in life. But I find meaning in life – and here I come back to the question with which we started – not in my isolated self but only in the midst of human relationships. That means that my self finds my meaning in life only if it is open to a you, an us: to a beloved person, to the family, colleagues, circle of friends, fellow human beings who live with me and on whom I am always dependent. I find meaning in life only when I transcend myself, rise to embrace a person, a community or a cause in whose service I put myself. But it would be wrong here to think only of the great and noble and forget trivial everyday tasks.

## The 'lesser' meaning

From the beginning I have emphasized that the questionability of human life is by no means done away with by my fundamental trust in reality. This applies to the world as a whole. So when I am travelling by plane I often think how proudly some cities, for example in the United States, present themselves to a bird's-eye view with their skylines in the sunlight, but what immense economic, social, political, cultural concerns oppress them. And how beautiful our whole blue planet is from the perspective of the space traveller, but what natural catastrophes, plagues, conflicts and wars keep threatening the inhabitants of the various regions of the earth.

However, even my little world is not whole, but often threatened. My health, though robust, is constantly put in danger; my professional career is never immune from a fiasco. A certain fragility, questionability, finitude, indeed a meaninglessness threatening time and again is characteristic of all human life. It follows from this that the decision to trust in life that I once made in principle has to be constantly renewed in changing situations.

So what is the 'meaning', the 'purpose' of life? I fully understand that many people today content themselves with a 'lesser meaning' in life. They accept one of the many offers of meaning in the various partial spheres of human life: they find meaning in culture, art, music, or through necessity in therapy and the psychological aids to life. All this should not be belittled.

But it seems to me that despite all the partial experiences of meaning there remains an insatiable desire for comprehensive meaning, though this is often concealed, suppressed, stifled, submerged or 'put to rest'. There is the question of the meaning of the whole that has not yet been settled: the whole of our living and dying, the whole of our world, the question of the wider spiritual context, the 'larger' meaning. It is not surprising that in psychotherapy Viktor E. Frankl's logotherapy found such attention alongside Freud, Adler and Jung. He wanted psychotherapists to ask spiritual questions and especially the question of meaning.

## The 'greater' meaning

However, quite a number of people dispute the 'greater' meaning. Here I return to the dispute between 'realists' and 'nominalists' that I mentioned earlier. In the present-day discussion I stand at a distance from two tendencies of thought, both of which have a kernel of truth, but seem to me to be insufficient as a fundamental answer to the great question of meaning. I do not want to be either a 'naturalist' or a 'constructivist' in respect of my life.

I am left dissatisfied on the one hand by that scientific naturalism which is disseminated not just among natural scientists. For the naturalists, as a human being I am simply part of nature, a product of evolution. It is true that with such naturalists I share reverence for nature, solidarity of human beings with nature. And I unconditionally respect the recognized results of science, especially the theory of evolution; it may not be ignored or even dismissed for religious and ideological reasons.

Nevertheless, I cannot be satisfied with an understanding of human beings according to which I am simply there and otherwise nothing, having a particular biological structure, needs and interests, but without deeper meaning and value. As a being endowed with the spirit, I ask myself, am I not qualitatively more than the animal, which can raise no question about value and meaning? Am I in fact subject to the same becoming and dying? Bertolt Brecht put forward this view, summed up in his four-strophe poem 'Against Temptation'. Years ago in my book *Eternal Life?* I indulged in a respectful rewriting of this poem, without betraying its seriousness and dignity. In this way an alternative becomes clear which has at least as many reasons in favour of it. I quote 'Against Temptation' with my rewriting in the right-hand column:

| | |
|---|---|
| Do not be misled! | Do not be misled! |
| There is no return. | There is a return. |
| Day goes out at the door; | Day goes out at the door; |
| You might feel the night wind: | You might feel the night wind: |
| There is no tomorrow. | There is a tomorrow. |
| | |
| Do not be deceived! | Do not be deceived! |
| Life is very short. | Life is very short. |
| Quaff it in quick gulps! | Do not quaff it in quick gulps! |
| It will not suffice for you | It will not suffice for you |
| When you have to leave it. | When you have to leave it. |

| | |
|---|---|
| Do not be put off! | Do not be put off! |
| You have not too much time! | You have not too much time! |
| Leave decay to the redeemed! | Does decay seize the redeemed? |
| Life is the greatest thing: | Life is the greatest thing: |
| Nothing more remains. | There is still more to come. |
| | |
| Do not be misled | Do not be misled |
| To drudgery and wasting disease! | To drudgery and wasting disease! |
| What fear can still touch you? | What fear can still touch you? |
| You die like all the animals | You do not die like the animals |
| And nothing comes after. | There is not nothing after. |
| (*Gesammelte Werke*, Vol. II, p. 527) | (*Eternal Life?*, pp. 42–3) |

So there is a distance from a pure naturalism. But I am also left unsatisfied with an idealistic, materialistic or structuralistic constructivism that regards meaning and value in life merely as human constructions. For such constructivists, as a human being I am simply whitewashing reality and my existence with a conceptual or linguistic construct.

Now like such constructivists, I affirm human freedom, creative power and autonomy. Nevertheless I find it problematic when the individual or human society is to appear as the creator of systems of meaning, indeed of meaning itself, and no innate meaning is presupposed in reality. I find it problematic if I have to create my values myself, in the scheme of my existence and morality materialistically following Feuerbach and Freud, or existentialistically following Sartre, or structuralistically following de Saussure and the semiologists: meaning is merely a creation of human language.

Should I really make myself my own God and creator, as Friedrich Nietzsche expects of us human beings, after the 'madman' has proclaimed the 'death of God'? Here I see myself warned by Nietzsche himself when he finally sees the goal of life merely in the eternal recurrence of the same: an eternal 'life', which means suffering, passing away and coming into being and only in this way is eternal:

> The world is deep,
> Deeper than day can comprehend.
> Deep is its woe,
> Joy – deeper than heart's agony:
> Woe says: Fade! Go!

> But all joy wants eternity,
> Wants deep, deep, deep eternity.
> (*Thus spoke Zarathustra*, III,
> The other dance song, 3)

So should I believe in an infinite turning in a circle, which nature's cycle of coming into being and passing away seems to anticipate? This is the old myth of the Eternal Return, which Nietzsche takes up again, but cannot verify in any way. Certainly, in nature there are indisputably periodic courses such as movements of the stars, seasons, day and night. But the specific details are not repeated; on the contrary, from the atomic nuclei to the stars nature undergoes a history. Even stars can die. There is an irreversibility of becoming, but happily on the other side also authentic newness.

So for me the great question remains whether at least the history of humankind is not orientated on something that ultimately constitutes the fulfilment of human life. I do not by any means want to dispense with the question of an all-embracing, definitive, 'greater' meaning of life, the meaning of the whole. For what is the ultimate fate of the hundreds of millions of people who in the slums of London, New York, Mumbai, in the barrios of Colombia or the favelas of Brazil lead a life of suffering and misery which literally cries out to 'heaven'? Can one have no hope at all for these people? And what about the countless millions who perished wretchedly in the concentration camps of the Nazis, the Soviets and Mao? Or complete innocents who have been murdered, or who died as children without having lived a real life? 'Is there no justice?', I ask myself. Why indeed were they on earth? And why are we, who fare relatively well, on earth?

I admit that I cannot be content with all the wretchedness, injustice, meaninglessness in this world and therefore I look for an ultimate meaning, both in the life of others and in my life. However, I do not want to be immunized and comforted by a meaning in heaven. I am looking for a meaning on this earth. I take quite seriously Nietzsche's admonition, 'My brothers, remain true to the earth' (*Thus spoke Zarathustra*, Preface 3).

We must be content in finding a meaning in life for the here and now. And all of us, every man and every woman, must find that meaning for ourselves, in our own circle, however large or small. Any job, regardless of position, can become a real calling, can give satisfaction and fulfilment. Commitment to voluntary work – whether social, charitable or political

– can be more meaningful than some full-time jobs. Looking after and caring for relatives, despite all the labour that this involves, can change one's view of life and make new, unsuspected meaningful experiences possible. So I do not want anyone to be spared a crisis of meaning, but I want them to test and preserve the meaning of life through all kinds of crises or possibly even to seek it and find it again.

This must be a definitive, final meaning, which includes a meaning in dying. And here I know that I am at one with countless others in an unquenchable longing for final justice, eternal peace and abiding happiness. Can this longing ever be fulfilled? I shall attempt an answer to this question in the next chapter, in which I turn to the foundation of life.

## Chapter 5

# Foundation of Life

*What do I know about God and the purpose of life?*
*I know that this world exists.*
*That I am placed in it like my eye in its visual field.*
*That something about it is problematic, which we call its meaning.*
*That this meaning does not lie in it but outside it.*
*That life is the world.*
*That my will penetrates the world.*
*That my will is good or evil.*
*Therefore that good and evil are somehow connected with the*
   *meaning of the world.*
*The meaning of life, i.e. the meaning of the world, we can call God.*

The philosopher Ludwig Wittgenstein
in his diary on 11 June 1916

We go on the way of life with trust, joy and meaning in life. But what is the foundation of life?

It was a few months before the quincentenary celebrations of the University of Tübingen founded in 1477: the University President Adolf Theis confronted me with the wish of the committee responsible that I should give the ceremonial speech on this occasion. For me this was a triple surprise: they were not asking a historian, an orator or a philosopher but a theologian. They did not want a Protestant theologian to give the speech in the Protestant Stiftskirche, where the university was founded at that time, but a Catholic. And they did not want a theme from the history of the university to be treated, but a central question of human existence. I accepted this distinguished but difficult task in the awareness that I had to give the speech in an explosive social and political situation – 1977 was the climax of the Red Army Faction crisis. My question already at that time was:

## Does belief in God have a future?

Now on our ascent of the mountain we come up against a sheer wall, which we have to surmount, to 'transcend'. Some will perhaps shy away, but some know that one cannot reach the summit by any other route. So I will attempt at least to hammer in some pitons.

Let's look back. Beyond question religion has a great past. Research into the history of culture has shown that so far in the whole history of humankind no people or tribe has been found without any marks of religion, even if it is often indistinguishable from magic. Religion is omnipresent, both historically and geographically. But if we look forward, may we conclude from the past that there will also be religion in the future? Not necessarily. Religions can die: Egyptian, Babylonian, Roman, Germanic . . . But can the whole human phenomenon of religion die? Presumably no more than the human phenomena of art or music.

However, in modern times Western and Northern Europe have undergone a special development, with world-wide effects. I have already mentioned the Enlightenment. In the seventeenth and eighteenth centuries fundamental social spheres were detached from the religious context in a process of 'becoming worldly', 'secularization': philosophy, science, medicine, law, the state, art and culture. They became worldly, 'secular', i.e. independent, autonomous, within their own laws. Actual secularization initially aimed only at 'secularity', at worldly autonomy, independence from domination by religion and the church, without suppressing religion. It by no means necessarily meant an ideological 'secularism', it did not mean godlessness, championed theoretically or only lived out in practice. But in this development the question becomes increasingly clear, not least to our universities: does belief in God have a future?

With my speech at the university jubilee I wanted to do a service to my university, but also to 'God's cause', which is the object of 'theo-logy', talk of God. I felt well prepared; my more than four years' work on an 'answer to the question of God today', under the title *Does God Exist?*, was almost complete. So on 8 October 1977 – after a long critical-sympathetic 'greeting' from the Federal President Walter Scheel on the student movement – I gave a lecture on 'Can we still believe in God today?' Both were published together soon afterwards.

What I argued there remains my conviction: if today we want to make a case for a future for belief in God on rational grounds, we must know the arguments which tell against belief in God and take them seriously.

It is indisputable that often people were against religion because they were against institutionalized religion; they were against God because they were against the church. Through their own failure theologians and representatives of the church made an essential contribution to the spread of a scholarly and a political atheism: in the eighteenth century with some intellectual precursors, in the nineteenth century with numerous educated people, and finally in the twentieth century among great masses from Spain to Russia. The future of belief in God remains in danger in the twenty-first century. This is also because the old confrontation of belief in God with modern science and democracy has not been completely overcome.

## Belief in God versus science and democracy

As a member of the 'Tübingen Republic of Scholars' – thus the subtitle of Walter Jens's history of the University of Tübingen – I regretted then and still regret that people keep referring to God in order to combat modern science. The case of Galileo and the case of Darwin, but in our day also the case of sexual morality (against the pill, condoms, artificial fertilization) have burdened and poisoned the relations between religion and the sciences. How could I not understand that in the face of so many decrees from Rome and evangelical pamphlets many people reject a belief in authority, the Bible, the church, which seems to them to be contrary to reason, anti-philosophical and hostile to science? Today many believers understand that 'God' cannot be used as an argument in science, if science is to keep its method pure and exact. Notoriously difficult ethical questions such as those of abortion, stem cell research or euthanasia should be brought to a practicable humane solution: differentiated, scientifically backed answers with philosophical and theological reflections.

As a convinced Swiss Democrat I regretted then and regret today that people also keep referring to God to attack modern democracy. Certainly in our day political and religious confessional tutelage by the churches as in the *Ancien régime* is no longer conceivable. However, in newly reinforced fundamentalist circles, whether of Christian or Islamic provenance, the Enlightenment is still hated and the slogan of the French Revolution, 'Liberty, equality, fraternity', is taboo. But to keep to my own Catholic Church – not only the reactionary-traditionalist admirers of popes Pius X, XI and XII, but also many in the Vatican would dearly like to re-establish the church's condemnations of liberalism and socialism, of freedom of conscience, religion and the press from the nineteenth and early twentieth centuries and entrust the decisions on 'the truth' in all questions of faith and morality to an ecclesiastical 'magisterium', as is still called for in the most recent encyclicals on faith and reason. In this anti-modern spirit, people in papalist Rome still think that they may put pressure in the direction of Roman Catholic morality on democratically elected governments and parliaments, behind the scenes and sometimes in the open.

When I see the church, in the spirit of the Middle Ages, using 'miracles' as proofs in beatifications, proclaiming old legends as historical facts, promoting dubious pilgrimages and often hoodwinking pious people, and ask myself, 'What do I believe?', my clear answer is: I don't believe all this and no theologian in the world will be able to convince me that this sort of thing should be an essential part of my belief in God, indeed the Christian belief in God. On the contrary, we need to ask how far a false, wrong picture of God and sometimes an inhuman anti-social 'Christian' picture of human beings have contributed to atheism.

But now I must also go on to ask: how good are the arguments against belief in God? Two arguments above all need to be examined critically, first the psychological argument that God is only a projection of human beings, and then the argument from the philosophy of history and culture that the end of religion is near.

## God – a projection of longing?

Already as a student of philosophy I felt the absence of the lives and fates of the philosophers in the lectures on the history of philosophy of religion; only their arguments and systems were discussed. After Descartes and Pascal, Kant and Hegel, I was particularly fascinated by the great atheists Feuerbach, Marx, Nietzsche and Freud. I wanted to investigate their lives, what provoked them and their quite personal motives. Why did they in particular come to deny God? I was particularly interested in:

- Ludwig Feuerbach, a Protestant theological student whose first idea according to his own testimony was God, the second reason and the third human beings;
- Karl Marx who, born a Jew and brought up as a Christian, finally became a doctor of philosophy as a left-wing Hegelian;
- Friedrich Nietzsche, son of a Lutheran pastor brought up by overly

pious women, who became a critical philologist and adherent of the pessimistic philosophy of Schopenhauer;

* Sigmund Freud, son of Jewish parents, repelled by Catholic ritualism and antisemitism, who, shaped by medical materialism, developed into a psychiatrist and psychologist.

Just a year after my arrival in Tübingen, in the summer semester of 1961, I had to substitute for one of my colleagues in the philosophy lectures. For the first time I treated at length the philosophical theology of Georg Friedrich Wilhelm Hegel and then the anthropological anti-theology of Feuerbach, the social-revolutionary atheism of Marx, the nihilistic atheism of Nietzsche and atheism in Dostoievsky. And I well remember a later session of the seminar. I was discussing with the students Ludwig Feuerbach's theory of projection and the question whether prayer was only a matter of talking to oneself. Suddenly it dawned on me that I must not reject the argument for projection but must generalize it. For projection is in play everywhere, not only in the knowledge of God but also in any knowledge – even the knowledge of a beloved. My power of imagination is at work everywhere; everywhere I put something of myself into the object of my knowledge, I project something. But the question is whether my projection does not nevertheless correspond to something in reality.

Of course something does not exist simply because I wish it or desire it. But the reverse is also the case: it does not necessarily not exist because I wish it. This in particular was the false conclusion of the projection argument of Feuerbach and his countless followers: they think that God does not exist because I only want him to exist. I ask in return: why should something that I wish, hope for, long for, *a priori* not exist? Why should what has been proclaimed, venerated, worshipped for thousands of years in thousands of temples, synagogues, churches and mosques be sheer illusion? Why should the quest by the Ionian pre-Socratic thinkers for an initial foundation (Greek *arche*), a primal ground of all things, *a priori* be senseless activity, like Plato's reflection on the idea of the good, Aristotle's on a first mover and a goal of all things, or Plotinus's on the great One? Is it all 'non-sense'? And should the tremendous longing of people for eternal peace, an ultimate meaning, definitive justice really remain without any fulfilment?

I have nothing against people who criticize 'metaphysics' if this is understood as 'the world behind' or 'superstructure' conditioned by interests. And I have nothing against people analysing my belief in God psychologically or neuro-physiologically. But that does not prove the slightest thing in respect of an absolute reality independent of my psyche. That means that my wish for God can perhaps correspond to a real God. And conversely, couldn't the wish of some for no God to exist be a convenient projection conditioned by interests, which is ultimately grounded in particular prejudices?

So I have taken a good deal of trouble to illuminate widespread prejudices about belief in God, for example the prejudices that those who believe in God cannot engage in science with intellectual honesty; that faith and knowledge are exclusive; that science definitively replaces religion. Or there is the prejudice that someone who believes in God cannot be a genuine democrat; belief in God and liberty, equality and fraternity cannot be reconciled; politics has to take the place of religion. Finally there is the prejudice that with religion one cannot be truly human. God is necessarily believed in at the expense of human beings, indeed is an expression of alienation of human beings from themselves; humanism can therefore only be atheistic. Certainly such prejudices cannot be refuted purely theoretically, but effectively only by better practice on the part of religious representatives and institutions. But an enlightened religious sense is a presupposition for a practice that is friendly to life. However, what about the second argument against belief in God: is the end of religion in sight?

## Religion – an outdated model?

What I have only alluded to here I have substantiated point by point in my book *Does God Exist? An Answer for Today*. It appeared in German in 1978 (ET 1980) and was an invitation to a demanding argumentative process of thought. More deeply than is usual in theology I had felt my way into the rise of the great atheists and grappled with their arguments. The book was translated into the major European languages and later even published in the Russian underground in a samisdat edition, as was still the practice at the time; my Russian friends weren't running the slightest risk.

One could have expected that Rome and the German bishops would have praised this book as a service to God's cause and also as a further clarification of the constructive attitude to the christological dogmas that I had also taken. But these men of God were not interested in putting my answer to the question of God for today on record. They wanted to silence the critic of the pill encyclical *Humanae vitae*, papal infallibility and the Roman system. A year after the publication of *Does God Exist?*, on 18 December 1979, in a piece of skulduggery they removed the church's permission for me to teach.

This case of the Inquisition did not exactly help 'God's cause'. It occupied the media throughout the Christmas holidays. It was overshadowed only by the invasion of Afghanistan by Soviet troops, who had to be recalled ignominiously ten years later, something that essentially contributed to the implosion of the programmatically atheistic Soviet system and the return of religion to the Soviet bloc.

What was even more important for the subsequent period was that in 1979, my year of destiny, the secular regime of the Shah of Persia, hostile to Islam, collapsed and the opposition leader Ayatollah Khomeini returned to Tehran in triumph. By the establishment of the Islamic republic of Iran and its consequences, religion once more became an explosive factor in world politics. *Does God Exist?* was read even in Tehran. Later I was the first Western theologian to be able to carry on serious dialogues with leading religious scholars, including the later president Mohammad Khatami. It is a pity that the West no longer supported him.

So I could feel confirmed in my refutation of the second atheistic argument, which forecast an imminent end to the religions. Such a prognosis proved to be an ultimately unfounded extrapolation into the future. There was neither the 'transcending of religion' by atheistic humanism (Feuerbach) nor the 'dying out of religion' in atheistic socialism (Marx) nor the 'replacement of religion' by atheistic science (Freud). Rather, atheistic humanism, socialism and faith in science all came under the suspicion of being projections. But of course the dispute over religion continues.

## What speaks against religion?

In contrast to the great 'classical' atheists I have mentioned, the 'new atheists' emerging from the natural sciences are imitators. I cannot see any serious new scientific arguments against the existence of God. Instead of this there is sweeping polemic against religion in general and Christianity in particular. There is no discussion that gives pleasure because it has produced new results.

However, what I understand is that the occasion for the heightened attacks of unbelievers on belief in God is often given by the believers themselves. Many people are rightly hostile to Islamic fanatics and devastating terror attacks, even if they understand the lasting Muslim resentment about Western colonialism, imperialism and capitalism old or new. Others, particularly Catholics, take offence at the personality cult surrounding the Pope, contrary to the gospel, and his retrogressive church-political direction in liturgy, dogmatics, sexual and bioethics, in relations with the Protestant churches, Judaism and Islam and with Indios and Africans. Yet others are alarmed by the activities of Protestant creationists in various American states and schools and by unqualified statements by church people on the theory of evolution. Finally, others are offended at over-religious politicians, such as former American president George W. Bush and his neo-conservative helpers, who on the basis of an almost Orwellian structure of lies thought that they had God on their side in the invasion of Afghanistan and Iraq and in their methods of torture.

Truly there are many serious grounds for opposing religion and especially its misuse. And in all modesty I may point out that, more than many theologians in the past decades, I have systematically discussed the negative aspects of religion in all my books. For example in *Judaism*, the first volume in my trilogy 'The Religious Situation of Our Time', you can find precise and critical information about the mediaeval persecutions of the Jews, Lutheran and papal anti-Judaism, the Holocaust and the Palestinian problem. In the second volume, *Christianity*, about the Crusades, Inquisition, witch hunts, Christian wars of religion and Roman anti-Judaism. In the third volume, *Islam*, about Arab civil wars and wars of conquest, the problem of human rights and minorities, the question of women and violence, and much more.

So I find it almost incomprehensible that when the scientist Richard Dawkins, in the guise of enlightenment, writes about the God delusion and the scandalous history of the religions he does not take the trouble to make himself as informed on those questions as I have done on scientific questions. No one should ignore the relevant philosophical and theological basic literature and replace serious arguments with cheap smugness and irony. Moreover not only religions but also totalitarian atheistic ideologies – such as Nazism, Stalinism and Maoism – have produced pseudo-religious myths, and with the help of science and technology have committed horrific crimes against humanity at the cost of countless millions of victims.

So I would prefer that, instead of arguing against or for religion in a one-sided and superficial way, we learn from one another. The enlightened, whether religious or non-religious, theologian or scientist, should act together against any violence and war which has a religious or political motivation, against the oppression of minorities and discrimination against women, against obscurantism, superstition, addiction to miracles, but also against the misuse of science and scientific credulity.

In the long run religion has shown itself to be more powerful and long-lived than its critics and those who deny it. But I am confident that the overwhelming majority of Muslims will not allow themselves to be forced back under the yoke of a mediaeval penal law nor will the overwhelming majority of Catholics return to the Latin mass and the sexual morality of the Middle Ages, to the confessional and to papal infallibility.

Religion has a future only if it shows its philanthropic face, an inviting face, and not caricatured and repellent features. Only if Christianity and particularly the Catholic Church renews itself can the present loss of religion in Europe be overcome, church attendance rise again and the shaping power of religion in everyday life, which has declined markedly since the hopeful time of the Council, be regained.

## What speaks for religion?

Criticism of religion rightly points to the failure of the religions, which is catastrophic in many respects. But criticism of religion cannot replace religion, although it often functions as a substitute religion. Not only the 'perversion' of religion, but also the essence of religion should be made clear. Hence my fundamental question: what speaks for religion? Why do countless millions of people throughout the world not want to dispense with religion, despite its questionable character? Where does the strength of religion lie, and what does religion offer me, who values philosophy highly, that even the best philosophy cannot offer?

A threefold plus for religion is important for me:

• First, more than philosophy, which with its ideas and theories usually addresses an intellectual élite, religion can also shape and motivate broad strata of the population.
• Secondly, religion addresses people not only rationally but also emotionally, not just with ideas, concepts and words but also with symbols and rites, stories, prayers and festivals, and thus produces a 'surplus value' of wholeness.
• And thirdly, religion is grounded not just on current insights, dominant opinions and the course of time, but on age-old holy

scriptures and traditions, which offer normative guidelines for human behaviour on the basis of religious experiences, which have often shaped human morality for millennia. The Sayings of Confucius for the Chinese, the Bhagavad-Gita for Hindus, the Torah for Jews, the New Testament for Christians and the Qur'an for Muslims offer abiding religious information and orientation which have been handed down unchanged through time and interpreted anew, inspiring and motivating.

But what content, what spiritual capacities do all the religions have if they function in a way that is friendly to human beings? It is evident that the religions are very different. But it is less known that religions also show fundamental common features. I described at length how all religions contain elementary ethical values and norms that as a global ethic act as a criterion for world society. Through their leading figures, their stories, images, parables and sayings they provide motivation in a variety of ways for involvement with fellow men and women and the community.

In addition, religion can interpret where our existence comes from and where it is going; how I am to deal with suffering, injustice, guilt and meaninglessness and how I can find an ultimate meaning in life even in the face of death. Even ideology-critical philosophers such as Jürgen Habermas have recently acknowledged that in the age of 'post-metaphysical' thinking religious convictions can give self-knowledge and comfort for a failed or a redeemed life.

Finally, through the experiences and narratives, symbols, rituals and festivals that it hands down, religion can provide a home of trust, faith, certainty and thus also give strength, security and hope to the self. This can give rise not only to a feeling of togetherness but also of protesting against and resisting circumstances of injustice. In this sense religion is an expression of an unquenchable longing for a better world, indeed for the 'wholly other'. But is not such religion despite everything remote from all reason, a hotbed of irrationality? That is not my experience.

## A spirituality with rationality

My spirituality always had less to do with sentimentality than with rationality. I always wanted not just to 'believe' but to understand my faith. As a theologian I also understood myself to be a philosopher, and I allowed myself to be trained and be active as a philosopher. I did not have the aversion to philosophy that can be observed in Protestant theology since the time of Martin Luther. On the other hand, I could not see why the philosophers of the twentieth and twenty-first centuries did not want to raise the questions of 'metaphysics' any longer and largely left the stewardship of this great heritage of Western philosophy, beginning with the Greeks, to the theologians.

Through my theology can I remedy the way in which philosophy has forgotten God and theology has forgotten philosophy? At any rate my theology is not meant to be a secret science for those who already believe, which hides behind mysteries at decisive points, mysteries that theologians have themselves made in the course of a problematical history of dogma. Rather, my theology is meant to be understandable, capable of being followed and credible, so that even non-believers are led to the only really great mystery, the mystery of reality that we designate with the name of 'God'.

Here I am surprised how non-believers in particular, perhaps in order to exclude themselves, cite – and reject – the *credo quia absurdum*: I believe because it is absurd. It does not come from the great church teacher Augustine, as is often claimed, but goes back to the initiator of Latin theology, the lawyer Tertullian. I cannot and will not exclude my reason in questions of faith. All that is absurd – unexplained, infantile, from the backwoods, reactionary – is alien to me. And so too is any pseudo-religious mass hysteria or indeed global hysteria, for example over the accident to a beautiful princess or the unexpected death of a pop star surrounded by scandal or the public dying of a Pope transmitted by the media.

I am no less critical than the critics of religion. Indeed as far as I am concerned the critical rationalists need to be more critical, and even more so the uncritical dogmatists. An absolutized rationality, an ideological rationalism, can also be a superstition, just like theological dogmatics. At any rate I take little pleasure in holding discussions with rigid rationalists or immovable dogmatists. More than once I have noted that both show themselves incapable even of reproducing my view correctly in polemic. In such cases their reason is disturbed by their passion.

Like any human person, I consist not only of reason and rationality, but also of feelings and will, imagination and heart, emotions and passions. I deliberately strive as far as possible to attain a holistic view of things. I learned methodically clear thinking, the '*esprit de géometrie*' in the spirit of René Descartes, the founder of modern philosophy, but at the same time cultivated an intuitive holistic knowing, feeling and sensing, an '*esprit de finesse*' in the spirit of Descartes' opposite, the equally excellent mathematician Blaise Pascal.

At grammar school in Lucerne we were sometimes amused at our excellent teacher of the history of art who, when we were looking at works of art, at something unquantifiable but aesthetic and beautiful, rubbed his thumb with his index and middle fingers and said: 'You have to feel it, feel it.' And he was right. So many specifically human phenomena such as art, music, humour and laughter, and even more suffering, love, faith and hope, cannot be grasped in their different dimensions by rational criticism alone, but only felt holistically. The most recent brain research with its gigantic computer tomographs can explain the functioning of the neurones, but it cannot discover the content of our thoughts and emotions.

Already as a young professor I found it fascinating to enter into exchanges with important scholars of other disciplines. I did not just speak of 'interdisciplinarity', I practised it wherever I could. Of course I took a basic attitude of respect for granted, respect for the greatness of their disciplines, their immense knowledge, their assured results, their different methods and their objective judgement. In theology I also had to do with philosophers, lawyers, historians and medical experts, and increasingly also with psychologists, sociologists and political theorists. I always wanted to take especially seriously science orientated on mathematics and experiments, with its independence and autonomy. I determined that it should not be put in question by any theologian or churchman with reference to a higher authority, for instance God, Bible, church, or Pope.

But it was equally important to me that if questions of science must be treated in accordance with the methods and style of science, on the other hand questions of the human psyche and society, and also questions of law, politics and historical research, and even more questions of aesthetics, morality and religion must also be treated in accordance with their own method and style. Today quite legitimately we are also concerned in the humanities with the analysis of phenomena, operations, courses and structures. But we should not forget that there are also justified scholarly questions about last or first interpretations of meaning, values, ideals, norms and attitudes that require answers. As a philosopher and theologian I cannot be content with the surface of problems but must attempt to penetrate to the depths. How else would an answer to the question of the foundation of life be found?

## Getting to the foundation of things

During my academic work I was interested not only in the logical ground, the ground of knowledge, the ratio, but also in the ontological ground, the ground of being, the substantive ground, the real ground, the cause. Philosophers have set alongside the principle of contradiction, the statement of contradiction ('Being is not not-being') the principle of sufficient cause: 'Nothing is or happens without a cause.'

On this presupposition it seems easy to produce 'conclusive proof' for an ultimate ground, a first cause, for God. But is it so easy to say 'God'? I have already said that the objections of the critics of religion to the frequently misused word 'God', most recently in analytical philosophy or linguistic analysis, are familiar to me. And I accept that I myself often have reservations about using the name 'God'. Hardly any name has been so misused, abused or light-heartedly joked about, not only in politics and business but also within political parties, religions and churches.

The Jewish philosopher of religion Martin Buber expressed this in a moving passage:

> God? Yes, it is the most loaded of all words used by men. None has been so soiled, so mauled. But that is the very reason why I cannot give it up. Generations of men have blamed this word for the burdens of their troubled lives and crushed it into the ground; it lies in the dust, bearing all their burdens. Generations of men with their religious divisions have torn the word apart: they have killed for it and died for it; it bears all their fingerprints and is stained with all their blood. Where would I find a word to equal it, to describe supreme reality?
>
> ('Gottesfinsternis', *Werke* Vol. 1, pp. 509f.)

The first petition in Jesus' prayer 'Our Father', completely in the spirit of the Hebrew Bible, is 'Hallowed be thy name' (Matthew 6.9, in the original Aramaic which Jesus used probably *yitkaddash shemak*). For Orientals the 'name' (*hasshem*) is not just an external designation but also an essential part of the personality, i.e. here God himself. The petition means that God's name should not be 'dishonoured', that one should not put oneself above God's will and shame his honour before humankind. Rather, one should 'hallow' his name, keep his commandments and fulfil them, and praise God before the world. Do Jews, who seem already to have shrunk from pronouncing the name Yahweh as early as the last centuries before Christ, and Christians, who often use the name *abba*, Father, for him, do enough to ensure that the name of God is honoured?

For me as a Christian this mean respecting those who in the present situation no longer use the word 'God' but express awareness of God in other ways. Rather than talking about God in the old way or not talking about God at all, it is important to me to talk of God in a new way, with respect and humility. For time and again in the history of humankind questions have been asked about God. Time and again there have been doubts in God. Time and again God has been denied. Time and again there have been struggles over God, belief in God, prayers to God, arguing with God. The question of God must be put anew, but it must be put correctly. Some non-believers have a notion of God which believers would dismiss as primitive, wrong, even beyond discussion. One does not *have to* believe in God, but *may* one believe in God? Or more precisely, can one be responsible, as a person in a modernity that is critical of religion, for believing in God?

Over the years I have spoken of, discussed, meditated on God with countless people everywhere, from all walks of life. I have been asked, 'Have you ever doubted the existence of God?' and have replied: 'Not God, but the proofs for his existence.' Immanuel Kant, who consummated and overcame the Enlightenment, convinced me at an early stage that 'pure' or theoretical reason has its limits. And that means that scholarly proofs of God are not possible. Why? Because God does not exist as an object in space and time exists. He is not the object of vision and knowledge that can be proved scientifically. Reason cannot rise beyond the horizon of our experience, to the real God, penetrating space and time through the power of thought. Human beings cannot build towers reaching to heaven, but only dwellings which are roomy and high enough for our business on the ground.

No, there is no compelling proof for the existence of God but – and many times I have referred to this often ignored other side of Kant's argument – there is no proof against! Why? Because a negative judgement would likewise go beyond the horizon of space-time experience. Anyone who concedes that we cannot peer behind the curtain of phenomena may not also assert that there is nothing beyond it.

All the statements of physicists refer to physical space, space-time. Physicists cannot and will not answer questions outside the possibility of physical measurement. If it is to remain true to its method, science may not go beyond the horizon of experience in its judgements. For such judgements and decisions one does better not to reckon with time measurable with the chronometer (Greek *chronos*), but to look for the favourable time (Greek *kairos*), the right moment.

Neither the superiority of a sceptical ignorance nor the arrogance of a know-all is appropriate to the natural sciences, to science generally. Perhaps there are events and interactions in our universe that are not visible in physical space, experiences in our human life that cannot be verified scientifically. 'So I had to abolish knowledge,' writes Kant in his preface to the second edition of the *Critique of Pure Reason* (1787), 'in order to make room for faith.'

No – and here we have come up against the sheer wall – there are very different possibilities of 'transcending', of 'going beyond' the sensible, empirical world of experience, all of which end up in a rational trust. There are various ways to 'transcendence', to a meta-empirical reality beyond the senses, to that great mystery that we call God. I shall sketch just three approaches, not as proofs but as indicators, as a stimulus towards reflection, towards 'tracking' transcendence. The first is from biology, the second from mathematics and the third from music.

## Evolution towards humanity

In decades of tireless research work astrophysics has discovered what had to be balanced precisely (and by no means always symmetrically) so that after billions of years life could arise: the fine tuning of energy and matter, of nuclear electromagnetic forces, of the force of gravity and energy through nuclear reactions in our sun. It is more than understandable that physicists and non-physicists ask whether all this developed completely by chance towards life, indeed towards human beings. Only on our planet in the whole solar system did life, including spirit, finally develop from the animal kingdom after billions of years. According to all that we know on the basis of the most recent research, human beings are alone in the universe. Science fiction is fascinating in the cinema but is pure fiction; there are no aliens to be seen. I do not believe in extraterrestrials.

But an evolution towards humankind is a scientific fact. Is everything chance? Are so many 'chances' chance? And is not such chance an empty principle of explanation? It is natural, indeed inevitable, to ask whether this tremendous development ran according to a 'very special recipe', as I heard from the Astronomer Royal Martin Rees of Cambridge, i.e., as astrophysicists and biologists assume, something like a meta- or super law behind, over or in all the fine tunings and natural laws. Some call this super law an anthropic principle. It guarantees that the initial conditions and natural constants are such that life and finally an 'anthropos', a human being, could and did come into being.

When we say 'can' or 'could', it means that something can be demonstrated scientifically. There is no proof for a 'had to': if believers rapidly make this 'anthropic principle' a scientific proof that God must exist and have willed human beings into existence, that is a short cut on the basis of faith, an ideologization which is not orientated on the subject but on certain interests.

But the other side of the problem is that science is incapable of giving an empirical, mathematical foundation for such a meta-natural law. One does not have to be a Kantian to recognize that science is no longer competent on this question of a 'transcendent' and at the same time 'immanent' super principle which transcends everything empirical. And philosophy is competent only if it accepts the question. Otherwise, the only alternative is religion.

At this point it is evident how even more foolish is the opposite conclusion, that it follows from this grandiose process of development that there can be no God who willed human beings into existence. This is a short-cut on the basis of unbelief, which likewise stands under the suspicion of being an ideology: that what may not be – in the interests of someone or another – cannot be. One cannot exclude God even with the Darwinian principle of evolution (nor was that Darwin's intention): science is, as I have described, no more responsible for the negation of God than for the affirmation of God.

That is not surprising, for no science can embrace the whole of reality. Each has its own perspective and competence that it should not absolutize. There are several explanations even for so simple a thing as a table or a bicycle: physical and chemical, functional, culture-historical, sociological . . . It is important that one explanation does not exclude another, but can supplement it and enrich it.

These different perspectives of the sciences are grounded not just in the limits of human knowledge, which no individual science can transcend. The reality of the world and human beings shows different aspects, levels, dimensions, and anyone who absolutizes a single dimension becomes blind to the others. It would be better to discover new dimensions. The conclusion is that physics invites us to be open to the great mystery of the cosmos, where the constants of nature and the anthropic principle are. And mathematics invites us too.

## Is the infinite a real dimension?

From the time of Greek mathematician Euclid in the fourth century BCE, physical space has been defined as three-dimensional (in length, breadth and height). But since Albert Einstein's theory of relativity at the beginning of the twentieth century it is understood as four-dimensional time-space or space-time – time combined with space. That is not a purely mathematical construction such as the speculations about many worlds, but a new model of the universe that is confirmed by measurements and space travel, but cannot be depicted as a four-dimensional entity.

In fact the speculations of cosmologists who produce highly complex mathematical models and calculations about further universes and further dimensions with the help of computers are irrelevant to our considerations. This is because, as I described in my book *The Beginning of All Things* (2005; ET 2007), these have no support in the world of experience. By contrast, reflections on the dimension of infinity which is constantly but invisibly present in mathematics and introduced into its systems do seem to me well worth engaging in; any figure can be endlessly projected, multiplied, divided, but need not be calculated into everyday equations. The question arises whether there could not be something like a real dimension of infinity present in all things, even if, like four-dimensional space, it cannot be depicted tangibly, because it is a reality beyond space and time.

However, one may not conclude from the idea of such an infinite reality that it exists, i.e. from a perfect or absolutely necessary being to his real existence, as Anselm of Canterbury, the father of scholasticism, and also Descartes and Leibniz did. This real dimension of infinity would no longer be a category of space-time but of eternity, which mathematical scientific reason cannot attain. Amazingly the Renaissance thinker Nicholas of Cusa in the fifteenth century already contributed to making infinity rationally accessible. He expressed the infinity of God as a 'coincidence of opposites' and represented this notion symbolically in mathematics. If we think, say, of the radius of a segment of a circle extended to infinity, the circle approaches a straight line; so the opposites of straight and curved come together in the infinite.

In the late nineteenth century the inventor of the theory of masses, Georg Cantor (died 1918), refers to Nicholas of Cusa in his reflections on the category 'infinite'. His theory of masses led in mathematics to antinomies, paradoxes, contradictions: certain statements which have to do with the concept of infinity can be mathematically proved and refuted at the same time. For mathematics, this has resulted in a fundamental crisis that has even now not been overcome. In view of the freedom of contradiction in the basic structures which still has not been proved, I have heard from mathematicians the *bon mot*: 'God exists because mathematics is free of contradiction, and the devil exists, because the freedom from contradiction cannot be proved.' As I do not believe in a personal devil, I advise all lovers of mathematics that it is better to hold on to God.

The conclusion is that in the problem of its foundations mathematics in principle comes against limits. But the very number infinity can be an occasion to reflect on the possibility of a qualitative ascent into quite another dimension, a real infinite, a real transcendence. And because mathematicians are also good musicians, I propose a third way towards approaching the great mystery of reality: music.

## 'Tuning in' to music

As is well known, music and mathematics belong together, but so do music and religion. Music has a mysterious mathematical structure. Since the Pythagoreans in antiquity this structure has been noted and expressed in the note system and the infinite possibilities of using it. But there is something that the mathematician cannot do, which is to produce a mathematical proof that can demonstrate music to be beautiful and compel people to listen to it. I can simply reject music, particularly classical music, which calls for understanding. I can simply switch off, outwardly or inwardly. Music invites me to listen but does not compel me. Listening to music is an act of freedom. And in quite another way that also applies to saying yes to a meta-empirical reality: even more this is a matter of a free assent. But music, which is uniquely powerful in arousing and strengthening feeling, can be a special help here.

In some circumstances musicians, and also poets, artists and religious people generally, can sense, trace, hear and express in their works realities that break through physical space, the space of energy and time. Like any sound, music is a physical phenomenon, and physics has made a thorough investigation of it in acoustics. But it is not just a physical phenomenon that can be grasped by physics alone. I must turn to Mozart again.

Fifty years ago in my Paris garret, Mozart's clarinet concerto KV622, his last orchestral work, for all its gloomy features of resignation, of unsurpassable beauty, intensity and inwardness, completed exactly two months before his death, every day delighted, strengthened and comforted me afresh. In short, it gave me a little bit of 'bliss', the word that Mozart himself used. And someone else listening to Mozart's music may sometimes have felt such short moments of 'bliss'.

But even Mozart's music can hardly communicate harmony and beauty to cynics and nihilists. And it can be heard in different ways. Sometimes when studying or relaxing, I open myself to the music, let it flow into me, and abandon myself completely to it, not only with the intelligence of the head, which is necessary for scholarship, but with the intelligence of the heart which binds, integrates, communicates totality.

It is this experience that draws me back to this music time and again. If I am listening to Mozart's music utterly and intensely, without outside disturbances, alone at home or sometimes at a concert, my eyes close and I suddenly feel that the body of sound is no longer outside me but part of my being. It is the music that now embraces me, permeates me and resounds from within. What has happened? I sense that I am wholly turned inwards with eyes and ears, body and spirit: the I is silent and everything external, any subject–object split, ceases to exist. The music is no longer outside me but is what embraces me, permeates me, brings me happiness from within, fulfils me completely. The phrase that occurs to me is: 'In it we live and move and have our being.'

This is a saying from the New Testament, from the apostle Paul's speech on the Areopagus in Athens, where he speaks of seeking and finding God, who is not remote from any of us, in whom we live and move and are (Acts 17.27f.). Truly more than any other music, with its sensual-nonsensual beauty, power and clarity Mozart's music seems to show how fine and narrow the boundary is between music, the most unobjective of all arts, and religion, which has always especially had to do with music. Both, though different, point to the ultimately unspeakable, to the mystery. And though music must not become a religion of art, the art of music is the most spiritual of all symbols for that 'mystical sanctuary of our religion', of which Mozart once spoke, the divine itself.

The conclusion is that Mozart's music is not a proof of God but even more not a pointer to pessimism and nihilism. On the contrary, sensitive listeners will sometimes find themselves opening up, in that reasonable trust which transcends reason. With this fine hearing they may then perceive a wholly Other in the pure, utterly internalized sound, say, of the adagio of the clarinet concerto; the sound of the beautiful in its infinity, indeed the sound of the infinite that transcends us and for which 'beautiful' is not a word. So music is a 'tuning in' to a higher harmony.

## Traces of transcendence

There are ciphers, traces that give us an inkling of another reality than the purely physical, physiological or empirical. One *need* not perceive these traces, but one *may* perceive them; there is no demanding evidence here, no compelling transparency.

Many people have made an effort to see basic experiences of human existence and human history as an occasion for transcending the one-dimensionality of modern life to a completely different reality, the reality of God, the ground of meaning of everything. Here I would like to recall three important figures with whom I have felt a personal link:

First is the Austro-American sociologist of religion Peter Berger, who has interpreted the little signs and gestures of human life as *A Rumour of Angels* (1970) in our everyday life: gestures of protection and comfort, when a mother calms her anxious child, but also our remarkable tendency towards restoring order, our impulse to play, our humour, our hope – all that is part of the expression of the nature of human beings yet points to more than human beings, to something that rises above them, transcends them.

Then there is Karl Rahner, who has written in exemplary fashion about the frequent basic experiences of human existence. It was an honour for me as editor of the series 'Theological Meditations' in 1964 to publish his reflections on 'everyday things': a person's everyday life is full of everyday things: we work, walk and sit, see and laugh, eat and sleep – everyday things from which the heedful person can infer a hidden, rich depth.

And finally there is the founder of liberation theology, the Peruvian Gustavo Gutiérrez, who passionately refers to basic experiences in human history in society and politics: to the possibility of experiencing God in the history of human oppression and liberation – and particularly of the poor of this world. He wants to open our eyes to them: that God can be experienced everywhere that alienation is overcome, injustices removed, peace restored and love lived out.

So there are remarkable facts, signs, events, situations, 'chances' in the history of the life and suffering of every human being which can be an occasion for reflection, for religious contemplation. Our experiences are too precious for them simply to be thrown away instead of being preserved and thought about. And perhaps it will help if at the end of this chapter, I indicate what experiences were particularly important for me, which made me pause, reflect and think beyond them. There are two key and inter-connected experiences: the experience of being stopped and the experience of being supported.

One can be brought to a standstill in things great and small and as I know personally, the experience of being stopped can become harsh and bitter, robbing one of sleep for a long time. For me there was suddenly no way forward in an undertaking that seemed highly important to me and to other people and my, our, enemies rejoiced. 'They've stopped him!' Someone – whoever or whatever that is – prevented me, us, from going forward and that changed my situation completely. I knew only one thing: things would never be the same again. I didn't know what would happen. I should have become resigned, but I could not and would not: the cause had to go on. Yet I had been stopped, with no way out.

So what was I to do? Did I consider this yet another instance of the absurdity of life? Be this as it may, being stopped like this was a very tangible demand not just to stop but to look deeply into myself. Regardless of whether the stop comes in professional life, in an unexpected illness or in the collapse of a human relationship, it can be an occasion to reflect on the depth dimensions of one's life, to open oneself anew in trusting faith. Then one can have the comforting experience that there is a support even in this enforcement that rests in the basic reality of our life, in the reality of God, our ground of life, who can create new prospects even in hopeless situations. From this trust we can draw new strength and become capable of seeing our lives anew, taking up new standpoints, correcting our course and taking up a task again.

The second such key experience is the experience of being supported. At present everything is going smoothly, not just work; everything is going like clockwork. Is this because of the weather or my horoscope or my biorhythms? At any rate, I am making progress, achieving something. I am in a good mood. Of course it will not always be like this, things will certainly change. But that doesn't bother me here and now: this is a fulfilled moment. Why waste time with other thoughts, feelings, moods ... *Qui vivra verra*.

And yet something doesn't quite fit here. At such times it isn't that one is in a good mood that would be corrupted by moral indignation. It isn't that here one senses success which later might turn bad. It is that this sense of success, this untroubled mood, is often coupled with indifference, overestimation of oneself and superficiality. There is no sense of the deep dimension of our life, the knowledge that thinking has to do with thanking. One has only to reflect for a moment that success and happiness do not just depend on one's work; one has certainly achieved a lot, but one has received even more, happiness has come, perhaps not unhoped-for but, if one is honest, often undeserved.

So for me there is always reason for gratitude, not only to fellow human beings but to another authority, which makes my life meaningful despite all that is contrary to meaning. This represents the primal ground for a renewed trust in the dispensation and guidance in my life's work, the gratitude for our existence, the reason for joy being that for all I am driven I am still guided and supported safely. And what is true of me is certainly true of countless others.

In short, those who in a reasonable trust say *Yes* to a primal foundation and primal meaning, to God, know not only what but why they can ultimately trust in life. The *Yes* to God means a trust in life that is consistent and has an ultimate ground. It is a primal trust rooted in the ultimate depth, the ground of grounds, and directed towards the goal of goals, God as the name for the supportive ground of meaning of the whole. Despite all the uncertainty of life, a radical knowledge and security is given to me.

It must have become clear that fundamental trust and trust in God show a similar basic structure; they are a matter not only of human reason, but of the whole human being with spirit and body, reason and drives. Trust in God is beyond reason, but not irrational. It can be rationally justified in the face of rational criticism, not with compelling proofs but with convincing reasons.

For this trust the Bible uses the great word faith: 'Faith is the substance of things hoped for, the conviction of things unseen' (Hebrews 11.1). 'What do I believe?' I have now given an answer. I believe in God, origin and primal meaning of all things. I understand faith here in the full and radical sense. I do not just believe that God exists; I do not just believe God, believe his words, but I believe *in* God, put my whole unconditional and irrevocable trust in him.

In the creed this 'in' is avoided in association with the 'church'. For the church is the community of faith which believes not in itself but in God. Augustine could still say that he believed in God 'because of' the church. Many people today would say that they believe in God 'in spite of' the church, which does not seem credible to them in its present form.

The eternal God bestows ground and meaning on all that is temporal, and today no one need make excuses for an enlightened faith in God. But what if it proved at the end that I had been deceived in my faith? In that case my conviction is that I would nevertheless have lived a happier life with God than without him. That should all become clearer when now, building on the foundation of life, I enquire about the power of life.

## Chapter 6

# Power of Life

*From ancient times down to the present, there is found among various peoples a certain perception of that hidden power which hovers over the course of things and over the events of human history; at times some indeed have come to the recognition of a Supreme Being, or even of a Father. This perception and recognition penetrates their lives with a profound religious sense. Religions, however, that are bound up with an advanced culture have struggled to answer the same questions by means of more refined concepts and a more developed language.*

Declaration of the Second Vatican Council on the Relation of the Church to Non-Christian religions

We go the way of life with trust, joy and meaning in life. But what is the power of life?

For me personally there is a link between the Second Vatican Council (1962–5) with its 'Declaration on the World Religions' and the second Parliament of the World's Religions (1993) with its 'Declaration toward a Global Ethic' which came three decades later. I played an active part in both great religious events. I will always be grateful to the Dalai Lama for being the first, after a difficult debate, to sign the Declaration in Chicago on 4 September 1993 and present it to the public. After the ceremonial opening of the Parliament it was Buddhists under the leadership of the Dalai Lama who had made a written objection: with the best of intentions, Christian, Jewish and Muslim dignitaries had addressed in speeches and in prayers the 'unity of the religions to be striven for as God', and even unwittingly identified the Buddha with 'God'. They should have known that Buddhists reject the term God, but that they accept a last and pure spiritual reality (Ultimate Reality) that they call 'Great Being' or 'Power of the Transcendent' or 'Higher Spiritual Authority'. They could also have spoken of Nirvana, the goal of the way of redemption, or of the Dharmakaya (body of teaching), the law that determines the cosmos and human beings. In any case I felt confirmed because, as the one who drafted the Declaration and a committed believer in God, I had from the start refrained from referring to God.

## A new look at the religions

'What I believe': we have now climbed the sheer wall to the transcendent, transempirical, unconditional reality and we can hopefully look around without vertigo, get our breath back and draw on inner strength for the way forward.

A couple of months before the Parliament of the World's Religions in Chicago I had celebrated my 65th birthday. For a long time I had been taking trouble to get to know the diverse and often contradictory world of the religions through journeys, lectures, conferences and encounters. I was always convinced that there is a tremendous spiritual power in the religions that the declaration of Vatican II also speaks of. But I was also aware that this power may unfortunately be greatly misused. Recently sociologists and political theorists have noted that religious faith is perhaps the most strongly motivating power in the history of humankind. Religious convictions, attitudes and inspirations have now settled at the deepest level of humankind and can set powerful changes in motion – or block them. The conflict over the 'Holy Land' waged for decades in six wars is an impressive and sorry example of this.

The religions have always wanted to be both an interpretation of life and a way of life; the second aspect has become increasingly important to me.

- As an interpretation of life religions, at any rate the ethical high religions, start from the same eternal questions which open up behind what can be seen and grasped by the natural sciences and in one's own limited lifetime. Where do the world and its order come from? Why are we born and why must we die? What determines the destiny of the individual and humankind? How are we to explain moral awareness and the presence of ethical norms?
- Over and above the interpretation of life and all psychology the religions also seek to be a way of life, to open up a practical way for everyday life and in limit situations, a way that leads from the distress and torment of existence to liberation, to salvation. The guidelines of ethical behaviour offer themselves as orientation on this way. They all regard murder, lies, theft and sexual misconduct as guilt and put

forward as a universally valid practical criterion something like a 'Golden Rule'.

Since the Second Vatican Council and corresponding initiatives by the World Council of Churches, Christians have worked hard to gain an undistorted look at the world religions. They no longer want, as was customary for centuries, to judge by Christian dogmatic criteria. They want to understand them as they understand themselves. I had always been aware that in spite of all the agreements among the religions there are fundamental differences, many opposing views, despite all the similarities.

There are countless gods of the religions in history and the present, the divine nature figures and forces of nature, the plant, animal and human gods, gods of equal rank and gods in hierarchies. We have to face the question: Which is the true God? Is he to be found in the original tribal religions that still have a simple structure, or in the highly-developed religions? In those which have grown up slowly or those which have been founded? In the mythological religions or the enlightened religions? And there are other questions: Are there many gods, polytheism, or an individual supreme God among many gods, henotheism? Or is there only one God, monotheism? Is God to be thought of above or outside the world, deism? Is God completely included in the world, pantheism? Or is the world completely in God, panentheism?

I realized long ago that to examine these questions at every level and within all religions we need to have friendly and pleasant discussions together, having provided ourselves with the necessary factual knowledge. The more I read, travel, speak, listen, experience, the clearer it has become to me that dialogue between the religions is no remote academic affair. Rather, dialogue is a political and religious necessity – a foundation for peace between the nations. As early as 1984 – as a keyword for the 'Introduction to the Dialogue with Islam, Hinduism and Buddhism' under the title *Christianity and the World Religions* – I formulated the principle: 'No world peace without religious peace'. This later became the foundation for the first symposium that UNESCO ventured in Paris in February 1989 with representatives of the world religions. A good decade later, after a debate and a resolution at the UN General Assembly after 11 September 2001, on 9 November, the 'Dialogue of Civilizations' also became the programme of the United Nations Organization – against Samuel Huntington's conflictual thesis of the 'clash of civilizations'.

But if the dialogue is to bear fruit, knowledge of the other religions or confessions or churches is as necessary as the goodwill of the political and religious authorities. So the dialogue should extend not just to the monotheistic religions – Judaism, Christianity and Islam – but also include the Asian religions that have a mystical or wisdom orientation.

## Mystical spirituality?

'Tell me, what is mysticism?' One of my famous Roman professors, a social expert, and recognizable as a clergyman, was asked this question in the street in Berlin by a person unknown to him. And he gave the answer – he told me – which one usually gives if one is at a loss: 'Mysticism can mean very different things . . .' Indeed, he was right.

Mysticism is in fashion once more. Evidently to compensate for a theology and liturgy that is mostly governed by reason, intellectualized, and to combat a reduction of religion to social practice, people are again calling for religion as experience. Old and new classics of Christian mysticism fill the shelves of the bookshops. Serious and not so serious gurus promise religious experiences in ashrams, meditation centres and on quiet days. People want to experience faith, feel it. But aren't some of these people speaking as blind people speak about colour?

'Mysticism' is a highly elusive term, used even by theologians in a very arbitrary way. First, I first want to give it a precise definition. 'Mysticism', understood in the original sense of the word, comes from the Greek *myein* = close (the mouth). 'Mysteries' are therefore 'secrets', 'secret teachings', 'secret cults', about which one is silent in the presence of the uninitiated. So a religion is 'mystical' when it closes its mouth about its hidden secrets to profane ears, in order to seek salvation in its own inner depths. And silence is expected of those who want to approach the mystery. Turning away from the world and turning inward, immediate union with the Holy, Absolute, Divine, Deity – this has always been regarded as a characteristic of 'mysticism'. But that is only the start of today's problems.

Mysticism is more than the religious experience that, alongside its doctrinal system, ethic and rite, can be found in any religion. There are countless kinds of religious experience which are not mysticism at all, such as an elated feeling at a beautiful service, being moved when contemplating a natural or cultural wonder, the feeling of security in a holy place, the experience of togetherness in a religious mass occasion, a conversion experience, a childlike intimacy with God, and so on. A sentence by Karl Rahner is often quoted unthinkingly: 'The Christian of the future will be a mystic or will not exist at all' (*Theological Investigations* XX, 1981, p.149). This remark is at best correct if one understands mysticism in a broad sense as religious experience. But it does an injustice to many committed but by no means 'mystical' Christians and in some circumstances deters more sober people from being Christians.

Mystical experience tends towards unity, and mysticism precisely defined is direct and intuitive experience of unity. But the problem is that such intuition of a great unity which does away with the difference between subject and object can be attained in very different ways. However, I have never felt a temptation as the writer Aldous Huxley did to provoke abnormal expansions of consciousness with the help of mescaline or other experiments. For me this sort of thing is part of 'parareligious' mysticism: the unity of myself with nature, the cosmos, life, which can be understood in visionary cosmic or vitalistic terms. Even less did I ever want to have anything to do with a 'pseudo-religious' mysticism which functions as a substitute religion: to feel oneself at one with an entity such as people, nation, party or leader, especially in acts of intoxicated, hysterical fusion on mass occasions, including papal appearances.

Authentic religious mysticism means the experience of the unity of myself with the great All-embracing, the Last of all or Highest of all reality, the Absolute – understood as God, Brahman, Dharma or Nirvana. It exists above all in Indian spirituality, in the Vedanta, in Samkhya Yoga and in Mahayana Buddhism, but also in Chinese Daoism. Indeed it also exists in the Jewish Kabbalah, in Muslim Sufism and in branches of Christianity, above all monastic.

I believe in an all-embracing and permeating Last of all, First of all reality. Yet I question whether unity with God is possible. Does God allow himself to be attained by me from a unity that is more than imagination? At any rate I could not say that I agree with that American colleague who became a Hindu monk and to attain unity with the Absolute recommended not only fasting and meditation but also intoxicating drugs, not only self-denying asceticism but also sexual libertinism. Even religious ends do not justify all means, if the human being is to remain a human being and God remain God.

In the mystical tradition there is a call to allow oneself to be touched by the mystery of God. But anyone who argues for mystical unity with the divine should always keep in mind the dark side of mysticism. In the Christian tradition the naïve pre-modern explanation of paranormal phenomena of consciousness by demonic or divine influence has long since given way to a differentiated psychological diagnosis. Visions, auditions, inspirations are familiar to psychiatrists from their work with schizophrenic, manic or over-excited patients and are no longer given religious interpretations. What was once interpreted as the 'dark night of the soul' is now diagnosed as depression, the dryness of the soul as a burn-out syndrome. States of anxiety, guilt feelings and problems in making relationships can be treated as neurosis.

I have noted such phenomena in people around me: are they in fact illnesses? Both good psychiatrists and good theologians are cautious here. What is decisive is the long-term effect on the personality as a whole. It can be that a psychosis proves to be a breakthrough experienced on the way to healing. Maturing is not always a linear process without breaks and deviations. Psychological drugs and shock therapy are no substitute for working through thoughts in psychotherapy and a sensitive assimilation through behavioural therapy. If for example a hitherto successful writer or scholar does not want a new project to succeed, or perhaps will not even embark on one, for whatever reason, psychological drugs at best are only of provisional help.

However, in some mental illnesses religious problems are beyond psychiatrists and psychologists. Therefore pastors too have their independent role within the therapeutic team. Clinical pastors should certainly have a clinical training alongside a solid theological training, but their task is not to slip into the role of psychiatrists or psychotherapists. They are not equipped for medication or depth-psychological analysis but for the interpretation of religious meaning and guidance. So 'extraordinary' spiritual experiences should not all be therapied away as diseases; they remain dangerous and warnings have been given about them in the churches. One can accept them but should not seek them.

Of course there are also genuine religious mystics in Christianity. I have great admiration for the Benedictine monk Bede Griffiths, whom I visited during a lecture tour in his Sat-Chit-Ananda Shamtivanam in Tiruchirappalli in southern India. He showed by his life how one can be a Christian fully acculturated into Indian culture, and boldly criticized the centralized Roman system. I also treasure the Jesuit H. M. Enomiya-Lassalle, who lived in Japan and had an exceptional gift for combining Zen meditation with Christian spirituality. He was present at the opening of the Second Vatican Council and was the first Christian Zen master to suffer under the Roman system. Unfortunately I was unable to meet the world-famous Trappist monk Thomas Merton on my visit to Kentucky because of pressure of time. All the great mystics of Christian provenance are now dead, but they still have a great following.

I admire the great Hindu unitary vision of the all-embracing nameless Whole in which the separation of the individual (*atman*) from his origin, the all-penetrating world-principle (*Brahman*) can be overcome. For Hinduism, mysticism, at least since the late-Vedic period of the older Upanishads, stands at the centre of the religion. I also believe that one can find God not only 'in the heights' but also in the heart, in a purified inner self. Then it is more inward to me than I am myself.

And yet, the fundamental difference between mystical and prophetic religion needs to be noted. One often hears that all religions are the same because the same mystical experience underlies all of them. But that is a statement for which there is no kind of empirical proof. This is not about different interpretations of the same experience but about different experiences and thus different basic types of religion.

Whenever I speak with people immersed in Indian religion I become aware that like Christians, Jews and Muslims generally, I am rooted deeply in the prophetic tradition. Whether one looks to Abraham, Moses, David and the Israelite prophets, or to Jesus the Messiah (Christ) of the Christians or to the Prophet Muhammad, for all of them there is no unity but an irreducible difference between the holy God and creator and his fallible sinful creature. That is shown by Moses, who veils his face before God in the bush that burns but is not consumed. It is shown by Jesus' remark to an admirer: 'Why do you call me good? No one is good but God?' (Mark 10.18). It is shown by Muhammad who knows the essence of religion in Islam = subjection, submission to God. All this directs me to the infinite difference, which has often been stressed in the last century: God is wholly Other, different from man and the world.

But I do not exclude a convergence of prophetic and mystic religions. Various experiences in India and the Middle East can be interpreted in terms of each other, transferred from one cultural context to another and linguistically reformulated. All those who have had mystical experiences of unity in India with gurus, such as the physicist and philosopher Carl Friedrich von Weizsäcker, a conversation partner whom I prize highly, were already familiar with Indian wisdom.

Here it should be noted that mystical experience, too, is by no means uniform and orientated on unity, with no differentiation. In India, for example, the doctrine of the total unity of God and world, as in the mystical philosophy of Shankara (9th century), the most famous Hindu thinker, has not found the most adherents. Nor has the doctrine of the total split between God and world, the dualism of Madhva (13th century), Shankara's mystical opponent. The doctrine of differentiated unity as developed by Ramanuja (12th century), also a mystical thinker, reformer and founder of monasteries, is more widespread. As a Christian I personally believe neither in a total identification of God and the world nor in a total separation between them. Rather, I believe in God in the world and the world in God, in other words in unity in differentiation. But – one might object – is not a Jew, Christian or Muslim *a priori* attached to the personal image of the God of the Bible and the Qur'an? That is a difficult question.

## God – personal or apersonal?

Let me say clearly straightway: I do not know what God looks like, nor can I nor do I want to make an image of him. 'God' is other, breaks apart all our ideas. For me the decisive question is not whether God should be understood personally or non-personally, but whether he can be addressed or not. Why? Because in the end the possibility and meaningfulness of both prayer and worship depend on that, and both of these are essential for my spirituality.

Of course in my youth I had a simple, naïve, anthropomorphic, human-like understanding of God 'from above'. At the beginning of life that is normal. It is less normal that a grown man or woman should preserve his or her childlike understanding of God in spite of all their other further development and education. It has touched me but also irritated me to hear from a first-class specialist, a former director of the Tübingen clinic, that he still prays as before but still only one prayer: 'Angels come, make me pious, that I may come to you in heaven.'

Seen as a whole the Hebrew Bible, New Testament and Qur'an are beyond doubt shaped by a personal understanding of God. But the Indian mystical tradition also found its way in the West, into Greece through Asia Minor at an early stage. There are already individual mystical elements in Paul and John, who around the year 100 formulated as a saying of Jesus, 'I and the Father are one' (John 10.30). But Jesus also requires this unity from the disciples, 'That they may be one as we are one' (John 17.11). Later, mystical elements appear in the Alexandrian theologians Clement and Origen (3rd century), in the North African Augustine (4th/5th centuries) and above all – under the pseudonym of a disciple of Paul – in the mystical philosopher Dionysius the Areopagite

(5th/6th centuries). The term 'mystical theology', from which our word 'mysticism' derives, comes from him.

Conversely, in India the mystical religion of the Upanishads later fuses with more personally orientated cults: those of Vishnu, Bhagavan, Krishna, Rama. But in the Indian religions mysticism remains at the centre, in the prophetic religions at the margin. In the church, mystics often came under suspicion and were mercilessly persecuted by the Inquisition, for example the French religious Marguerite Porète (burnt 1310), the German Meister Eckhart and the Spaniards John of the Cross and Teresa of Avila. In Judaism and in Islam too it was easy to fall under the suspicion of the identification of human beings with God and be accused of blasphemy and self-deification. The most famous cases in the three prophetic religions are the Islamic mystic Al Halaj, who was hanged in Baghdad, probably for political reasons; the mystical thinker Giordano Bruno, who was burnt by the Inquisition in 1600 in Rome and the Portuguese–Dutch philosopher of unity, Baruch Spinoza, who was expelled in 1656 from the Amsterdam Synagogue because of his criticism of dogmas.

In today's industrial society orientated on rationality and technology a holistic understanding of human beings and God seems to me to be particularly important. I am trying to unite the two without contradiction: on the one hand to preserve my Christian faith orientated on a God who can be addressed, on the other to interpret all elements of human form (anthropomorphic) in the image of God symbolically. After its tremendous restoration I paid another visit to the Vatican Sistine chapel with its depictions of the creator of light, sun, moon and stars and finally of Adam and Eve, man and woman. In our era of space research, however, only a few people will understand these pictures realistically and imagine God still as a super-terrestrial male being with a grey beard. Images such as the sun or the sea, or concepts such as the supreme good, love itself, being itself, seem more appropriate.

Albert Einstein, inspired by Spinoza, expressed objections to a personal understanding of God. I take them seriously. If he speaks of cosmic reason or if Eastern thinkers speak of the 'One (*tad ekam*)', of 'Nirvana', 'void (*shunyata*)', 'absolute Nothingness', 'shining darkness' we have to understand this as an often paradoxical expression of veneration of the mystery of the Absolute which cannot be caught either in concepts or in notions – a *theologia negativa* over against all too human 'theistic' notions of God. Therefore, as I have said, the term 'God' is rejected by Buddhists, who do accept the one Supreme Reality (Dharmakaya, Buddhakaya, Nirvana).

Be this as it may, it seems to me indisputable that God is not a person as the human being is person: the all-embracing, all-permeating is never an object from which I can differentiate myself as a human being, in order to talk of it. The primal ground, primal support and primal goal of all reality which determines me as a believer, which is closer to me than my neck-vein, as the Qur'an (Surah 50.16) says metaphorically, is not a limited individual person among other persons. God is not a superman nor even a burdensome superego. The concept of person too is thus only a cipher for God: God is not the supreme person among other persons. God bursts open the concept of person. God is more than person.

But a second thing also seems to me to be indisputable: God is no less than a person. Precisely because God is no 'object'; precisely because, as is emphasized in Eastern wisdom, he cannot be grasped, seen through, kept at one's disposal, manipulated, he is also not impersonal, not 'sub-personal'. He is no thing among things, no cause among causes. God who makes possible the coming into being of the personal, also breaks open the concept of the impersonal. God is also no less than a person.

Instead of 'personal' and 'apersonal' one can use the theological terms 'transpersonal', 'suprapersonal'. But those who think that they have understood God with such terms forget that God is and always remains the incomprehensible, invisible, indefinable. Or one can speak of a '*coincidentia oppositorum* – a coming together of opposites', as the Renaissance thinker Nicholas of Cusa whom I have already mentioned did: as maximum also minimum and so transcending maximum and minimum. God is 'the wholly Other' and yet '*interior intimo meo* – more inward to me than my innermost being' (Augustine).

Have I perhaps taken all this far too theoretically? At any rate it will be easier to understand in the light of religious practice. Two basic forms of spirituality in the narrower sense are expressed in the prophetic and mystical basic form of religion: the prophetic in prayer, the mystical in meditation. I have practised both.

## Pray or meditate?

Praying is literally child's play. I learned to pray in the family as a matter of course, above all before meals and before going to bed. Unusually this took place in specific formulae addressed to 'dear God'. They were usually prayers to be heard and helped, for mercy and forgiveness, and also thanksgiving and praise.

In church at that time praying was still more fixed on particular formulae and rites, liturgically stylized and refined. If I did not understand the Latin (before the Second Vatican Council liturgy was in Latin), I got bored. But soon after I started school my parents gave me a thick bilingual 'People's Missal' in which I could read the German translation and with growing knowledge of Latin also the Latin original text, which was often very tortuous. I never liked long services, and the Rosary with the more than fifty Ave Marias and more than five Our Fathers which was recommended to us was not my favourite prayer. What was worst, though, say in Lent, was the 'Psalter', which consisted of three Rosaries and lasted at least three-quarters of an hour.

In my seven years in Rome prayer was thought particularly important and there was a great deal more of it. I joined in everything with complete seriousness, day after day, from the 'silent mass' through the Latin choral office and the German sing-and-pray mass to the pontifical masses of bishops and the bombastic papal masses in St Peter's. Along with the daily celebration of the eucharist, other services were obligatory in the German College: silent morning and evening prayer in the chapel and the adoration after lunch and supper which had already been opened and closed in the refectory with the grace. Before the evening meal there was the litany, sometimes also sung vespers or compline. Truly, prayer did not fall far short of study; it could also have fitted well in any contemplative religious order.

Yes, praying can be simple – but meditation? Meditation has to be learned; in the mystical tradition in Hinduism and Buddhism, it is fundamentally different from the kind of prayer I have described. A psychologically complex method of meditation has been developed, especially in meditative or Zen Buddhism: attention to one's own breathing, supported by slow ritual walking or the monotonous recitation of Buddhist sutras.

I have taken part in various meditation exercises in Burma, India, Japan, Tibet and on Hawaii. I understand how Christians too can experience peace, relaxation, forgetfulness of the self, a true liberation also from church ritualism and liturgical business. This practice of the monastic tradition comes about essentially through being detached from the world and one's own passions and turning inwards. Methodologically and systematically it is meant to lead to the ultimate reality – in Hinduism understood as 'fullness', in Buddhism more as 'emptiness'. Meditation (*zen* = immersion) is meant to become concentration of the will through a breathing technique practised and observed in strict discipline in 'sitting' (= Japanese *za*), and from there to released, passively grasped, contemplation forgetful of the self and finally to complete wakefulness without content and the experiences of illumination. But Western people too can sit in silence with a quiet, level breathing and attempt not to think of anything, or recite the holy syllable OM, which for Indians is the most important mantra (Sanskrit 'tool for thought'), so as to calm the spirit and pacify the soul.

## A higher form of praying?

There is also meditation in Christianity, usually called contemplation. I practised it at the German College for seven years, every morning, half an hour before breakfast and the eucharist, prepared for the previous evening by so called 'contemplation points'. In addition there were 'spiritual exercises', either three days or eight days each year to be spent in complete silence. However, this daily meditation was not about focusing on one's own breath, nor about not-thinking, but about contemplating a scene in the Bible (above all from the life of Jesus), or a biblical saying, or generally reflecting on a religious festival or special event.

We were also introduced to the 'higher forms' of prayer. The Christian mystics too – the founder of the Jesuit Order and the German College, the Spaniard Ignatius Loyola was one of them – have described a 'ladder of prayer' which has various stages, presented and practised above all in Christian monasticism and the Ignatian Exercises. So I too learned different forms of prayer and through analysing the phases of prayer attained inner clarity; I could practise self-criticism and orientate myself completely on the Absolute. And I zealously strove to attain these higher stages and 'simple prayer'. A couple of times I was granted the emotion of being filled completely with the presence of God and inner joy.

But I also realized that a special religious gift is needed for the 'higher stages' which I possess only to a degree and which can in no way be expected of any businessman and industrial worker, of any housewife or teacher or student. Together with high mystical and spiritual ideals sometimes came guilt feelings; prayer was made difficult and at times impossible because we could not reach these highest stages.

So it was an inner liberation for me to realize while meditating that neither the Hebrew Bible nor the New Testament has a method, a system and psycho-technique of prayer: there are no stages of prayer to be gone through, there is no psychological reflecting on prayer, no self-analyses, no breathing techniques or ascetic efforts to attain a particular state of the soul extending as far as an ecstasy in which one forgets oneself.

Instead of this I found in the Bible a naïve, unreflected 'conversation with God', in which I simply give expression to my faith, hope and love, and utter words of thanksgiving, praise, lament and petition. And though it is reported that the carpenter's son from Nazareth sometimes withdrew to pray alone, he taught his disciples only the short petitions of the 'Our Father'. None of this presupposes any special religious gift.

Therefore the Bible offers no justification for designating particular forms of prayer as 'higher'. Certainly, spiritually demanding forms of prayer may be engaged in by Christians, but they need not be. In no way may they be made a sign of a particular Christian quality, even the esoteric affair of a spiritual élite that feels itself to be above the 'average person' in praying.

No particular method of praying or meditating has become the norm for me in my mentally and often physically demanding life – just one of my favourite sayings from the Sermon on the Mount: 'And in praying do not heap up empty phrases as the Gentiles do; for they think that they will be heard for their many words. Do not be like them, for your Father knows what you need before you ask him. Pray then like this: Our Father who art in heaven . . . ' (Matthew 6.7–9).

Following this advice I pray regularly and have often recommended such prayer to others, especially giving brief thanks and saying a prayer inwardly before every meal, quite simply addressing the good God and saying thank you for a night spent more or less well or a day which has been more or less successful. And at the same time I ask for a piece of work, a speech, a lecture or a journey to be successful, or simply for bright sunshine in my heart when there is rain and storm outside; often I remember particular friends or relatives in sickness or in other critical situations, and sometimes say a 'Rest in peace' for someone who has died or a 'Have mercy on us' for a country or a region of the world when there is natural catastrophe or a dramatic political turn of events. In the evening I give thanks for the day and say a prayer for the night.

Of course I also know what psychoanalysis and brain physiologists have discovered by painstaking research, that during the night the human brain incessantly works over the impressions of the day. Some of my dreams make me think. But I also know something that neither psychoanalysts nor brain researchers can tell me: I am in God's hands, and therefore – in spite of all the problems that there can be and are – I should have no unnecessary concern about the next day.

Mahatma Gandhi said that 'prayer is the key of the morning and the bolt of the evening'. It never needs many words, but sometimes I also use a short verse from the Psalms: 'O give thanks to the Lord for he is good; for his steadfast love endures for ever' (Psalm 136.1). And in distress or in a sleepless night I can also simply say, 'God, my God . . .' That comforts me, strengthens me. Any time in the midst of everyday life I can pause for a few seconds to draw breath and open myself to transcendence.

I usually do that quietly by myself. I do not normally pray in a restaurant or in other public places. I do not pray 'to show myself to people', as a saying in the Sermon on the Mount puts it, but follow the instruction, 'When you pray, go into your room and shut the door and pray to your Father who is in secret' (Matthew 6.5f.). The prayer which follows as a basic pattern is deliberately put in the first person plural: 'Our Father who art in heaven . . .' (Matthew 6.9–13). Therefore I also value praying in community as long as it is not mechanical and formalistic, but comes from the heart – a moving, authentic 'service of God'.

There is great power and much encouragement in liturgy if it is ordered well and the people gathered together play an active part in it, if texts are not intoned in a boring way and high and fine-sounding prayers are not reeled off according to instructions, but when, whether in traditional or modern formulations, the whole person can stand behind it. I have always kept to a fixed foundation and framework for the eucharist in particular. But space and times, ceremonies, vestments and gestures, hymns and forms of speech – none of these are unassailable immutable constants, but variables of worship. In principle I do not use any formula of prayer in which I do not believe, and would recommend this to any pastor (one should show tolerance when it comes to traditional hymns). My criterion is not arbitrary: the texts should first be backed by the Christian message itself and secondly be comprehensible to people of today. Like many others I also formulate some prayers freely even in worship, following the early Christian custom. But *Gottesdienst*, 'service of God', to use the German term, is the central question for me: what God should it be about?

## The one God and the many gods?

For me the Bible is not just a literary heritage of world culture, not just part of the Western canon of education, but a unique testimony to experiences of God in faith down the centuries.

Anyone who like me has been born into the monotheistic tradition takes for granted what the Hebrew Bible, the New Testament and the Qur'an all announce. There is only one God, the God of the fathers, the God of Abraham, Isaac and Jacob, but also of Ishmael, the God of the mothers, Sarah and Hagar, Rebekah and Rachel, the God of the people of Israel. This is also the God of the Christians and the God of the Muslims. He is one and the same God. Such a monotheism could in no way be taken for granted from the beginning; on the contrary. In Israel it took many centuries before people realized that alongside the one God there are not only no higher gods (such as 'fate') or equally high gods (say divinized human beings) or lower gods (tribal gods and fertility gods). There are no other gods at all. He is not only the supreme but also the only and incomparable God.

Here we have to do with narratives about God that are millennia old. On the basis of the patriarchal form of rule, at least 3000 years old, God is depicted and addressed above also as 'Lord', 'King' and 'Father'. In a time of the equality of sexes and the democratic principle this causes considerable difficulties to many women in particular. Bad experiences with the earthly father are easily transferred to the heavenly Father and 'Lord', and conversely the authority of the heavenly Father is claimed to strengthen the authority of the male over and against women and children.

It is not enough here just to point out that in the Hebrew Bible a feminine side to God is already evident. There is maternal sympathy and compassion. This insight must be taken more seriously, and expressed in the liturgy. 'Father' and 'Lord' do not represent designations of God as male. Rather, they are symbols and ciphers for an invisible reality that transcends masculinity and femininity. Whenever I have to introduce the 'Our Father' in a service I say, 'Let us pray to the unspeakable mystery in our life, who is both father and mother'. And then, in what Paul Ricoeur calls a 'second naivety', I can simply pray 'Our Father who art in heaven'. I need not emphasize that I strictly reject the Roman Catholic argument that because God is to be understood as male it is impossible or inappropriate for women to be ordained; there are scriptural and contemporary reasons for women's ordination.

Jews, Christians and Muslims are monotheists – are the other religions polytheistic? Whenever I speak with educated Indians I observe how they do not like being described simplistically as polytheists, as believers in many Gods. For in India too there are monotheistic religions. Thus for many Indians Vishnu and Shiva are God. And others see behind all the different gods of India the one and only deity whom they call *Brahman* and who dwells in every human soul (*atman*). This God is all-embracing and all-permeating for them. The individual gods are regarded as aspects or manifestations of the one primal principle who are responsible for individual spheres: a god for the fertility of the earth, a god for good fortune in war, a god for the tricks of fate, a goddess for the dangers of love ... Polytheism, particularly that of the Egyptians and Greeks, has its indisputable aesthetic and poetic attraction, but also its intellectual difficulties, which have led to the victory of monotheism.

Conversely, I observe that many Indian visitors, say to baroque Catholic churches, receive the impression that Christianity is by no means monotheistic, but a thoroughly polytheistic religion, although Catholics do not address all the intermediate beings between God and human beings as gods but as angels and saints and call on them for help. And the speculation of the church fathers and theologians on the Trinity, which put the man Jesus of Nazareth on the same level as the Father (who in the New Testament is always exclusively called '*ho theos* – the God' whose Son is Jesus) puts the unity of God in question not only for Jews and Muslims.

Today's 'milieu' theologians – theology of hope, of liberation, of revolution, feminist, black, indigenous, native – are often criticized for making God serve their own ends and thus privatizing him. But that depends on their political orientation and shaping. At any rate they do not want to go against the faith that God is one.

## The power of life and the other powers

For Jews, Christians and Muslims, God is the Lord of all. He is the great power of life, who gives and sustains all life, all that is good. He may therefore expect trust and dedication from human beings. This strict, living, passionate, uncompromising belief in one God managed to establish itself in Israel only in the 7th/6th pre-Christian centuries in the controversy with Babylon. It remains the distinguishing mark of Israel among the peoples and at the same time the gift of Israel to the peoples. This belief in one God also has political consequences if it is taken seriously by believers.

I hear the objection that these are negative consequences. Those very religions which tie themselves to a single God behave in a particularly intolerant way to all the others, and are therefore unpeaceful and ready for violence. This objection must be taken seriously; it rests on experience. In order to counter it, it is not enough to point out that human beings have always been involved in religion and violence. Or that the wars which Christians waged, say, against the original inhabitants of Latin and North America, Africa and Australia, or Jews waged in Palestine and the Lebanon, or Muslims in the Balkans or against the Armenians – that all these wars cannot be blamed on belief in the one God.

It cannot be proved that the monotheistic religions of the Middle East are particularly prone to intolerance, fanaticism and a terrorist faith and that Hinduism and Buddhism are *a priori* ready for peace. There is fanaticism and terrorist faith everywhere. However, each religion should examine its sources and note that not only the Qur'an but also the Hebrew Bible contain acts of violence that may in no way serve as justification for acts of violence and wars in the present. And in the New Testament? Particularly in the Gospel of John, which was written late, there are christological statements that are constantly cited by fundamentalists and, understood exclusively, easily lead to the damnation of non-Christians.

Against this, positively it must be emphasized that in the Bible, from Cain and Abel to the Apocalypse, violence is not passed over. It is made a theme and in this way unsparingly confronts human beings with their violent nature. Violence is still a problem today in every modern society. In New York, in front of the United Nations building there is a powerful sculpture which symbolizes the saying of the great Israelite prophet: 'They shall beat their swords into ploughshares' (Isaiah 2.4) – today that is understood in all nations and religions. Wars are inhuman and must be prevented by every means. And particularly Christian crusader ideologists in America and in Europe must be reminded of a saying of Jesus of Nazareth: 'Blessed are the peacemakers, for they shall be called children of God' (Matthew 5.9).

In the light of the common faith of Jews, Christians and Muslims in the one God – the foundation of all their holy scriptures – peaceful coexistence is what is needed instead of scandalous fighting against one another. Common faith in the one God already forms the basis for better mutual understanding and a deeper solidarity of the three faith communities, all of which belong to the great monotheistic religious movement. Each of the three cannot in fact really understand its nature and history without a look at the two others. How can they still regard one another as 'unbelievers' (the Christian attitude towards Jews and Muslims), or as 'apostates' (the Jewish attitude to Christians and Muslims), or as 'superseded' (the Muslim attitude to Jews and Christians)? They should learn to understand themselves – and many already do so – as 'sons' and 'daughters', as 'brothers' and 'sisters' in belief in one and the same God. But another aspect of belief in the one God is no less important.

## The fall of the gods, ancient and modern

Belief in the one God is a guard against the divinization of natural power and the divinization of political power and those who hold it. Granted, belief in the one God does not contain any topical social programme, but it has decisive social consequences: it dethrones the divinized world powers in favour of the one true God.

This is still important for the tribal societies. Belief in the one God means a radical renunciation of the super-power of threatening or benevolent natural forces in an ever-returning cosmic dying and coming to be. But it is above all important for our secular, apparently atheistic age, where substitute gods have been and are constantly worshipped. Here belief in God means a radical renunciation of all dictators in state, religion and society who attribute to themselves God's properties or functions and claim quasi-divine worship and unconditional obedience. This was expressed in exemplary fashion in the Barmen Theological Declaration of the Confessing Church (1934) – inspired by Karl Barth – in the face of the claim of National Socialism to absoluteness.

But a lived-out belief in God also means renouncing other powers that are being divinized today. It is ultimately unimportant whether the idolatrous modern man and woman – be they 'monotheist' or 'polytheist' – sing their 'Great God we praise you' to the great god mammon, the great god sex or the great god power, to the great god science, nation or football, for which they are prepared to sacrifice everything. The fact remains that belief in one God stands as a contradiction to any pseudo-religion which subjects human beings to a non-godly power that enslaves them and robs them of human dignity.

But let's be self-critical – even some of the characteristics we attribute to the one true God are not unproblematic, for instance 'the Almighty'. I find a different attribute of God more important, indeed central for my 'spirituality', our spiritual existence.

## God as 'spirit'

'Almighty' (Latin *omnipotens* – 'capable of anything'; Greek *pantokrator* – 'ruler of all') is not my favourite attribute of God. In the Greek translation of the Hebrew Bible this word is used for *zebaot* (Lord of 'hosts') but in the New Testament – apart from the Apocalypse (and a quotation in Paul) – it is strikingly avoided. As a divine predicate it takes on importance only in the theology of the church fathers and the mediaeval Scholastics. And it appears even in modern state constitutions, which are proclaimed in the name of 'God, the Almighty'. This is manifestly a legitimating of political power, but at the same time it shows the limits to the politically powerful – especially after the deification of the Führer in National Socialism.

Enlightened belief in God can in fact form a well-founded counterbalance to the delusion that human beings are omnipotent, what the psychotherapist Horst Eberhard Richter calls the 'God complex'. In principle I would prefer other predicates of God from the New Testament such as 'all gracious' or (as in the Qur'an) 'all merciful'. Or even, if the word had not been so degraded, simply 'dear God' as an expression of what from a Christian point of view must be the deepest description of God: 'God is love' (1 John 4.8,16).

I think that it is an all-too-external, anthropomorphic notion to imagine God as a mighty 'Lord' and 'Ruler' who controls or 'guides' all the events in the world, even those which are apparently fortuitous, even the indeterminate sub-atomic processes. In that case, what about all the waste and dead-ends of evolution, the extinct species, the animals and human beings who perished miserably? And the infinite suffering and all the evil in this world, past and present? The conception of an almighty Lord God has no answer to this.

The opposite to this anthropomorphic notion of God is for me the biblical understanding of God as spirit; this is particularly helpful in the context of an evolutionary world-view. The biblical evidence for spirit is rich in metaphors and pictorial representations: tangible yet not tangible, invisible yet powerful, as important to life as the air that one breathes, as loaded with energy as the wind, the storm – that is the spirit. All languages have a word for it but the different gender attached to it shows that the spirit cannot be so easily defined. *Spiritus* in Latin is masculine, as too is *Geist* in German; *ruach* in Hebrew is feminine and the Greek knows only the neutral *pneuma*. So at any rate spirit is quite different from a human person. The *ruach* is that breath of air, 'breeze' or 'storm' of God that moves over the waters at the beginning of the account of creation in the book of Genesis. And the *pneuma*, according to the New Testament, stands in opposition to the flesh, that is, to created transitory reality.

The spirit is not – as often in the history of religions – a magical, substantial, mysteriously supernatural fluid of a dynamic nature. It is not a spiritual 'something', a magical being of an animistic kind, a spiritual being or ghost. 'Dove' and 'tongues of fire' are only images for its effect. So what according to the New Testament is the Spirit, the Holy Spirit? It is none other than God himself. God as power, force, grace. The power that goes out from God that touches but cannot be touched. A life-giving but also a judging power. A giving grace, but a grace that is not at our disposal. And what is the 'Holy' Spirit? It is holy in that, as God's spirit, it is different from the unholy spirit, that of human beings and their world, and must be regarded as the spirit of the only one who is holy, God himself.

In a spiritualized understanding of God in an evolutionary world-view many earlier options of Greek or Scholastic origin seem to me to be outdated. I do not understand God as Spirit as an unmoved mover, who works over or behind the world. Rather I understand God as the dynamic spiritual reality that makes possible, permeates and consummates the quite ambivalent process of the development of the world from within. Not exalted above but in the middle of the sorry processes of the world: in, with and under human beings and things. The origin, centre and goal of the world process is God himself.

Nor do I understand God as spirit as a miracle-working God of the gaps, who is at work only at particularly important individual points of the world process and my human life. Rather, I understand him as a creative and consummating primal power and support of the world that is constantly at work. So he is a controller of the world who is immanent in the world and at the same time above it, omnipresent also in chance and disaster, completely respecting the laws of nature and my freedom, whose origin he himself is: 'Where the spirit of the Lord is, there is freedom' (2 Corinthians 3.17).

So I do not want to decide. World or God is not an alternative! There can be neither a world without God nor a God identical with the world. Against atheism and pantheism I advocate a differentiated unity: God in the world and the world in God. Thus I understand God and world, God and human beings not as two competing finite causalities where one gains what the other loses. I am convinced that if God really is the all-embracing infinite spiritual foundation, stay and meaning of the world and human beings, the infinite God loses nothing if human beings in their finitude gain. Rather, God gains when human beings gain.

Of course this spiritualized understanding of God has consequences for my understanding of evolution, creation and consummation, of belief in providence and miracles.

## Creative origin: no particular model of the world

God is not evolution, as Pierre Teilhard de Chardin misleadingly put it, but God is in evolution. Yet I feel great sympathy for this Jesuit who as a theologian and palaeontologist was the first creatively to bring together theology and science to reflect on the problems they have in common. The leaders of the church did not thank him; on the intervention of Rome he had already lost his chair at the Institut Catholique in Paris before I went there for my doctorate. There was a ban on his publications and he did not see any of his main works published before his death. Banished to New York, he died there in solitude in 1955. It was only with difficulty that during my guest semester there in 1968 I found his grave on the Hudson north of New York. Only after the Second Vatican Council, in which my friend Léon-Arthur Elchinger, Bishop of Strasbourg, still vainly called for Teilhard's rehabilitation, did theologians take any interest in his works.

Like so many modern insights, the notion of evolution became established in Catholic theology despite the constant opposition from Rome. Today we know that our universe is in all probability infinite in space and time. It came into being 13.7 billion years ago from the explosion of a tiny unit of extreme density, temperature and initial thrust, in which the potential for millions of galaxies was contained. And this universe is still expanding on the basis of the conditions that seem to have been set from the very beginning, including space and time.

Now I am not a scientist, but if I were an astrophysicist I would ask myself about the very first beginning. This Big Bang, about the cause of which physics has not yet been able to say the slightest thing, seems to be an impassable barrier for human knowledge. So physics cannot explain where the universal natural constants come from which were already given in the first hundredth of a second after the Big Bang and which govern all physical events to the present day. As a physicist I would appeal to the philosopher Kant, who argued that science no longer has any competence beyond the horizon of experience and therefore cannot ask the fundamental questions of human beings about the origin of the universe. But it is also not competent, I would immediately add along Kant's lines, to dismiss this question as meaningless.

With philosophy, which already sought the basic principle of reality from the pre-Socratics on, religion is responsible for the question of the origin of the universe. But it is hardly possible for the religious scholar to consider the ideas of the origin of the cosmos (cosmogony) that often precedes the origin of the gods (theogony). There are cosmogonies according to which the world and human beings owe their existence to the movement of impersonal forces. There are others in which several gods created everything – or just the one creator God.

For most scientists the references in the prophetic religions to a creator God cause difficulties. That is understandable, since the two biblical accounts of creation in the book of Genesis were written around 900 and around 500 BCE. Neither gives scientific information about the origin of the world and human beings. But they communicate an impressive testimony of faith about the ultimate origin of the universe that the scientist can neither confirm nor refute. At the beginning of all things is God. From the chaos ('the earth was without form and void') God makes the ordered 'cosmos' and produces the elements and all creatures. That God created the world 'from nothing' is a late insight in the Bible; it only comes from the Hellenistic period. This philosophical statement may not be understood as making nothingness independent, as if it were so to speak a black hole before or alongside God. Rather, it is an expression that the world and human beings, along with space and time, owe themselves to no other power but God alone.

Have these age-old accounts of creation, which do not speak in mathematical formulae and physical models but in images (metaphors) and likenesses (parables), still something to say about the origin of the universe? Certainly there are truths on which scientists too should reflect, because they are relevant not only to science but above all to our lives:

- that God is the origin of each and everything;
- that in world history God does not compete with some evil demonic principle;
- that the world as a whole and in detail, that matter, the human body and sexuality are fundamentally good;
- that the human being is the whole of the process of creation and that God's creation already means his gracious care for the world and human beings.

Astrophysics in particular teaches me that the years of my life are nothing by comparison with the age of humankind. And even the years of humankind are nothing in comparison with the whole of the Milky Way, which comprises over a billion individual stars, one of which is the sun. And this Milky Way is in turn a speck of dust by comparison with those piles of galaxies, first understood as 'nebulae', each of which contains

10,000 galaxies, so that the number of observable galaxies runs into the hundreds of millions. Here even the scientist must ask the one question: What am I in the universe? What does it all mean? Where does it all come from? From nothing? Does the nothing explain anything and is our reason content with that? What could a possible alternative be? The only alternative, which of course pure reason cannot give me because it transcends the experiential horizon of space and time, is that the whole comes from that first creative ground of grounds that we call God, the creator God. And although I cannot prove it, I can affirm God with good reason in that trust which for me is so rational, tested and enlightened, in which I have already affirmed God's existence. For if the God who exists is truly God, then he is not just God for me here and now but is already God from the beginning, God from all eternity.

But to avoid misunderstandings that suggest themselves to scientists, I immediately add that belief in creation by no means requires me to decide for this or that one of the changing physical models of the world. It names the presupposition for all models of the world and the world in general and is reconcilable with different models of the world. To believe in a creator of the world means only in enlightened trust to affirm that the ultimate origin of the world and human beings does not remain inexplicable, that the world and man are not thrown meaninglessly from nothingness to nothingness, that despite all that is meaningless and valueless as a whole they are meaningful and valuable, not chaos, but cosmos, because they have their first and last security in God, their primal ground, author, creator. How good it is that nothing compels me to this belief. I can freely decide for it myself.

Belief in a creative ground of grounds changes my position in the world, my attitude to the world. It roots my basic trust and makes my trust in God concrete. However, it also requires practical consequences: to perceive my responsibility for my fellow human beings and the environment and to approach my worldly tasks with deep earnestness, more hope and greater realism. But I hear the objection: aren't the biblical miracle stories a constant stumbling block, quite unrealistic and absolutely unacceptable to scientists?

## Belief in miracles today?

I am not a scientist, but I find the most recent results of microbiology as convincing as those of astrophysics. However the transition from inanimate to life may be explained in detail, it rests on biochemical regularities and thus on the self-organization of matter, the molecule. Just as ever more complex molecules and systems have formed from primal matter through electrical charges, so life based on carbon has developed from nuclei of hydrogen and proteins. I have understood that already at the level of molecules the principle established by Darwin first in the world of plants and animals of 'natural selection' and 'survival of the fittest' reigns. This tendency towards fitness drives development 'upwards' at the cost of the less well-adapted molecules. Thus there is the development from single-cell to multi-cell living beings and finally to higher plants and animals.

As a believer I simply have to note that according to the most recent results of biochemistry these extremely complex processes did not need a special intervention by the creator God. Although many questions are still unexplained, the origin of life is an event understood through physics and chemistry. For this I need not assume any cosmic power of life or energy that was still presupposed by Pierre Teilhard de Chardin, whom I have already mentioned, in the direction of an omega point. In the individual process the event is governed by chance as in quantum mechanics, but at the same time runs from the beginning according to guiding laws of nature.

Were I a biologist I would of course also ask myself: doesn't self-regulating evolution make God superfluous? But as the physicist had to concede to the biologist, the existence of God can neither be postulated nor excluded on the basis of this evidence from molecular biology. The process of evolution as such reveals no meaning. Human meanings must provide the meaning themselves. So for the biologist too there is no intellectual compulsion but freedom of choice. But he will hardly believe in God if he understands God in evolution as a person above history who by virtue of his creative power from time to time descends on and overcomes the world with miracles, even contrary to the laws of nature.

So of course the question arises: can we still believe in miracles in this world of evolution? The Bible, from beginning to end, is full of them. The question already bothered me when writing my *On Being a Christian*: how do I reconcile these miracle stories with the strictly causal process of development if 'nature miracles' break the elementary laws of nature? Now of course I can understand that today people who are little affected by the results of science want to take literally these biblical 'nature miracles' which violate the unbroken causal connection. I am against 'compulsory enlightenment'. But enlightened believers in God do not have to seek ingenious scientific explanations for the 'nature miracles' but must take the results of modern biblical scholarship seriously. This is vitally important, for scientists as well.

That means that scientists, too, will be able to draw a distinction. First, there are miracle stories involving historical events that can hardly be disputed, especially the many charismatic healings of Jesus that include the expulsion of demons that bring sickness. A second genre of miracle stories is simply about amazing but not completely unusual natural events, for example, the plagues of flies and locusts and other plagues in the expulsion from Egypt. A third genre, however, evidently involves stories with legendary elaborations, for example, the sun which according to the book of Joshua stands still over Gibeon, but also in the New Testament: the walking on the water, the stilling of the storm, the miraculous feeding of thousands, the three raisings from the dead. These are the real 'nature miracles', which we need not take literally. Preachers should be more honest here.

It is also helpful for scientists to know that no breaking of the laws of nature can be demonstrated historically in the Bible. Why? Because the people at the time of the Bible were not at all interested in the laws of nature. They did not know them. They did not think scientifically and consequently did not understand the miracle stories as breaking the laws of nature.

For the people of biblical times these were simply great 'signs' through which God reveals his presence in the world: 'God's mighty acts'. Miracle stories set out to interpret and confirm God's word, they seek to strengthen belief in God. Nowhere in the Bible is belief in miracles required, belief that there are miracles or even that this or that event is a miracle. Rather, it is simply expected that people should believe that God is at work in history.

Rather than taking the miracle stories literally, I would prefer to try to explain them and put the emphasis in the right place. It is not the shaking of Mount Sinai that is important but the message of the covenant with God and commandments that Moses receives on this occasion. It is not the plagues of Egypt that are important but the testimony of God who demonstrates his saving power. It is not the wonderful journey through the Red Sea that is important but the message of God whom the people experience as the God of liberation. So unlike the historical healing miracles, the so-called 'nature miracles' stand in the Bible as metaphors, and as in poetry, so too these metaphors do not seek to break the laws of nature.

But what then – and the question cannot be avoided – about those biblical narratives which announce a terrifying endtime?

## Consummation: our last hour?

Much that has been taught by physicists about the 'last three minutes of the universe' is speculative: 'Conjectures about the ultimate fate of the universe' is the subtitle of the physicist Paul Davies' book *The Last Three Minutes*. Most cosmological physicists begin by assuming that our world is anything but stable, immutable, eternal. However, they differ as to whether the expansion of the universe which began with the Big Bang will one day come to a standstill and then move over to contraction (for which there is no evidence) or whether it will go on constantly to a definitive end.

Today the overwhelming majority of astrophysicists support the second hypothesis: the expansion will go on without being braked and even accelerate until the matter in the interior of stars is burned through core processes into 'star ashes'. Unlike contraction, this process can already be observed precisely, and the different stages of the development of the stars have been verified by astronomers in terms of physics and mathematics in an amazingly precise way. But I ask myself whether I should worry about something that will not happen, if it happens at all, for 500 billion years, when the store of hydrogen in the interior of the sun is exhausted and coolness, silence and death enter our cosmos.

Today we are threatened by the imminent expectation of an end to our earth, more precisely an end to the human world – brought about by human beings. Science provides dramatic empirical warning signs of this: the amount of $CO_2$ is rising, the atmosphere is getting warmer, glaciers are melting and permafrost is disappearing. The hole in the ozone layer is getting wider, and the climate is changing more quickly than expected. At the same time over-population and catastrophic pollution threaten. Infected air, poisoned ground, water polluted with chemicals, a shortage of water can all lead to conflict. Prominent physicists such as Martin Rees are asking: Is this our final century? Not to mention that we are the first human generation capable of putting an end to humanity in the shortest possible time through unleashing nuclear power.

I am not surprised that in the face of such catastrophic development, fundamentalist Bible believers in particular are attempting to instil fear and terror into people with the fearsome apocalyptic visions from the New Testament (cf. Matthew 24.6–8, 29). In the United States in recent times there has been a boom in 'Christian' endtime literature which has replaced the technological novels about the future which were so optimistic; this has also had a political effect, especially in the notion of a final biblical battle called 'Armageddon' against the 'realm of the evil one'.

But just as the biblical narratives of God's creative work have been taken from the environment of the time, so too have those of God's final work been taken from contemporary apocalyptic, that current of time stamped by expectations of the end in Judaism and in early Christianity. In fact the spectral visions of the Apocalypse are an urgent admonition to humankind and the individual to recognize the 'signs of the time', the seriousness of the situation. Just as the biblical protology cannot be a report of events at the beginning, so too the biblical eschatology cannot be a prognosis of end events. We look in vain for a revealed screenplay of the last act of the human tragedy. Here too the Bible does not speak a scientific language of facts but a metaphorical language of images which are not to be taken literally but must be understood contemporaneously.

Do these poetic images and narratives about the beginning and end still have any meaning today? They stand for what cannot be investigated by science, for what is hoped for and feared. The biblical statements about the end of the world give me a testimony of faith to the consummation of God's work on his creation. What I mean is that at the end of the history of the world and above all at the end of my life is not nothingness, but God. According to the message of the Bible the history of human life leads up to that last goal of goals, the ultimate culmination that we call God. We do not come to an end, either as individual beings in death or as the human race in an end to the world, but are completed, we hope, in the consummation of the kingdom of God, however that is to be imagined.

I cannot prove the God who brings all things to fulfilment any more than I can prove the creator God, but I can affirm him in that trust in which I have already affirmed God's very existence. For if the God who exists is truly God, then he is not only God for me here and now but also God at the end, at the end of my life and the end of the world. If alpha, then omega. Or as it says in the liturgy: God for ever and ever.

But who wouldn't like to know more about God and his ways? Moses once expresses the wish to see God's glory. But the answer he is given is: 'You cannot see my face, for no man can see me and live' (Exodus 33.20). However, he may place himself in a cleft of the rock and God will hold his hand protectively over him as he passes by: 'Then I shall take away my hand and you will see my back. But my face will not be seen' (Exodus 33.23).

And so it will remain until the end of our earthly life. We can always only recognize God's power and glory and his 'providence' afterwards.

If I look back on my life in retrospect, I can recognize that I have been especially supported and guided, and where. That must be enough for me, and it is.

# Chapter 7

## Model of Life

*Had God so willed, he would have made you a single community. But he wills to test you in what he has given you. Be zealous then in the good.*

(Qur'an, Surah 5.48)

A way of life with meaning in life, supported by a power of life – but following which model?

When I made my first journey around the world in 1964 and experienced Asia with wondering eyes, I was utterly fascinated by the diversity of faces: Indian, Thai, Chinese, Japanese women, men and children. It was almost boring when I then saw predominantly white faces in San Francisco.

### Religions in competition

Now that on our spiritual tour of the mountain we have got over the steep wall of transcendence, we note that there are different ways to the summit. The diversity of peoples and cultures is expressed weightily right at the beginning of the first book of the Hebrew Bible. After the flood 'the tribes of the sons of Noah are listed according to their descent into their peoples'; from them the peoples of the earth branched off. However, because of their arrogant delusion of unity at the building of the tower of Babel they were dispersed all over the earth and their languages were confused (Genesis 10–11).

In the New Testament the narrative of Pentecost in the Acts of the Apostles (Acts 2) gives an answer to the confusion of languages. The various peoples with their different languages, explicitly also the Arabs, are mentioned. In their different languages they understand one and the same message through the working of the spirit.

But especially the Qur'an recognizes explicitly the different religions and sees them caught up in competition for the good. Religions are essentially responsible for human beings taking very different ways to salvation. The different contents are in global rivalry and have shaped very different cultural and religious profiles which today more than ever can be compared. Given all the process of economic and political inter-weaving a unitary religion is not in sight.

When I stayed in other continents, I often reflected what would have become of me had I not been born in Europe but in another cultural circle. Perhaps I would then have shaped my life according to quite a different model, a quite different pattern of feeling, thinking and acting. For example, according to the Hindu model.

## The Hindu model

Assume that I was born in India as one of the almost 1.2 billion people there. Originally 'Hindus' and 'Indians' were the same. But today 'Hinduism' describes the Indian religion, to the various currents of which around four-fifths of all Indians belong. The culture of Indians, their way of living and world of ideas are governed by it. Were I a Hindu (or indeed an adherent of the Indian reform movements of Buddhism and Jainism) as a matter of course I would believe in the age-old teaching of the cycle of rebirths, in a cycle in the courses of nature and in the different periods of the world, a cycle also in the reincarnation of human beings. And I would certainly believe that morally right or wrong action (Sanskrit *karma*) in my previous life would govern my present life and my positive or negative action in the present life my state in the next.

Presumably I would also have studied the ancient holy scriptures, the Vedas (the holy 'knowledge'), and the writings that interpret them. Even if I hadn't, I would certainly have the conviction that an 'eternal order' (*santana dharma*) prevailed: an all-embracing cosmic and moral order which governs all life and which all human beings should observe regard-less of what class or caste they are born into. However, here defined dogmas and formal orthodoxy would be unimportant to me; Hinduism knows no binding magisterium. Rather, right action would be important: the correct rite, custom, the living out of religion. And I would not be primarily concerned with particular human rights but with being what God has made me and to that extent with the duties and responsibilities that I have to family, society, to the gods or God.

Possibly I would feel at home in a religion of eternal *dharma*. Why? Because this order is grounded in the cosmos. Therefore it transcends space and time and with rites often lasting over centuries is extremely stable. But at the same time this eternal order shows itself flexible enough to adopt and accept the most opposed religious forms and shapes and to show different ways to salvation:

- the way of doing (*karmamarga*);
- the way of knowledge (*jnanamarga*);
- the way of surrender (*bhaktimarga*).

All are ways of purification, moral, spiritual and religious.

To take my thoughts further: as in Christianity, if I was educated to the same degree, presumably in Hinduism too, I would be dissatisfied with some rites and teachings, precepts and practices. I would be one of today's Hindu critics. I would have no time for the social élites preferred by the 'eternal order' who all too readily – with a reference to the cosmic law – insist on their given rights and privileges and miss out on social involvement. Without any tendency towards fundamentalism I would certainly be one of the critical thinkers and reformers of India who fight the caste system which, though officially abolished, in practice still functions, and I would fight for an improved position for women and the around 150 million out-castes.

Moreover, because I would be antipathetic to the apparently insuperable caste system, like many Indians in former centuries I might turn my back on Hinduism and incline towards Buddhism. A famous example of someone who did this is B. R. Ambedkar, the first minister of justice in independent India, who in 1956 led a mass conversion of around half a million 'untouchables' to Buddhism. He is still highly respected in India today.

## The Buddhist model

Had I been born in Sri Lanka, Thailand, Burma or Japan, countries that I know and admire, I would probably have been one of the many hundreds of millions of Buddhists in the world. I would then share with Hindus the world-view of a cycle of births and eras, and also the notion of determination by *karma*, earlier deeds. But as a Buddhist I would reject the authority of the Vedas and thus the rule of the Brahmans, bloody sacrifices and the Hindu caste order.

My religion would not simply be comparable to the organically flowing Ganges, as the 4000 years of Hinduism are. Rather, it would be orientated on the epoch-making Indian Siddartha Gautama, named the Buddha, the 'Awakened', the 'Enlightened'. Since the seventh century before our era he has offered men and women a way of spiritualization, internalization, immersion. Through his teaching (*dharma*) he gives them answers to the four primal questions, the 'four noble truths': What is suffering? All of life. How does it come about? Through 'thirst for life', greed, hatred, blindness. How can it be overcome? Through not clinging on and thus through conquering the thirst for life. What is the way to achieve this? The 'eightfold path' of the Buddha.

The Buddha does not seek to offer an explanation of the world but a doctrine of salvation and ways of salvation: how shall sufferers find liberation and redemption, overcome the crises of life, conquer suffering and come to terms with their limitations, finitude, mortality? In meditation human beings are to turn inwards. If they may experience illumination then they may unmask the inconstancy of things and realize that everything that they see is unstable, that nothing in the world lasts, that everything is changing, indeed that even my self to which I cling so tightly is without a core of being and is therefore transitory. From the Buddha I can learn to become free of a self. I can find the way from being imprisoned in myself in greed, hatred and blindness, from concentration on the self and entanglement in it, to selflessness. The eightfold path of the Buddha is a reasonable middle way, neither a quest for enjoyment nor self-chastisement, but rather right thinking and right disposition (knowledge), right speaking, right action and right composure (morality, ethics), right effort, right attention and right concentration. The eightfold path is the symbol for *dharma*, the Buddha's teaching of the eightfold path.

For me it is important that from knowledge a moral behaviour, an ethic, is possible which is expected of every Buddhist, and not just monks and nuns. It comprises four elementary basic demands: not to kill, not to lie, not to steal, not to surrender to sexual profligacy. Therefore perhaps as a Buddhist, too, I might have come upon the idea of a common ethic for humankind that, according to the Declaration of the Parliament of the World's Religions of Chicago 1993, likewise builds on these four ethical constants. Only the fifth Buddhist directive, to refrain from all intoxication, finds no consensus in the religions and therefore cannot be the ingredient of a global ethic.

I go on thinking this through to the end. I would have to become a monk to attain meditative composure through disciplining the spirit. That alone would enable me to rise out of the cycle of births, that alone would make possible the entry into 'Nirvana', into 'extinction', where greed, hatred and blindness end and perhaps not nothingness but bliss awaits me. I would not feel drawn to becoming a Buddhist monk any more than I feel drawn to becoming a Christian monk. Both call for the same thing: separation from the world, a strictly regulated life without possessions and with sexual continence. However, in Christianity monasticism stands more at the periphery, while in Buddhism it stands at the centre. I would not enter the Sangha, the Buddhist community of monks, any more than I would enter a Christian mendicant order. Instead of parting from the world I see my place utterly in the world. In this respect I am closer to the original Chinese tradition than to the Buddhist tradition.

## The Confucian model

Had I been born in China as one of the 1.5 billion Chinese, I would probably have become a Confucian. Only relatively late, in connection with journeys across China and dialogue lectures in the University of Tübingen with my Chinese colleague and friend Julia Ching in the 1980s, did I arrive at the insight that the difference between West and East is superficial. Alongside the prophetic religions of Near Eastern origin, Judaism, Christianity and Islam, and the mystical religions of Indian provenance, above all Hinduism and Buddhism, the religions of Chinese origin, Confucianism and Daoism, form a third independent religious system of equal worth. Their prototype is neither the prophet nor the guru, but the wise man. By comparison with Indian religion and its mysticism, abundant mythologies and strictly cyclically orientated thought, Chinese culture is shaped by observing rationality and historical thought. Historiography developed in China at a very early stage, unlike India.

Coming as I do from the West, I could certainly not have identified with Chinese Marxism and Maoism. But I could have identified with Chinese humanism, which began to develop as early as the time of the Greek pre-Socratics in the sixth century BCE. There was a transition from the magical religion of old Chinese culture to rationality: human beings and their rationality were accorded priority over and above the spirits and gods. Finally a spiritual breakthrough took place in the shape of a great interest in history, art and literature so that the scholars, men of letters and intellectuals advanced to the uppermost level of Chinese society.

For Confucius (or Kung-futse), initially one teacher among many, the traditional oracular sayings are less important than the ethical decisions of the individual. It is the moral powers in human beings that he wants to arouse rather than the mystical powers of nature. I would not find the Confucian orientation on a better past very congenial. Confucius wanted to restore the original order of society, one that is supported by moral principles resting on the observance of the old rites, customs, norms of conduct. However, this is not just a simple moral doctrine. Already in Confucius 'heaven' is an active force standing above law and order. Human beings, especially rulers, are to understand the 'will of heaven' and try to fulfil it. If they do not do that, they lose legitimacy, a motive for quite a few Chinese revolutions.

But beyond doubt I would find the humanistic wisdom of the doctrine of Master Kung very congenial. Human beings are to strive for a harmonious relationship with their fellows and show all people humanity (*ren*) within the framework of external norms of conduct. *Ren* is human goodness, concern, goodwill. And in this sense the inner renewal of the individual is to be sought, along with the external consti-tution of the state.

According to Confucius, the word that is meant to serve as a guideline for me all my life is mutuality (*shu*). It is an abbreviation for the Golden Rule, which he formulates for the first time in human history: 'What you do not wish for yourself, do not do to others.' Humanity could very well be the basis of a fundamental ethic even today – not only in China but in humankind as a whole. Humanity instead of the inhumanity so often practised everywhere.

No one wants the return of the Confucian state religion that came into being after him and ceased with the last emperor in 1912. That permanent dominance of parents over children, men over women and a patriarchal order of society generally has no future. But the humane values of Confucianism still have importance: community, which comes before the individual, but respects and supports the individual; the family as the basic building block of society; the resolution of problems through consensus and not through confrontation; and ethical–religious harmony as an ideal for both the individual and society.

Near though this Chinese humanism stands to the European Enlight-enment and to me personally, I was not born into the Chinese or Indian religious systems, but into the Middle Eastern prophetic one. Much in these alternative systems is not exclusive. In inter-religious dialogue today we are less confrontational than complementary. But it is also clear that the ways of the religions are different and cannot all be taken contemporaneously. I was born a Christian. And to this degree the Jewish model of life is closest to me after the Christian.

## The Jewish model

Christianity is rooted in Judaism, the religion founded by Moses. In my youth I did not know about these roots, though a Jewish family with whom we were friends lived in the house opposite my parents' house. But we didn't talk about religion. The churches and many faithful had largely forgotten that Jesus of Nazareth, to whom Christianity refers as its Messiah, its Christ, was a Jew. His disciples and female followers were also Jews. I only became fully aware of this with the Second Vatican Council in the early 1960s. And in all this of course is the basic conviction of the people of Israel: 'Yahweh (in the first centuries still spoken as the name of God) is the God of Israel and Israel is his people.'

Since then the abiding common features have been of the utmost importance for me. They show me that in central perspectives the Jewish model of life has also become the Christian model of life. Judaism has had a cruel history, full of conflicts, especially since the time of the twelfth-century crusades. First it suffered the church's anti-Judaism and then racist–biologistic antisemitism, which reached its nadir in the Holocaust. However, Judaism and Christianity have common features that have lasted to the present day.

Like the Jews, I believe in the one God of Abraham, Isaac and Jacob in whom human beings may put believing trust as the one who creates and sustains the world and history and brings them to their culmination.

Like the Jews, we Christians use in our worship psalms, prayers, readings and acclamations such as Hallelujah from the Hebrew Bible.

Like the Jews, we Christians accept the collection of Holy Scriptures (the Hebrew Bible, the Tenach or the 'Old Testament') that form the foundation document of the common faith and of numerous common values and thought structures.

Like the Jews, we Christians are committed to an ethic of justice, truthfulness and peace on the foundation of love of God and love of neighbour.

At that place in Tel Aviv where the former Israeli Prime Minister and Nobel peace prize-winner Yitzhak Rabin, who had fought for peace with the expelled and oppressed Palestinians, was murdered by a Jewish fanatic in 1995, in a statement about Judaism in the film 'Tracing the

Way' I emphasized the religious and ethical heritage of this religion: 'There is hardly any other people which has something as substantial and striking to offer as Judaism with its Ten Commandments. As the German writer Thomas Mann explained after the terrors of National Socialism, these are the "basic instruction and rock of respectable humanity", indeed the "ABC of human behaviour". The rabbi and head of the Abraham Geiger College in Potsdam, Walter Homolka, has clearly described the Jewish sources for an ethic of humanity in a book produced with me, *How to Do Good and Avoid Evil* (2009). And I had already edited with the Mainz pastor Angela Rinn-Maurer 'Global Ethic – Understood in a Christian Way' in 2005.

But what specifically is Christian spirituality? First of all I need to draw a distinction.

## Falsified Christian spirituality

'Spirituality', often distinguished from religion, can mean all kinds of things. Christian spirituality should not be based, as it is today for some 'spiritual' persons and movements, primarily on pious impulses, feelings and mass gatherings, but on rational faith, solid knowledge and well-tried insights. I at any rate do not want to believe everything possible and even mix contradictory elements with my spirituality. Because I am a believer, I am not superstitious. I do not believe in the stars of the horoscope nor have I deified stars in the media, sport and politics. My ideal is not a superficial 'patchwork' religion but a religion with a solid foundation and clear profile.

Christian spirituality is based not only on assertions and claims but also on plausible arguments. Nothing is true for me simply because I hold it to be true, and I cannot require that others accept statements of faith without proof. Because I am a believer, I would also like to give rational reasons for why I am. Therefore I do not believe either in fictional constructions such as *The Da Vinci Code* or in other conspiracy theories of suppressed Gospels and the concealment by the Vatican of documents that might cause a scandal. Because I studied the original documents of Christianity collected in the New Testament, I have no need for sensational religious novels and pseudo-scholarly treatises in order to be regarded as informed and 'enlightened'.

Anyone like me who has seen much coming and going, will time and again wonder at the number of people, including serious Christians, who readily allow themselves to be influenced by barefaced inventions, for example that Jesus, who was not crucified, married Mary Magdalene, fathered descendants and died peacefully in India or Kashmir, not to mention hackneyed conspiracies about murderous secret associations with cults of the Grail. This gullibility is around not least because the church authorities (not just Roman Catholic) have neglected the necessary work of enlightenment, indeed sometimes have even hindered it. For all too long in official doctrine, in encyclicals, catechisms, pastoral letters and sermons, they have withheld the results of historical biblical criticism and for example left people in the dark about the origin of the Gospels and different genres of biblical narrative. To the present day there are not many people with knowledge of the foundations of the Christian message and tradition – which is now easily available. So they have often been exposed to the producers of sacral thrillers and the infotainment of post-modern society.

Shouldn't people in the Christian churches reflect critically and self-critically on the foundation of Christian spirituality, with the aim of going on the offensive against the tremendous loss of trust in the churches that has been demonstrated statistically? Laments about the decline in values and the random pluralism of the time are not enough.

Yet it is reasonable to ask, can Christianity still offer orientation? With the church as it is, don't we have reason to doubt Christianity? Hasn't it, at least in the European countries, perhaps even world-wide, lost plausibility and credibility? Isn't it more part of the problem than part of the solution?

More than ever there are trends away from Christianity towards the fascination of Far Eastern religions, towards esoteric movements or substitute religions of all kinds, within the framework of an 'experience and pleasure society', and also thus towards religious indifference.

The churches are not innocent here. Countless people still have oppressive experiences with the official Catholic Church: authoritarianism, discrimination against women, sexual complexes, refusal to engage in dialogue, intolerance to those with other views. But narrowness, provincialism and a lack of profile in the Protestant churches, too, are responsible for thousands leaving year after year, millions retreating into themselves and millions more, for example in the countries which have recently emerged from Communist domination, not even entering a church at all. The oppressive question arises whether the light of Christianity can still be an orientation in the twenty-first century.

On the other hand, many people who can no longer cope with the churches are asking, what if the ideals of Christianity simply disappeared?

What would a world look like which no longer knew the Ten Commandments and the command to love one's neighbour and one's enemy, the Sermon on the Mount and the parables of Jesus? So many people do not want to write off Christianity along with the churches. And many still testify inside and outside the churches that they by no means despair of Christianity; they bear witness that they have not given up hope that for them being a Christian is still a great option in life.

But in that case, in view of the secular and ecclesiastical falsifications of Christianity, we must ask again honestly: What does 'Christian' mean? How should we understand Christian spirituality today? How should we understand ourselves as Christians? What does being a Christian mean originally, really, essentially? It took me years as a theologian to realize fully that the foundation of Christian spirituality does not lie in often incomprehensible dogmas or noble moral commandments, does not mean a great theory or world-view, does not mean a church system, but – yes, what?

## The Christian model

Like countless other Catholics before Vatican II, I had grown up with the traditional picture of Christ from the creed, the Hellenistic councils and Byzantine mosaics: Jesus Christ as the enthroned 'Son of God', a benevolent 'Saviour', and even 'Christ the king'. In catechism instruction we learned dogmatic formulae without understanding them: Jesus Christ is the 'second person of the most-holy Trinity', 'one divine person in two natures', human and divine. In Rome I then heard a lecture series lasting a whole semester on 'christology', covering all the heresies that were condemned by the councils, and all the answers to the difficulties that were already given at that time and are still given today. Certainly I passed all the Latin examinations, which were by no means simple, without difficulty – but what about my spirituality? That was something else; that remained unsatisfied. For a long time my main interest was in the brilliant Pauline theology; the Gospels seemed to me too familiar and rather boring. The Christ figure only became really interesting for me when after my years in Rome, on the basis of modern biblical study, I was able to get to know him as a real figure of history. A thorough study of Catholic and Protestant exegetical literature in connection with my lectures, seminars and publications was driven on by my tremendous desire to get to know this 'unknown Jesus'.

For the essence of Christianity is not something abstract and dogmatic, some general teaching, but has always been a living historical figure: Jesus of Nazareth. Over the years, on the basis of the abundant biblical research of the last two centuries, I discovered for myself what is unique about the man from Nazareth. I thought everything through with passionate involvement, gave it a precise foundation and presented it systematically. It had shaken me that in my book *The Church* (1967) I constantly spoke of the church of 'Jesus Christ' but couldn't give a precise answer to the question what this Jesus really wanted, said, did. My questioning deepened when on my own suggestion at the International Theological Congress in Brussels in 1970 I attempted to answer the elementary question, 'What is the Christian message?' And I finally gave a comprehensive description of the preaching, conduct and fate of Jesus in my book *On Being a Christian* (1974, ET 1977), originally planned as a small volume and which became a big one. All in all this was an exciting undertaking. In this connection I even preached on the whole Gospel of Mark from the first verse to the last, and also on the Sermon on the Mount.

So I know what I am talking about when I say in a quite elementary way: the Christian model of life is simply this Jesus of Nazareth as the Messiah, Christos, anointed and sent. Jesus Christ is the foundation of authentic Christian spirituality. He is a challenging model for our relationship with our fellow human beings and also with God himself, and has become the orientation and criterion for millions of people all over the world.

So who is a Christian? Not someone who simply says 'Lord, Lord' and pays homage to a 'fundamentalism' – whether this is of a biblicist Protestant, authoritarian Roman Catholic or traditionalist Eastern Orthodox stamp. A Christian is rather someone who throughout his or her personal career (and everyone has one) makes an effort to orientate himself or herself practically on this Jesus Christ. No more is required.

This authentic Christian spirituality has seldom become so clear to me as after worshipping in the slums of San Salvador in the church where Archbishop Oscar Romero, a committed defender of the rights of his people, was gunned down at the altar directly from a car on 24 March 1980. In the film 'Tracing the Way' I reflected on the Christianity of the Protestant resistance fighter Dietrich Bonhoeffer (executed by the Nazis in 1945), the American civil rights activist Martin Luther King (shot in 1968) and the Polish priest Jerzy Popielusko (murdered in 1984 by the state security service). They all showed to me and the world that such a spirituality can be maintained even to the point of a violent death.

My own less dramatic life, with its heights and depths, and also my loyalty to the church and criticism of it, can only be understood from this perspective. My criticism of the church in particular comes most deeply from suffering over the discrepancy between what this historical Jesus was, what he preached, lived out, fought for and suffered for, and what is today represented by the institutional church and its hierarchy. This discrepancy has often become intolerably great. Can we imagine Jesus as the Pontiff in St Peter's? Or in prayer with George W. Bush and the Pope in the White House? Unthinkable. With Dostoievsky's Grand Inquisitor the authorities would probably ask him: 'Why do you come to disturb us?'

It is therefore most urgent and most liberating for our Christian theology to orientate ourselves as Christians theologically and in practice not so much on traditional dogmatic formulae and church rules as on the unique figure who has given his name to Christianity. Certainly, we can know Jesus over what Lessing called the 'gaping ditch of history', but always in a new context.

The criterion for this orientation may not be a dreamed-up Christ but only the real historical Jesus. We can recognize him from the New Testament in spite of the legends and unhistorical elaborations.

## A unique life

I cannot narrate the history of Jesus of Nazareth here; I have researched it and described it at length elsewhere. One can argue over many details of the New Testament witnesses, all of which were composed by people in the context of the first Christian communities. One can especially argue over what are authentic sayings of Jesus and what are not.

But on the whole Jesus' profile in the New Testament emerges in an utterly unmistakable way. I have also studied the leading figures of the other world religions and in other books have offered sensitive portraits of them, for each is a distinctive personality who at least deserves the respect of those of other faiths and of unbelievers. I therefore find it incomprehensible that in 2006 a sensation-hungry opera impresario in Berlin could misuse the great Mozart opera *Idomeneo* to present the decapitated heads of the founders of religions at the end without any supporting text or music, and that this was approved of by some simple politicians and journalists. Nor can I understand the praise given to a caricaturist and a newspaper which in the same year, 2006, for commercial and populist reasons published slanderous caricatures of the Prophet

Muhammad, as though for Danish politicians freedom of the press did not also include responsibility of the press. Adherents of other religions are often amazed by the extremes to which the media have gone in formerly Christian Europe, in which nothing holy seems to be holy any more.

In a comparison with founders of other religions, the life, teaching and activity of Jesus of Nazareth clearly emerge for me as distinctive. Jesus was not educated at court as Moses seems to have been. Nor was he the son of a prince as Buddha was. Nor was he a scholar and politician like Confucius or a rich and widely travelled merchant like Muhammad. Precisely because his origin was so insignificant, his abiding significance is so amazing. He does not advocate any unconditional validity of a written law which was developed more and more (Moses); he does not call for a monastic retreat in ascetic immersion within the regulated community of an order (Buddha); he is not a rebel from the traditional morality and established society according to an eternal world law (Confucius); he did not make violent revolutionary conquests through battle against the unbelievers and establishment of a theocratic state (Muhammad).

Jesus, too, seems to me to escape all categorization. He cannot be put either among the rulers or the rebels, among the moralizers or among the silent in the land. He proves to be provocative, but towards both left and right. Not backed by any party, he is challenging on all sides. As Eduard Schweizer puts it, he is 'The man who burst open all schemes'. He is not a priest but is apparently nearer to God than the priests. He is not a political or a social revolutionary, but appears more revolutionary than the revolutionaries. He is not a monk but seems to be freer from the world than the ascetics. He is not a model casuist, but is more moral than the moralists. Time and again the Gospels show that Jesus is different. Despite all the parallels the historical Jesus of Nazareth shows himself as a whole to be unique – then as now.

For our way of life the decisive message of Jesus about the kingdom and will of God is quite clear: in sayings, similitudes and actions to match it is a joyful, welcome message of a new freedom. For me here and now this means:

- particularly in times of market fever and shareholder value not to allow oneself to be dominated by avarice and prestige;
- particularly in times of revived imperialistic politics not to allow oneself to be impressed by the will for power;

- particularly in times of an unprecedented removal of taboos and unbridled consumerism not to allow oneself to be enslaved by the sexual drive and the quest for enjoyment and contentment;
- particularly in times when only achievement seems to make up human value, to champion the human dignity of the weak, 'unproductive' and poor.

It is a matter of a new freedom: being freed by the greater reality of God which embraces and permeates not only me but all men and women, a reality that Jesus designates by the name 'Father'. And in the light of God and ultimately him alone we become free for fellow human beings.

I needn't become an ascetic; it is well known that Jesus drank wine and went to parties. But I shouldn't cultivate my own interests and satisfy my own needs in a selfish lifestyle. Rather, it is important in everyday life to keep in view the well-being of the neighbours who need us. This does not mean wanting to dominate them but attempting to serve them as far as we can, and in everything to do good and where necessary exercise restraint and renunciation. I admit that this is a continuous challenge – it has been so for me personally in the course of a long life.

Jesus himself took the observance of elementary commandments for granted. For him, too, to observe God's commandments means not to murder, not to lie, not to steal, not to misuse sexuality. In this he corresponds to the moral demands of the other founders of religions; these are the foundations for a global ethic. But at the same time he radicalizes these demands. In the Sermon on the Mount he far exceeds them. Instead of going the obligatory mile, in some circumstances one should go two miles. However, such a demand is not understood as a universal law. That could not be fulfilled; it would be unrealistic, as many Jewish critics rightly point out. Jesus' 'demands' are invitations, challenges, in each case to show a generous commitment to one's fellow human beings, following the example of the treatment by the Samaritan (for the Jews a heretic) of the stranger who had fallen among thieves. In practice this means to exercise a creative love that cannot be required by any law. 'Love' is a word that Jesus hardly uses but in practice is his key demand – as universal as it is radical: a love without sentimentality, which respects everyone, even opponents, and does not have the enemy as an eternal enemy.

For me and countless others, this is a joyful, liberating spirituality of non-violence, of justice, mercy and peace. It is even a spirituality of joy that does not place unnecessary moral burdens on people's shoulders, a spirituality that brings together and does not divide, but a spirituality that has a price.

## A unique dying

Time and again I have to reflect that Jesus of Nazareth was quite a young man when – possibly inspired by the preacher of repentance and baptizer John by the Jordan – he fearlessly entered the public arena. Neither the earliest Gospel (according to Mark) nor the Fourth (according to John) is interested in his childhood story as it is reported in the Gospels according to Matthew and Luke, with many meaningful and touching, but also legendary features.

And this Jesus was active for at most three years; according to the chronology of the Gospel of John, which evidently uses old sources, perhaps only a year. Whereas the Buddha, Confucius, Moses and to some extent also the Prophet Muhammad went to sleep in advanced old age, at only 30 years of age Jesus died a shameful death on a cross, a punishment which the Romans inflicted only on non-Romans and above all on political rebels and slaves as the severest punishment.

But was Jesus a political rebel? There is no mistaking the fact that his words and actions inevitably resulted in conflicts. It strengthens and comforts me, and certainly not only me, to know that even the one on whom we as Christians call came into confrontation with the religious–political establishment of his time on the basis of his message and conduct. His criticism of traditional religion and the exercise of power by the rulers was too radical. His charismatic healing of the sick was too suspicious. The way in which he dealt with the religious law, with the Sabbath, with regulations about cleanliness and food were too liberal. His solidarity with the despised, the sick, the poor, the wretched 'poor devils', with the outcast, women and children, was too scandalous. His behaviour towards heretics, schismatics and the politically compromised was not 'politically or religiously correct', indeed he did not pity the high priest but the people. He showed too much concern for the despised, the law-breakers, tax collectors, and 'sinners' and this offended the self-righteous pious.

It follows from this that Jesus' message and his conduct form an unprecedented challenge to the religious and social system and its representatives, the hierarchy. He puts the usual Jewish model of life in question. His protest action against the temple commerce and its beneficiaries was probably the decisive provocation that finally led to his arrest and condemnation as a false teacher, pseudo-prophet and blasphemer. Jesus was not any of these, nor was he a revolutionary leader with a political agenda. But he was condemned by the Roman authorities as a political revolutionary who led the people astray.

His fate is well known. He died on the cross, betrayed and denied by his disciples and adherents, mocked and scorned by his enemies, forsaken by God and his fellow human beings. He passed away with the loud cry '*Eloi, eloi, lema sabachthani*', which means 'My God, my God, why have you forsaken me' (Mark 15.34).

Since then the cross has been the remarkable hallmark of Christians. Only Jesus' message, life and activity as a whole make it clear what distinguishes the cross of this one man from, say, that of the slave leader Spartacus and the many crosses in world history. But from then to now the great question remains: how can such a sign of shame be a sign of salvation for me?

From the beginning, a conviction of believing Christians, provoked by spiritual experiences, was that his death was not the end. 'Resurrection' does not mean the ghost story of a revived corpse but the Easter message that Jesus is with God, that he did not die into nothingness but into the most real reality. So the 'resurrection' of Jesus, which was soon surrounded by legends, is not a continuation of or a return to life in this space and time but rather about his acceptance into God's eternal life that transcends all human ideas. Moreover, this belief was testified to by witnesses who were not afraid to die for it.

## A model of life in person

Thus the crucified Jesus becomes a sign of hope. In the light of Jesus' acceptance into God's eternal life his adherents begin to see the person of the master from Nazareth differently and interpret him in a different way. He appears more and more as the living embodiment of his cause: the embodiment of a new attitude to life and a new lifestyle. Since his resurrection to new life it is manifest that Jesus Christ is the foundation of Christian spirituality.

As the apostle Paul puts it clearly: 'For no other foundation can anyone lay than that which is laid, which is Jesus Christ' (1 Corinthians 3.11). Or as the Gospel of John puts it: he is 'the way, the truth and the life' (John 14.6). In this sense as a Christian I believe not only in God but also in Jesus Christ, the one sent by God. No emperor, no philosopher, no statesman, no general, he is the Christian model of life in person.

Christian life is life in the spirit of Christ; life in the spirit of Christ is discipleship of Christ.

So this is what Christian spirituality means in practice: not the confession of a dogma or a doctrine but following him, the Christ, in one's own way. Good and bad, I always add, as is human nature. But time and again driven on by his spirit, the spirit of God.

As the spirit of Jesus Christ this spirit cannot be confused with any other spirit, with any spirit of enthusiasm, ministry, evil. It is the *Spiritus sanctus* which is the inspiration, the driving force of Christian spirituality. So I believe in the Holy Spirit. And I can understand in biblical terms the dogma of a Trinity formulated with Hellenistic categories and notions alien to us; not according to Augustine's trinitarian speculation as belief in 1=3 and 3=1 but according to the New Testament as belief in the one God and Father, through Jesus Christ, the Son whom he sent, in the Holy Spirit, God's Spirit and Christ's Spirit.

Does this spirit change my life? Yes, in so far as I allow myself to be inspired by it.

- It gives me new motivations, why I should act in this particular way and not otherwise, why – and to this even Sigmund Freud had no answer – I should then be honourable, considerate and where possible gracious, even if I am harmed as a result and have to suffer the unreliability and brutality of others.
- It makes new dispositions possible for me, attitudes of unpretentious commitment to my fellow human beings, solidarity with the disadvantaged, the fight against unjust structures in state, church and society, dispositions of freedom, gratitude, generosity, unselfishness, joy.
- Everywhere it inspires new actions, new deeds small or great, which in the footsteps of Jesus Christ begin where no one is helping. These are not just general programmes that change society but concrete signs, testimonies, witnesses to humanity and the humanization of men and women and of human society.

But I do not present myself as one who has achieved all this! I am not a model Christian nor a candidate for beatification. But for me there is no doubt that this spiritual driving force has formed my spirituality. And it is a comfort to me that with increasing age this driving force does not necessarily decline, but can even become stronger. Indeed in each new period of life it can time and again give meaning, energy and joy in life.

Finally it shows me a last horizon of meaning and a last destination, so that we can bear not only the positive in our life but also the negative. We shall have to think more closely about joy and suffering in the next chapter.

In this chapter I have of course as a Christian given the largest amount of space to the model that is determinative for me, the Christian model. But it should not be forgotten that the Christian model is not the last in the history of humankind.

## The Muslim model

In the course of half a millennium the originally simple Christian message had become a highly complex Greek–Hellenistic dogmatics in the framework of a state-church Byzantine system – with not a few 'heretical' splits. It was not one that had readily attracted the desert-dwellers, the Bedouins and traders of the Arabian peninsula. It took an Arab prophet, influenced by Judaism and Jewish Christianity, to convince these polytheistic tribes of belief in the one God and the need for social justice.

Seven centuries after Christ, surprisingly and with tremendous speed, a new, the newest, world religion developed: Islam. And had I been born somewhere in the 'green belt' between Morocco and Indonesia, Uzbekistan in central Asia and Mozambique in Africa, I would have been one of the 1.3 billion Muslims who follow the Prophet Muhammad.

As a Muslim, with Jews and Christians I would believe in the one and only God of Abraham, the gracious and merciful creator, who sustains all human beings and brings them to consummation. But whereas Israel as God's people and land is central to the Jewish model of life and Jesus Christ as God's Messiah and Son is central for Christians, so for me as a Muslim the Qur'an as God's word and book would be central.

I would have few difficulties in accepting the Qur'an as an originally Arabic book, but at the same time a living and holy book for Muslims throughout the world. However, like many Muslims even of former centuries I would have difficulty in understanding the Qur'an as a literally revealed book, as it were dictated by God. And I would ask whether the Qur'an as word of God was not also the word of man, the word of the Prophet Muhammad. Even so, the Qur'an could reveal itself to me as the truth, the way and the life.

The Qur'an is the basis for the Muslim model of life, for law, rites and theology, the inspiration for the whole of Islamic art and culture. This includes the five basic pillars of Islam: the confession of the one God and Muhammad whom he sent, the obligation to daily prayer, social giving or giving to the poor, the fast month of Ramadan and the pilgrimage to Mecca once in a lifetime.

As a Muslim I would also beyond doubt learn from the Qur'an a deep respect for Jesus. He is one of the three messengers of God who received a revelation before Muhammad: Moses the Torah, David the Psalms, and Jesus the Gospel. He may be called Messiah and word of God and his miracles can be recognized. On the other hand, as a Muslim I would have difficulties about what is attested unanimously and clearly in the Gospels and the letters of Paul, namely the death of Jesus on the cross. For the Qur'an such a death seems shameful for so great a prophet. Therefore the Qur'an says that another was crucified in place of Jesus but Jesus was exalted directly to God.

So as a Muslim I could emphatically affirm Jesus' exaltation to God. I could relatively easily identify with the Jewish–Christian understanding of Christ, which the Prophet Muhammad evidently knew. Granted, Jewish Christianity, out of which Christianity grew, would have been represented at the first ecumenical council of Nicaea in the fourth century when the creed was laid down. But Jewish Christians certainly would not have accepted some Hellenistic formulae that the Prophet Muhammad could not accept later. No Jewish Christian would have subscribed to 'of one being with the Father' ('*homo-ousios*'), the christological formula introduced by the emperor, and no Jew or Muslim can accept it to the present day.

So like any Muslim I would have had objections to an elevation of Jesus to God, which made the one who is the son of God simply God (Greek *ho theos*), whom Jesus himself named his and our Father. The New Testament itself speaks of an empowered 'appointing' and 'enthronement' of Jesus – on the basis of his resurrection by God himself – as 'Messiah (anointed king) in power' (Romans 1.3–4; Acts 2.36). A Muslim can also accept this.

With the sharp Qur'anic saying, 'They are unbelievers who say "God is Christ, the Son of Mary"' (Surah 5.27), the Prophet Muhammad has become a 'warner' for educated Hellenistic Christianity in which the understanding of Christ of the early Jewish Christians had no chance against the new Hellenistic interpretations. No Jewish Christian would probably have had anything against the notion that Jesus was Son of God, since he was God's representative: 'The Lord said to my Lord, sit at my right hand' (Psalm 110.1; Acts 2.33–35). In Christian interpretation this became one of the most important christological statements: Jesus is God's representative and the representative can also be called son in the tradition of Israel rightly understood: 'You are my son, today I have begotten you' (Psalm 2.7; Acts 13.33). This is to be understood as is stated in the Bible – for the day of the enthronement of the king: God has 'begotten' the king of Israel.

The Islamic model could also have been understood as a corrective of the paradigm of the Hellenistic dogmatization of Christ. The Qur'an in fact refers back to the original Jewish–Christian model as I have described this in my book *Islam* (2004, ET 2007). The task of church preaching would be to translate into the thought world and language of today central concepts of Christian faith which were expressed with the Greek and then Latin vocabulary of late antiquity.

## Steadfastness and readiness for dialogue

However, I do not want to continue the old dogmatic dispute but to be guided by the one who for me is the way, the truth and the life. The fine words of the Protestant theologian Dorothee Sölle, which have always impressed me, have confirmed this for me.

> Compare him calmly with other great figures
> Socrates
> Rosa Luxemburg
> Gandhi
> He can stand that
> But it is better
> For you to compare him
> With yourself
> (*Meditationen und Gebrauchstexte*, 1969)

Jesus as a model of life is above all a challenge for me, as I want to be a respectable Christian. I can talk with those of other faiths about this centre of Christian faith. I am in dialogue with Jews and Muslims and members of other religions. But I do not want to force Christ as a model of life on anyone, not even on a Jew, who has so much in common with Jesus and possibly regards him as the last Israelite prophet. I am not carrying on any mission to the Jews. Nor on any Muslim, who in Jesus recognizes the great prophet before Muhammad. I am not carrying on any mission to the Muslims either. However, I am convinced that Jews and Muslims can learn much about Jesus in the New Testament writings that is not to be found in their holy books.

What I set out at length in my *Global Responsibility* (1990, ET 1991) remains my conviction:

- We can learn from one another, not just tolerate one another, but attempt to understand each other in order to understand ourselves better and 'co-operate'.
- We may also dispute over the truth if this is done in truthfulness. As a Christian I have no monopoly of the truth, but I am also not ready in the face of untruth to give up confession of the truth. Dialogue and witness are not exclusive.
- We all may continue along our own proven way to salvation, but should grant that others can likewise attain salvation through their religions.
- Seen from outside, so to speak from the history of religions, there are different ways to salvation, different true religions. But seen from within, i.e. for myself as a believing Christian, there is only one true religion: the Christian religion, which the others accept as a true religion only with reservations.
- That is because for me Jesus Christ is and remains 'the way, the truth and the life'. But I respect the fact that 'the way, the truth and the life' is for Jews the Torah, for Muslims the Qur'an, for Hindus the Dharma, for Buddhists the eightfold path and for Daoists Dao.
- An ecumenical attitude means both steadfastness and readiness for dialogue: for me personally to stand fast in loyalty to the Christian cause, incorruptibly and without anxiety about being discredited by the church, but in unlimited openness to others.

# Chapter 8

# Suffering in Life

*I cry to you and you do not answer me;*
*I stand and you do not heed me.*
*You have turned cruel to me.*

Job 30.20f.

A way of life with joy in life and meaning in life – but not without suffering in life.

During all the decades of my life I have hardly ever been seriously ill. But fate would have it that I am writing the first stages of this chapter towards the end of a week in the Tübingen University Clinic – a small routine operation that need not worry me. But at the same time this is an opportunity to reflect again on suffering, this dark basic theme of life, not so much in the medical context, where I am receiving the best possible care, as in a theological context, where an answer is especially hard to give – in the face of the higher authority before whom one brings one's life.

## A fundamental question: Why do I suffer?

Like every human being I have had a good measure of suffering, but more mental than physical. I have experienced crises in life, larger and smaller – some of them can be read about in my memoirs. I have had experiences of failure; I have often been left in the lurch by people who seemed to be my friends. And I know anxiety, above all at being alone, anxiety at losing people who are dear and important to me. 'Why do I suffer? That is the rock of atheism,' the writer Georg Büchner makes one of the figures in his play *Danton's Death* say. Yes, why do I suffer, why is it I who suffer, why now, why in this way? That is a question asked by believers and unbelievers.

The question hardly arises if I believe in an unalterable and unfathomable destiny or in a monistic mysticism in which everything is one. Nor does the question arise for me if conversely in a dualistic religion – such as the ancient Persian and later Manichean religion – I attribute all evil to a second, evil primal power alongside the good God.

But in the face of all the suffering and evil in this world, anyone who believes in a living good God is confronted with a riddle that from earliest times throughout human history has been put as a loud or soft question, as a bitter or weary complaint, indeed as an indignant and cynical enquiry. Why hasn't God prevented evil? As far back as 300 BCE the Greek philosopher Epicurus posed this question to religion. And in the Enlightenment the French rationalist Pierre Bayle gave it a classic formulation which has been repeated countless times to the present day: 'Why has God not prevented evil?'

> Either God cannot: then he is not really omnipotent.
> Or he will not: in that case he is not good, just and holy.
> Or he cannot and will not: in which case he is powerless and hostile.
> Or he can and will: but then why all the evil in this world?

Christian theology's answers, from Augustine to Thomas Aquinas, have never completely satisfied me, answers such as: evil has no substance of its own but is merely a lack of good; it does not presuppose an efficient cause but only a deficient cause. That is said by a church teacher, Augustine, a former adherent of Manichaeism, a belief which thinks dualistically. He passed on to all Latin theology the pernicious idea of an original sin transmitted by sexual intercourse, which makes sexuality *a priori* appear as a demonic, evil power. Mustn't one find another way of taking the negative force of evil seriously?

By contrast Thomas Aquinas formulated a clear answer in three brief clauses: '*nec vult, nec non vult, sed permittit*'.

- God does not will evil: he is infinitely good, just and holy.
- But God does not not will evil: otherwise there would in fact be no wickedness in the world.
- However, God allows evil. He allows evil to educate us and punish us.

But wisely though it is formulated, in the end of the day this solution does not convince me either.

## Justifying God in the face of suffering?

The theologian, jurist, historian and mathematician Gottfried Wilhelm Leibniz grappled with Pierre Bayle's argument. To him the world owes the term 'theo-dicy', justification of God. His work published in 1710 rapidly became a classic: *Essais de théodicé sur la bonté de Dieu, la liberté de l'homme et l'origine du mal* ('An attempt at a justification of God. On the goodness of God, human freedom and the origin of evil').

Leibniz was realistic enough not to belittle the manifold suffering and evil in the world. For him the world is by no means perfect, by no means simply good. Rather, he distinguishes three kinds of evil:

- metaphysical ill or the limitations of being. This is grounded in human finitude;
- physical ill or pain. This is given with human corporeality;
- moral ill or evil. This exists because of human freedom.

Moreover the present creation is by no means perfect. For Leibniz it is only the best of all possible worlds. A world without sin and suffering and thus also without human freedom would not be *a priori* better. God allows evil for the sake of harmony and the whole.

Leibniz's *Theodicy* became the textbook for educated Europe. But the enthusiasm for the best of all possible worlds was fundamentally destroyed fifty years later by the earthquake in Lisbon on 1 November 1755, All Saints' Day, with the death of tens of thousands. It was then easy for Voltaire to make Leibniz's theology look ridiculous in his philosophical novel *Candide, or Optimism* (1759).

And in 1791 Immanuel Kant wrote a work on theodicy with the strikingly cool title: 'On the failures of all philosophical attempts at theodicy'. If one doesn't get on so easily in the face of the sharp logic and comprehensive system of Leibniz's theodicy, in the concrete individual instance, in a quite specific illness, a professional or human fiasco, in disloyalty or treachery or in death – such a theodicy is no real comfort for someone despairing in suffering. Arguing in such a skilful intellectual way is like giving a lecture on food chemistry and nutrition to the hungry and thirsty.

On the other hand chain smokers should not complain to God because of lung cancer or emphysema. Often we are too little aware how much harm human beings constantly do themselves, not least through their moral failures, from hatred and envy between neighbours or colleagues at work to wars between races and nations. But we also know how much suffering human beings bear completely innocently. Above all the undeserved suffering of children cannot be justified by any argument. What is the freedom given by God to human beings if it leads to such monstrosity? Because of it, as is well known, Dostoievsky's Ivan Karamazov wants to give back his 'entry tickets' to creation. Albert Camus' doctor in *The Plague*, Dr Rieux, grounds his 'No' to God in the experience of children dying on their sickbeds. And then there is the tremendous suffering that famines and natural catastrophes bring to hundreds of thousands of innocent people.

During my years-long studies on Judaism (completed in 1991 with my book *Judaism*, ET 1992) I had to grapple with a new dimension of suffering. In the so-called 'permissive' twentieth century humankind has experienced evil to an unprecedented degree: the totalitarian state and the industrialization of murder in the Shoah. And there the question arises yet again with quite different urgency: how could God allow something like this? It has taken me many years to find an answer to this that convinces me.

## The dialectic of suffering in God himself?

At the end of my studies in Rome I sought the solution to the riddle of suffering not with Thomas Aquinas and Leibniz, but in another direction. Already in Rome I had been enthused by the philosophy of Hegel, and immediately after the early completion of my theological dissertation on Karl Barth I began a philosophical dissertation at the Sorbonne in Paris on Hegel's christology, a christology which culminates in a 'speculative Good Friday'.

Hegel had discovered dialectic, development in opposites – statement ('thesis'), counter-statement ('antithesis') and reconciliation ('synthesis') – as not only a rhythm of thought but as a necessary rhythm of the universe as manifested in nature and in history, indeed of the Absolute, God himself. So it seemed to me one could also solve the riddle of suffering in this way: 'that the human, finite, frail, weak, negative are themselves a divine element, that this negative is in God himself; that finitude, the negative, i.e. otherness is not outside God and as otherness does not prevent unity with God' (*Philosophie der Religion*, II, p. 172).

So according to Hegel God's destiny was itself fulfilled in the painful fate of Christ and in his death the death of God and at the same time the death of death is fulfilled: 'God has died, God is dead – this is the most fearful thought, namely that all that is eternal, all that is true is not, that negation itself is in God; the greatest pain, the feeling of complete lostness, giving up all that is higher, is bound up with this. However, things do not stop here but now a change takes place. God receives himself in this process and this is only the death of death. God comes to life again and thus there is a turn to the opposite' (II, p. 167).

How should I still complain at my suffering and death if God's destiny is reflected in me? In joy at this discovery while I was in Rome, I composed a short account of the dialectic of the properties of God and presented it to my dogmatics professor. He had no objections to it, but didn't really know what to make of it. As I couldn't complete my philosophical dissertation in Paris because of my call to the chair of fundamental theology in Tübingen, I later revised the whole manuscript twice more and finally published it in the Hegel anniversary year 1970 under the title *The Incarnation of God: Prolegomena to a Future Christology*. I still get angry when looking through the book yet again I see what infinite trouble I took in studying the history of the dogma of Christ in the early church and in mediaeval theology, and how little those who are fond of presenting themselves as guardians of orthodoxy have ever bothered with these questions. But in the last edition I put all my learned investigations into the history of dogma at the end of the book as an excursus. For in the meantime something else had struck me.

In studying the most recent exegetical literature, especially research into the historical Jesus, it had become clear to me that like Hegel one cannot identify the fate of Jesus with the fate of God himself. I had to see that this christology 'from above', as also advocated by Karl Barth and Karl Rahner, as it were hangs in the air without a christology 'from below' based on the concrete Jesus of history. Twenty years later Karl-Josef Kuschel worked out this shift in my christological thinking in his monumental investigation *Born Before All Time? The Dispute over Christian Origins* (1990, ET 1992). Of course with Hegel I still wanted to understand God as a living God who, unlike the rigid God of Greek metaphysics, moves, changes, undergoes a history, a God who does not persist in himself above the world but who emerges from himself, empties himself.

But if one starts from the historical Jesus of Nazareth one can in no way identify his suffering and dying with the dying of God. After all, with him the 'Son' of God and not God the Father himself died. Rather, the Son is raised from the dead by God, his Father, and taken into his eternal life. But in Hegel's philosophy of religion God himself of necessity moves almost automatically from death to life again in a dialectical reversal.

## God's impotence in the face of the Holocaust

The Holocaust, the systematic murder of 6,000,000 Jews and an estimated 500,000 Sinti and gypsies, this event of unique human brutality, brings the question of God and suffering to a nadir hitherto unattained. I remember the gripping address given in 1984 by the Jewish philosopher Hans Jonas, who was driven by the Nazis from Germany and whose mother was murdered in Auschwitz, at the University of Tübingen on 'The Concept of God after Auschwitz'. Instead of starting from God's majesty, his answer began with the suffering of God since the creation of the world and instead of God's omnipotence he talked of God's impotence. God was silent in Auschwitz and did not intervene 'not because he did not want to, but because he could not'. With this answer Hans Jonas put himself in the tradition of Jewish mysticism, the Kabbalah, which already in God's creation saw a 'contraction' (Hebrew *zimzum*), a voluntary withdrawal and self-limitation of God. Is that a satisfying answer, for Jews, for Christians?

With all due respect to Hans Jonas, to whom we are also indebted for his extremely important book *Das Prinzip Verantwortung* ('The Principle of Responsibility'), in my reservations about this solution I see myself endorsed by theologians such as Louis Jacobs and Joseph Soloveitchik. That God has to concentrate himself in human fashion, contract, in order to give existence and essence, time and space, to another alongside him seems to rob God of his infinity, eternity and perfection – always maintained in the great Jewish Christian tradition. The finite cannot *a priori* limit the infinite, indeed even an infinite universe could not limit the infinite God who is in all things. It would be better to understand the creation as an 'unfolding of God' (Nicholas of Cusa, *explicatio Dei*) than as a limitation of God.

In the face of Auschwitz (and of other twentieth-century horrors such as the Gulag Archipelago and Hiroshima) post-modern understandings of God by Jews and Christians seem to me to correspond in two important points: on the one hand both Jews and Christians reject an uninvolved, unhistorical, cruel God without compassion who does not suffer, and on the other they both believe in a God who is nevertheless present in a hidden way, truly taking part in history, merciful, indeed sharing in suffering. From this it seems to me to follow that God's 'omnipotence', too, must not be understood to mean that an 'absolute' holder of power, detached, untouched by anything, guides, does or could do anything. But on the other hand God's power may not simply be replaced by impotence, nor his wisdom with folly. That would no longer be the God of the Bible.

So it remains my conviction that a monstrous reality such as Auschwitz, but also the thousands of deaths caused by a tsunami or an earthquake, cannot be 'dealt with' by such bold speculations. Muslims, who are rightly even more concerned with God's transcendence, make ironic critical commentaries on such 'condescending', 'merciful' images of God. And the christology which is often used excessively for the image of God proves to be particularly prone to criticism. I may not avoid another question.

## A crucified God?

After the Second World War, with reference to a remark of Dietrich Bon-hoeffer, Christian theologians have often attempted to cope with the problem of suffering by assuming a 'suffering God'. God is said to be 'impotent and weak in the world' and precisely in this way, only in this way, is he with us and helps us: only the 'suffering God' can help. In view of the Holocaust some have concluded from this that the 'inexpressible suffering of the six million is also the voice of the suffering God'. Yet others have even thought that the problem of suffering can be coped with in an extremely speculative way by a divine history of suffering which is played out between God and God, even by God against God, within the Trinity (of Father, Son and Spirit). But all this is without reference to the Hebrew Bible or the New Testament.

An attentive reader of the Bible will hardly understand these specula-tions, which culminate in a humbling of God. Karl Rahner once rightly said to me, 'Why should it be better for me if things are going badly even with God himself?' According to the New Testament the man Jesus, the Son of God, cries to God his Father because he believes that he has been abandoned in the depths of his suffering. But nowhere does God cry to God, nowhere is God himself weak, impotent, suffering, crucified or even dead. If we identify human suffering so closely with that of God that there is even a suffering of God, if the cry of human beings becomes the cry of God, then we would really have to make human sin (say the crimes of the SS thugs) God's sin.

A 'crucified God', then? I cannot agree with this thesis of Christian theologians. I prefer to follow the New Testament and the Hebrew Bible and not Gnostic–kabbalistic speculations. In the cross of Christ the one who has been crucified is not the God, *ho theos*, who throughout the New Testament is the Father, *Deus Pater Omnipotens*. How otherwise could the crucified Jesus have been able to cry to God in his godforsakenness, 'My God, my God, why have you forsaken me?' (Mark 15.34f.)? No, according to the New Testament, what takes place here is not a 'speculative Good Friday' (as Hegel put it), 'a reversal', a 'mortal leap' of God himself. Despite the tempting voice in Elie Wiesel's famous Auschwitz story of the young man on the gallows, it is not God who hangs on the cross but God's 'anointed', his 'Christ', the Son of Man, God's 'Son'.

To put it a different way, the words often spoken to children, 'The good God hangs here', are not right. For the great Christian tradition, the cross, is not the symbol of the 'suffering', 'crying' God or even 'the symbol of God suffering the distress of death', but the symbol of the human being suffering the distress of death. An unbiblical 'patripassianism', the view that God the Father himself suffered, was rightly condemned by the church at an early stage. And if Jewish theology likewise rightly protests against a sadistic, cruel view of God according to which a bloodthirsty God required the sacrifice of his son, so Christian theology hopefully protests no less emphatically against a masochistic understanding of God according to which a weak God has to torment himself through suffering and death to resurrection if he is not to suffer for ever. It is here that the deepest distinction between Jesus the Christ and Buddha the Enlightened becomes evident.

## The Enlightened and the Crucified

We get a view of the decisive difference only if we venture to put side by side the figure of the smiling Buddha, sitting on a lotus flower, and that of the suffering Jesus, nailed to the cross. Only from this historical perspective can the far more comprehensive significance of the Buddha for Buddhists and the Christ for the Christians be rightly understood.

I have often in Japan and South East Asia nodded my head in respect to a statue of Buddha before whom the Buddhists prostrate themselves. Through his enlightenment the Buddha Gautama entered Nirvana – already accessible in this life – and after that lived as the 'Awakened', Enlightened, for decades, until he finally entered the final nirvana, parirnirvana, through an unspectacular death. He lived, though not without pain and suffering, cheerfully and seriously, harmonious and successful, finally respected by the mighty. His teaching spread and the number of his disciples grew tremendously. He died at the great age of 80 from food poisoning, but he died peacefully, surrounded by his disciples. All over the world even now the statues of this Buddha announce his repose, his clarity, his peace, his deep harmony, indeed his cheerfulness. I can understand how for many Asians the Buddha represents the more sympathetic figure.

How different is the man from Nazareth! His is a history of suffering which includes arrest, flogging and finally execution in the cruellest, most shameful form, at the age of only 30. Nothing sorted out and completed marks this life. It remains a fragment, a torso. Is it a fiasco? At any rate there is no trace of success during his lifetime; according to the accounts we have this man dies slandered, vilified and cursed. His is a lonely end in the utmost torment, avoided by his mother and his family, forsaken by his disciples and followers, evidently forgotten by his God. The very last thing we hear of him is his cry on the cross. Here is *the* image of the suffering human being – a heavy burden for Buddhists and indeed sensitive Christians – from thenceforward irreplaceable.

Truly this is one who suffers, who does not radiate compassion but himself invokes compassion, who does not rest in himself but totally surrenders himself. So in this way, according to the Christian understanding, as the one who suffers in self-surrender and love this Jesus differs from the Buddha, the benevolent, the compassionate. And he also differs unmistakably from all the many gods and divinized founders of religions, from all religious geniuses and gurus, heroes and Caesars of world history as being the one who suffers, who is executed, who is crucified. But does all that mean that there is no answer to the question of suffering?

## The insoluble riddle of theodicy

Life is suffering. That is the deep insight of Buddhism that one can also affirm as a Christian. By that I mean suffering in the broadest sense, all the negative elements that burden our life. Life is also suffering in our day, and even with the best technology and medicine, with effective psychotherapy and all the social reforms, people have not succeeded in simply abolishing suffering. The old illnesses are followed by new ones, former abuses by modern ones, physical illnesses by psychological ones . . . And everyone can find themselves in situations in which they ask themselves a question that cannot be answered. For decades I have studied all past attempts at theodicy, at justifying God, in philosophy and theology. And I have arrived at the clear conviction that there is no theoretical answer to the problem of theodicy.

That does not make a basic attitude of faith impossible. So I can and must say this, especially in response to the horror of the Holocaust: *if* God exists, then God was also in Auschwitz! Believers of different religions and confessions prayed to God even in this factory of death. In their suffering and dying they maintained that despite everything, God lives. But there remains no answer to the question: how could God be in Auschwitz without preventing Auschwitz?

Despite all pious apologetic it has to be soberly conceded that anyone who as a theologian wants to get behind the mystery which is the mystery of God will at best only find his own projected wishes or his own theological construct. At this extreme point, on this most difficult question, a theology of silence seems more appropriate. 'If I knew Him I would be He' is an old Jewish saying. And some Jewish theologians who in the face of all suffering prefer to dispense with a last justification of God, simply quote the terse word of scripture which follows the account of the death of the two sons of Aaron killed by God's fire: 'And Aaron was silent' (Leviticus 10.3).

None of the great spirits of humanity whom I studied – neither Augustine, nor Thomas nor Calvin, neither Leibniz nor Hegel nor Karl Barth – solved the fundamental problem. In 1791 Immanuel Kant wrote 'On the failures of all philosophical attempts at theodicy' when in Paris people were thinking of deposing God and replacing him with the goddess Reason. But conversely I would like to ask the atheists: Does reason, indeed atheism, offer the solution, an atheism that sees its ultimate support in Auschwitz? Is Auschwitz *the* rock of atheism? Then the question presses in on me: Does atheism explain the world better? The world's grandeur and its misery? Does unbelief explain the world as it is now? And may unbelief take its comfort from unmerited, incomprehensible, meaningless suffering? Doesn't all unbelieving reason have its limit at such suffering? Anti-theology here is no better than theology.

So it is my insight, which has grown up over many years and to which I have so far found no convincing alternative, that suffering – excessive, unmerited, meaningless suffering, both individual and collective – cannot be understood theoretically but at best can be endured practically. For Christians and Jews there is only a practical answer to the question of suffering. And if one asks about their practical attitude, Jews and Christians point to different traditions, yet ones that hang together.

In the utmost suffering Jews, but also Christians, have in view the figure of Job – from the biblical didactic narrative of the fifth to second pre-Christian centuries. This innocent man, who lost his possessions, his family and his health, a beggar inflicted with leprosy, complains to God and rejects all the arguments to justify God that his friends produce for him in a long conversation. He has shown that human beings need not simply accept suffering, they need not spare God. They may rebel, protest, revolt against a God who seems to be cruel, capricious and sly. It is finally conceded to Job that he has spoken rightly before God. But this is not the end of the story; finally Job is given everything back again.

The suffering human being cannot get behind the mystery of the counsel and plan of the Creator for the world. The riddle of suffering and evil cannot be violently broken open with the keys of reason. The darkness of suffering and evil cannot be changed to light by psychologizing or philosophizing or moralizing. The theodicy of Job's friends, who attempted to carry through the justification of God with their logical arguments, has failed. But the theodicy of Job itself, which attempted with its self-justification to achieve the justification of God indirectly, has also failed. And yet in the end it seems appropriate for people to put unshakable, unconditional trust in God in spite of everything. They may protest, but that should not be their last word.

For Christians – and why not also for Jews? – in extreme suffering, beyond the (ultimately fictitious) figure of Job there appears the truly historical figure of the suffering and dying 'servant of God', the man of sorrows from Nazareth. As an American Jewish woman once explained to me, the way in which he is delivered up, flogged and mocked, his long dying on the cross, has anticipated the thrice-fearful experience of the victims of the Holocaust, namely that all-permeating experience that one has been forsaken by all people, that one is even robbed of humanity, that one can be abandoned even by God.

The first Christians took a great deal of trouble to interpret Jesus' shameful death as a saving death. They used juridical categories: Jesus' death as proclaiming the sinner righteous. Or cultic concepts and images: Jesus' death as representation, sacrifice, sanctification. Or even financial terms: Jesus' death as the payment of a ransom. And finally even military terms: Jesus' death as a weapon against evil powers. This diversity of biblical interpretations leaves every coming generation much freedom for interpretation. There has been a unitary theory of the cross only since the Middle Ages. But this doctrine of satisfaction put forward by Anselm of Canterbury (died 1109), who wanted to prove with logical strictness that the sacrifice of the Son of God on the cross was to assuage the wrath of God the Father, has found increasing contradiction. In other publications I have criticized the evidence in the history of dogma. It is manifest that in the 2000 years of Christianity the cross of Christ has been the occasion for many misunderstandings.

## The cross misunderstood

Many Christians have evidently lost a sense of what a provocation the message that salvation was given by a crucified man still represents for non-Christians, not just for Buddhists but also for Muslims. Otherwise in 2009 a German cardinal and a Protestant church leader would not have rejected a shared inter-religious award with Navid Kermani, a highly-respected Muslim writer and Islamic scholar from Iran who was born in Germany, because he had criticized the depiction of the crucified Christ as 'blasphemy and idolatry'.

The two theologically educated Christians should have recalled that the apostle Paul had already termed the message of the cross a 'scandal for the Jews' and 'folly for the Greeks' (1 Corinthians 1.23). To the Romans the message that a crucified man brought salvation seemed to be a simple dumb-ass message, expressed by the first pictorial depiction of the crucified Jesus: a graffito scratched in the third century on the Palatine, the imperial precinct in Rome. The one suffering on the cross, given an ass's head, has underneath a kneeling figure and the inscription 'Alexamenos worships his god'. So this is a mocking crucifix.

I admit that in my study and living room there is a beautiful Greek icon of Christ, but there is no crucified figure. Why? Because I share the restraint of the first Christians. In the first three centuries Jesus was depicted as a youthful 'good shepherd' without a beard. The two earliest depictions of the crucified Jesus come only from the fifth century: Christ in the form not of one who suffers but of one who conquers or prays. It was late Gothic art, at the end of the Middle Ages, that first made the suffering of the crucified Jesus the dominant theme. The most shocking depiction is that of Mathias Grünewald in Colmar on the eve of the Reformation, which I have often looked at there – and the unique spiritualized depiction of the risen Christ connected with it.

In the present, I think one should deal in a more differentiated way with the shameful death of Jesus on the cross, both out of intercultural sensitivity and against the background of the negative experiences of history. Unfortunately I cannot overlook the fact that appalling actions were performed in church history in the name of the cross. When

Christianity took power in the Roman empire under Emperor Constantine with this sign, the cross of Christ, which was originally a sign of salvation and peace, increasingly became a sign of war and victory, above all for soldiers, statesmen and inquisitors. The Crusades and persecutions of heretics in the Middle Ages were horrendous, and no less evil are the campaigns of the American 'Crusaders' in the twenty-first century in Iraq and in Afghanistan, who in killing thousands likewise thought that they had God on their side.

Unfortunately the concept of 'discipleship of the cross' has also fallen into disrepute. Some pious people are responsible for the fact that 'creeping to the cross' today means giving in, not trusting anything, surrendering, diligently holding out one's neck. And bearing one's cross likewise for many people means humbling oneself, enduring passively, crawling away, not daring to do much while inwardly seething.

So the cross is not just a sign of warriors and those in power but also of weaklings and moral cowards. This fact already repelled the young Nietzsche. It is far removed from Jesus, the fearless and bold young man who was finally executed, and his message as we now have it from the New Testament. But there are three more subtle misunderstandings of the preaching of the cross in Christianity that have a negative effect on practice today and from which I want to dissociate myself.

I do not understand discipleship of the cross as cultic worship. I have nothing against a veneration of the cross in accordance with the gospel, for example in the Good Friday liturgy. But I do object to the thoughtless sign of the cross as a gesture of blessing, repeated thousands of times especially by those in office. And as for visual images, in the first Christian millennium up to late Gothic, as I have said, people hesitated to depict the crucified Jesus. We have got used to this depiction now but we should guard against a cheap commercialization by a clever devotional industry.

Nor do I understand discipleship of the cross as mystical identification. Again, I have nothing against the serious mysticism of suffering and the cross that arose in the Middle Ages with Francis of Assisi or the Spanish mystics. But I do object to an identification with the 'suffering of the One' that lacks a sense of distance and respect for the cross. It is particularly painful that Roman hierarchs, who bear the cross on their chests, in pompous ceremonies have recently been exchanging the traditional shepherd's staff that they carry before them for a crucifix, as if they themselves were a kind of second Christ.

Finally, I do not understand discipleship of the cross as literal imitation. I have respect for great figures such as Leo Tolstoy and Martin

Luther King, who directly followed this Jesus as a model by renouncing possessions and force and showed unmistakable programmatic signs of Christian action. But I do object to an imitation of Jesus which itself seeks suffering – up to self-flagellation or a cult of miracles and stigmatization (often deceptive) – in order to demonstrate discipleship. I do not believe in the miracles of Therese of Konnersreuth or those of Padre Pio, whom I knew personally. Jesus himself did not seek suffering; it was forced on him. Nor do I believe that human beings are nearest to God when they suffer. That would make heaven hell.

So if discipleship of the cross means neither *adoratio* nor *identificatio* nor *imitatio* – what then? Discipleship of the cross means bearing the suffering that I in particular endure in my own unique situation – in correspondence (*correlatio*) to the suffering of Christ.

## The cross in one's own life

'If any man would come after me . . . let him take up his cross' (Mark 8.34). So I am not to bear Christ's cross but to take my own cross upon myself, in accord with him. I am to go my own way in the risk of my situation and the uncertainty of the future. And each individual has his or her own way of life and way of suffering. So everyone should take their own cross upon themselves, which no one knows better than the person concerned. That includes the acceptance of oneself and one's 'shadow'.

Already as a child I understood that everyone must bear the cross destined for them. My mother told the story of someone who had complained about the cross that had been laid on him. Led by an angel, he was allowed to look for a new one in a great shop of crosses. But one seemed to him too heavy and another too light; after much to-ing and fro-ing he found one in between which seemed to correspond to his strength. 'You've chosen your cross,' the angel said to him. From then on he bore it with patience.

But there are many who find their cross all too difficult: professional failures, the incurably ill, those abandoned by their partners . . . A look at the crucified Jesus may show people in extreme need that they are not completely lost even when forsaken by fellow human beings and God.

But often there are also simply the constantly recurring efforts of everyday life which have to be borne patiently: the cross of one's job, of constant living together, difficult circumstances in life or unpleasant surroundings, all the daily duties, demands, claims, promises . . . Today no one needs to seek suffering like the old ascetics and chastise themselves.

For many people it takes enough strength – because of the frequency or duration this is often more difficult than an individual heroic act to bear – to endure the customary cross of everyday life.

But we should not just content ourselves with passively bearing the cross; we should fight suffering wherever possible and use our limited personal and social possibilities to change the miserable circumstances of others. In addition, where possible we should assimilate suffering inwardly. An inner freedom from suffering becomes evident whenever believers do not allow themselves to be oppressed by distress and oppression; when in doubt they do not doubt, when in loneliness they do not feel lost, when in all tribulation they do not lose cheerfulness and in all defeat are not wiped out.

But human existence remains an event permeated by the cross – by pain, anxiety, suffering and death. Yet in the light of the cross of Jesus such existence can take on meaning in discipleship of the cross – if one accepts it. No cross in the world can contradict the offer of meaning which is set up in the cross of the one who was raised to life, a sign that even extreme threat, meaninglessness, nothingness, forsakenness, loneliness and emptiness are embraced by God, who is in solidarity with human beings. So for the believer no way opens up around suffering, but through suffering. In active indifference to suffering they must be ready for the fight against suffering and its causes, in the life of the individual and in human society.

## Test question for humanists

I spoke of coping with the negative as the acid test of Christian faith and non-Christian humanism. Perhaps it has now become clear that in the light of the crucified Jesus the negative is overcome at a depth that seems almost impossible for non-Christian humanisms.

I admit that, even if I embark on the way of Jesus and soberly take my own cross upon myself in everyday life, I can never simply conquer and remove suffering. But I can withstand it and cope with it in faith. I will then never be simply oppressed by suffering and in suffering succumb to despair. If Jesus was not overwhelmed in the extreme suffering of being forsaken by God and his fellow human beings, then the one who holds to him in trusting faith will not succumb either. For in faith hope is given to me that suffering is not simply the definitive, the last thing. My ultimate hope is for a life without suffering, but this is a life which neither human society nor I myself will ever bring about. Rather, I may expect the fulfilment of this hope from the consummation, from the mysterious Wholly Other, from my God: all suffering definitively done away with in eternal life.

In suffering in life, in the negativity of human life, it becomes evident whether a humanism stands up. I have said time and again that Christians are no less humanist than any humanists. But – if they understand rightly what being a Christian means, namely being human, truly human – Christians see human beings and their God, together with humanity, freedom, justice, life, love, peace and meaning, in the light of this Jesus who for them is the concrete norm, the Christ. In his light I can confess a humanism that affirms all that is true, good, beautiful and human. Even when I was at school I acquired this humanism as the basis of my universal thought. As a Christian I can profess a truly 'radical' humanism, which goes to the 'radix', the 'root' of things and is able also to integrate and cope with what is not true, not good, not beautiful and not human; not only all that is positive but also all that is negative: even suffering, guilt, death, meaninglessness.

After 600 pages of fundamental consideration I have summarized this in my book *On Being a Christian* in a single sentence, not a word of which I would want to change now, many decades later.

> By following Jesus Christ
> men and women in the world of today
> can truly humanly live, act, suffer and die:
> in happiness and unhappiness, life and death,
> sustained by God and helpful to their fellow human beings.

But a sentence from the introduction remains important for me. 'This book was written, not because the author thinks he is a good Christian, but because he thinks that being a Christian is a particularly good thing.'

However, in the face of all the burdens and torments of life in this connection one more fundamental question remains to be answered.

## How does one hold on?

I am often asked, 'How have you held on?' Now it takes a great deal to hold on, and I would never condemn anyone who no longer had sufficient strength to do this. One needs good health, physical and mental, also a touch of humour and even a 'happy-go-lucky' attitude, above all friends who do not desert one in the hour of need, people who help to bear everything, even in trivial everyday matters. One cannot hold on alone.

But how does one maintain health of body and mind, humour and trust in people? An infinite amount could be said about that. I would simply mention what seems decisive to me, what in any case would support me and for me would be the final foundation for holding on even when everything else breaks, if for some reason I lost all sense of humour, if I was entangled in the deepest guilt, if all success abandoned me, if I also perhaps lost my good health and even trust in other people.

So what does it ultimately come down to in the life of a Christian? That is the question. What is decisive? Success, achievements? No, even if only success counts in our achievement society and everyone loves success and nothing is as successful as success. For me as a Christian in the end not everything depends on success. I am not concerned always to be proved right, to impose myself, to find approval for my views. I need not justify myself to my closer surroundings, to society, to any authorities, indeed even to myself.

Of course I will not *a priori* renounce success, or denigrate achievements. But I should be aware that human beings are more than their jobs, their work or the role that they have to play, and that while achievements are important they are not decisive. So I should achieve things, fight for my convictions, persuade others, seek their assent. But it is not achievements I can demonstrate that matter, however important they may be in daily life, in my job, even in the church.

Am I not also capable of mistakes, serious mistakes? Who would want to dispute that? But the second dimension of this message becomes evident in the fact that the Christian is concerned with neither successes nor mistakes. Even failure and defeat can take on another status for my life.

In the end something else is decisive and that is that even in limit situations, even in the greatest distress and guilt I do not despair, that I never despair, never. Or to put it in a positive way, that I always and unshakably maintain trust, an unshakable, unconditional and believing trust or trusting faith in God's grace.

That is what was decisive for Abraham and the patriarchs of Israel: 'Abraham believed God and that was counted for him as righteousness' (Romans 4.3). This trusting faith was also decisive for Mary and the first disciples: 'Blessed is she who has believed' (Luke 1.45). It is what Peter, so congenial yet so faint-hearted, learned as he walked on the water in trust, despite the storm and the waves, with his gaze fixed on Jesus. This trust is what ultimately the apostle Paul hammered into his fellow Christians: 'that we are not justified by our achievements, but are justified by faith' (Galatians 2.16; Romans 3.28).

That means, through unconditional trust in the gracious and merciful God. Here Paul understood most deeply what Jesus was concerned with and what had found expression in his message, in the parables of the Prodigal Son, the Pharisee and the Publican, the workers in the vineyard. Here he grasped what Jesus was concerned with in his teaching, fighting, working and suffering and finally in his death. It is the crucified Jesus for whom, hanging on the cross, there were no more achievements and successes and who had to regard his labours as failure that Paul puts before his eyes and the eyes of us all, justified solely by God, his Father and our Father. So he saw in the crucified Jesus that human beings are justified by trusting faith alone, which gives them a great freedom.

## The great freedom

'For freedom Christ has freed us' (Galatians 5.1). That does not mean the 'little' freedom, which in any case is limited in many ways, freedom of the will, the physiological processes of which are being investigated by more recent brain research, but which we take for granted in everyday life in ourselves and others. Even criminal law begins from it when it speaks of 'guilt': in our understanding of the law an action or a decision is 'free' when the one who acts could have acted otherwise or not acted at all.

This is the 'great' freedom that human beings can keep even when in chains. Fundamentally it is my inner freedom, not setting my heart on false gods, even on the gods of power, money, career, sport, sex or whatever, but on a true God as he has shown his face in Jesus of Nazareth. And because my heart depends on the one infinite God, I am and remain free over and against all finite, relative values, goods, powers and authorities. In the Sermon on the Mount, in which Jesus' ethical demands are collected together in short sayings and groups of sayings, Jesus calls the individual to obedience to God, and precisely in this way to become free for his or her neighbours.

But above all commandments, all behaviour decent or mistaken, stands the good and merciful God. And for this God we are always more than our role – as professional persons, scientists, businessmen, politicians, housewives. We remain affirmed even when the roles end in old age and merely living becomes a struggle.

As for me, I am before God as I am now – I remain valuable,

important, accepted. And this is the case even when I no longer find confirmation by work, when I can no longer shine before others by any achievements. Even when I become old and sick I am accepted, indeed loved, even when I am no longer 'productive'.

As a theologian and Christian I want to be like the great Protestant theologian Karl Barth who – as he once told me – when standing before his divine judge at the end would not point to his 'collected works', indeed not even to his 'good intentions' in justification, but with empty hands would find only one thing appropriate to say: 'God be merciful to me, poor sinner.'

So from beginning to end I put my trust in God's grace. But isn't that quintessentially Protestant? I think that it is quintessentially evangelical, i.e. in keeping with the gospel, and basically I have only spelt out the meaning of a scriptural text (which today sounds rather patriarchal): 'When you have done all that is required of you then say: We are no more than servants, we have done what it was our duty to do' (Luke 17.10).

Moreover, because all that is quintessentially evangelical, it is also quintessentially catholic, as we confess in the great Catholic hymn of praise *Te Deum Laudamus*: '*In te, Domine, speravi: non confundar in aeternum* – In you, Lord, have I trusted, I shall never be put to shame.' On the basis of this trust that supports me, my anxiety about life diminishes and my courage and joy in life increase. That is the basis for a real art of living.

## Chapter 9

# The Art of Living

*But test everything; hold fast to what is good, abstain from every form of evil.*
First Letter of the apostle Paul to the community of Thessalonica 5.21f.

We have followed a way of life through the joy of life and the suffering of life. But what is the art of living?

An infinite amount has been written about the art of living, *savoir-vivre*. The art of mastering life remains a task for life. I attempt to deal with the facts and make the most of them. But 'take it easy' isn't always the solution. Indeed I know of situations in which uncomfortable, unpleasant things, hostile to life, a sacrifice, is required of me. The art of life, the wisdom of life and the delight of life by no means exclude 'ascesis', training, discipline. The presupposition for the art of living must be a certain equilibrium between – to put it in the categories of Jung's depth psychology – introversion and extraversion, in some respects also between the animus, the spiritual disposition of the woman for the 'male', and the anima, the spiritual disposition of the man for the 'female'. The task of incorporating animus and anima in shaping life and cultivating them also extends to every kind of musical activity and then of course to the states of enthusiasm, being in love and love, and thus to the whole sphere of eroticism and sexuality. Here it is important to make distinctions everywhere, to examine everything and to keep the good.

## Eros and agape

In their reflections on love some theologians could not do enough to emphasize the difference between the desiring eros of the Greeks and the giving agape as Jesus understood it. I cannot go along with this sharp distinction: it damages both eros (Latin *amor*) and agape (Latin *caritas*).

I am against any devaluation and demonization of eros. This limits passionate love which desires the other to sex and thus at the same time disqualifies eroticism and sex. Both are important forces in life. However, hostility to the body and the suppression of sexuality have a long history which scholastic theology, ignoring the results of critical exegesis and the history of dogma, evades. This hostility already finds its expression in some ancient currents, above all in Manichaeism and Gnosticism. But it was powerfully furthered in the Latin West by the invention, which I have already mentioned, of an 'original sin' transmitted by the sexual act. It cannot be found either in the paradise story of the Book of Genesis or in the apostle Paul or in Greek theology. It was the brilliant Latin church father Augustine who transmitted it – a striking error of judgement – to the whole of Western theology, mediaeval theology and through Luther also to Reformation theology. Augustine, originally a very worldly man, fathered a child when he was seventeen and lived unmarried with its mother for thirteen years. For a time he was a 'hearer' of Manichaeism, which explained evil and sexuality with the help of an eternal evil principle. On the basis of his personal experience of the tremendous power of sexuality and his Manichaean past Augustine combines original sin – in an erroneous Latin translation and interpretation of a passage in Paul's letter to the Romans (5.12) – with the sexual act and the 'fleshly', I-seeking desire, concupiscence, connected with it.

So in Augustine's view any child that comes into the world is not innocent but – on the basis of the sexual drive of its parents – is from the beginning infected with original sin and destined to eternal damnation unless it is baptized in time. Therefore in his view any sexual intercourse is allowed only for procreation (Latin *generatio*) and not for sexual pleasure (Latin *delectatio*). Pope John Paul II still held the view that even in marriage a man could look on his wife 'unchastely'. No wonder that such hostility to eros and sex, particularly in the Catholic Church and in Catholic education, has done an infinite amount of damage not least with the prohibition of the pill. Eros is suspected even where it is not simply understood as an uncanny, overwhelming, blind and sensual passion, but as, say, in Plato's *Symposium*, as the urge towards the beautiful and philosophical knowledge rooted in friendship, as a creative force of the opening up of the sensual world to the world of ideas and the highest divine good. But many Catholics rightly expect their church to look at sexuality in a new, relaxed, loving and humane way, as a life-giving power of human beings created and affirmed by God.

Even Mary, the mother of Jesus, venerated at a very early stage, was still in the Latin West understood as tainted with original sin from her conception. This view prevailed until the thirteenth century, and was held by Thomas Aquinas. But in this period veneration of Mary increased more and more (*de Virgine numquam satis* – there is never enough praise of the Virgin!) and beyond doubt the veneration of Mary greatly enriched male-orientated poetry, art and music, indeed customs and the culture of festivals and the whole of popular piety.

Finally the Franciscan theologian Duns Scotus (died 1308) asserted a lasting 'pre-redemption', contrary to the whole of tradition hitherto, so that Mary was preserved from original sin. The idea of the 'immaculate conception' was invented and was now disseminated with every means, not least with the help of the liturgy. It was finally defined as a dogma in 1854 by that Pius IX who, after the loss of the papal church state, also had the papal primacy of jurisdiction and infallibility defined by the First Vatican Council. Since the 1854 dogma, in Catholic moral theology the tradition that the soul comes into being in the human foetus at a late point in its development, argued for by Aristotle, Thomas Aquinas and the Spanish baroque scholastics has increasingly been given up. This tradition had assumed that there is not a human person either in the vegetative or in the sensitive phase of the human foetus but only in the third stage, directed by the spirit-soul. Against this it was asserted – less on the basis of biological medical arguments than on theological–dogmatic ones – that a personhood is already indwelling before the fertilized egg. This latter view gives an added edge to the question of abortion.

Thus the Virgin immaculately conceived was raised as an asexual symbol above all other women, who are all tainted with original sin and burdened with sexual desires. At the same time the Virgin Mary was commended for sublimating or spiritualizing the sexual drive, an ideal woman not dangerous to the clergy, who from the eleventh century were obligated to celibacy. In this way Marianism, papism and celibacy mutually supported one another, especially from the nineteenth century on. But they are not included in any creed. On the contrary, Vatican II attempted to take measures against the excesses of Marianism and papalism, though only with limited success.

The devaluation and demonization of eros and sex on the other hand resulted in a heightening of agape, removing it from the senses. Agape (wrongly called 'Platonic love') is spiritualized: the ideal of a love without passion. The vital, emotional, affective elements are excluded. But where love is only a resolve of the will without a venture of the heart, it lacks genuine human depth, warmth, inwardness, tenderness. Such 'Christian caritas' can certainly do good deeds, but hardly radiates love.

Love takes many forms, from friendship, the love of parents, children, brothers and sisters, through the love of homeland, people and fatherland to the love of truth and freedom and finally to the love of neighbour, enemy and God. Rather than the distinction between eros and agape, another distinction is fundamental for me: between selfish love, which only seeks its own, and giving love, which seeks what is the other's good. The one who desires another can also give to him or her at the same time. And those who give themselves to other people may at the same time desire them. The desire of love and the service, play and fidelity of love are not exclusive.

## The power of love

To conclude from the Synoptic Gospels, Jesus himself uses the word 'love' both as a noun and a verb extremely sparingly in the sense of love for fellow human beings. Yet love of fellow human beings is present everywhere in his preaching. That means that for him love is above all an action. Love is not understood primarily as a sentimental–emotional affection, which it is impossible for me to show to everyone. Rather, it is understood as a benevolent being-there for others, ready to help. It is embodied by Jesus in all his teachings and behaviour, encouraging and healing, fighting and suffering. We can learn from Jesus of Nazareth what our present-day egotistical society, in which the weakest go to the wall, so much lacks, something that always delights us when we experience it ourselves: taking care and sharing, being able to forgive and repent, showing consideration, practising renunciation and giving help.

At the same time, Jesus combines love of God and love of neighbour in an indissoluble unity. Human love becomes virtually a criterion of piety and human behaviour pleasing to God. Jesus concentrates all the commandments on this twofold commandment to love God and one's neighbour that is already central in the Hebrew Bible. By it he does not mean to say something like 'You millions, I embrace you, this kiss for all the world', as in Schiller's and Beethoven's great Ode to Joy. Rather, he means love of 'neighbour' and sets up love of self as a yardstick for this love of neighbour. 'Love your neighbour as yourself.' This means being aware of, open to, ready for the fellow human being who needs me. For Jesus, that is the 'neighbour', not just the one who is close to me in the family, the clan or the nation, but the one who is in need, as that man attacked by robbers was for the 'good Samaritan' who selflessly helped him. Understood in this way, love seems to know no barriers. And in fact according to Jesus too it is to know no absolute frontiers. It is even to include enemies – that is the way in which Jesus characteristically sharpens it. The rigid frontier between kinsfolk and non-kinsfolk is to be overcome. Anyone can be our neighbour, even a political or religious opponent, a rival, an adversary or even an enemy. Despite all the differences and contradictions this means openness and compassion not just for the members of one's own social group or clan, one's own people, one's own race, class, party, religion, nation, to the exclusion of others, but unlimited openness and overcoming separations that do harm, wherever they arise.

So that is what the story of the hated Samaritan, the enemy of the people, of mixed race and a heretic, who is presented by Jesus to his fellow-Jews in a provocative way as a model, is about. It is not just about specific special deeds, works of love, 'Samaritan acts', but the actual overcoming of abiding frontiers – between Jews and non-Jews, neighbours and those remote, good and evil, Pharisees and tax collectors.

## Love as the fulfilment of the global ethic

A great freedom manifests itself in this love. Such a love is no longer directed towards commandments and prohibitions that are to be followed mechanically but towards what reality itself requires and makes possible. In this sense Augustine is right in his bold statement, which represents a radical renunciation of casuistry: 'Love, and do what you will.' Love quite naturally fulfils the principles of the global ethic which are binding on all men and women and at the same time transcends them, as the apostle Paul describes it in his letter to the community in Rome: 'He who loves his neighbour has fulfilled the law. The commandments, "You shall not commit adultery, You shall not kill, You shall not steal, You shall not covet," and any other commandment, are summed up in this sentence, "You shall love your neighbour as yourself." Love does no wrong to a neighbour; therefore love is the fulfilling of the law' (Romans 13.8–10). This is the specific Christian contribution to the global ethic.

Paul expressed what the power of love can do in his first letter to the community in Corinth in a way that is still valid today:

> Love is patient and kind;
> love is not jealous or boastful;
> it is not arrogant or rude.
> Love does not insist on its own way;
> it is not irritable or resentful;
> it does not rejoice at wrong,
> but rejoices in the right.
> Love bears all things, believes all things,
> hopes all things, endures all things.
> Love never ends.
>
> (1 Corinthians 13.4–8)

Can the power of love really change life? Some simple antitheses by an author unknown to me make it clear how much love as a basic attitude can change life.

> Duty without love is wearisome;
> Duty in love brings lasting fulfilment.
>
> Responsibility without love leads to carelessness;
> Responsibility borne in love results in care.
>
> Justice without love is harsh;
> Justice done in love is reliable.
>
> Education without love makes people refractory;
> Education received in love makes them patient.
>
> Wisdom without love brings divisions;
> Wisdom practised in love brings understanding.
>
> Friendship without love leads to hypocrisy;
> Friendship shown in love is gracious.
>
> Order without love makes people petty;
> Order in love makes them generous.
>
> Expert knowledge without love leads to pedantry;
> Expert knowledge shown in love makes people trustworthy.
>
> Power without love leads to violence;
> Power practised in love makes people ready to help.
>
> Honour without love brings arrogance;
> Honour kept in love brings modesty.

Possessions without love engender greed;
Possessions used in love show generosity.

Faith without love makes fanatics;
Faith lived in love makes peacemakers.

So the directives of a universal ethic of humanity, a global ethic, are affirmed and embraced by the specific Christian ethic, but at the same time they are radicalized and universalized by being applied concretely to all men and women, even enemies. But perhaps more important is whatever works out in everyday life. Countless stimuli to thought and action, stimuli for implementing the Christian programme in everyday practice, followed and follow from the basic Christian model as presented by Jesus in the Gospels. An infinite number of acts and sufferings of Christian love could be reported. However, I have been impressed by four concrete possibilities which the Christian ethic invites us to note: creating peace through renouncing rights, using power in favour of others, being moderate in consumption, understanding nurture in mutual respect. Here are some sketchy considerations.

## Peace through renouncing rights

I am thinking of the problem of war and peace. Every day I follow news events in the media. For decades it proved impossible to bring about peace in the heart of Europe, in the Middle East and the Far East. Why? Each side said it was because the 'other side' did not want peace. But the problem lies deeper. Usually both sides lay claim to the same territories (it used to be the Saarland and the German eastern territories, today it is Palestine or Kashmir) and can give historical, economic, cultural and political grounds for their claims. Now according to their state constitutions governments see themselves as obliged to preserve and defend the rights of their own states. Long-cherished hostile pictures and prejudices against other countries, peoples, cultures promote an atmosphere of collective suspicion. Of course the spiral of violence and counter-violence cannot be broken and peace restored in this way, since no one sees why they and not the other should renounce a position of right and power.

What does the Christian message tell me about this? Of course I know the Sermon on the Mount cannot be the basis for a state. One cannot derive detailed information and proposals for frontier conflicts and disarmament conferences from it. But it does say something that those who rule states cannot so easily ask of their people, but that religious leaders, bishops, theologians and pastors can say to the wider public, that renunciation of rights without anything in return need not necessarily do harm, but can serve peace. Go the second mile with the person who has only required one (Matthew 5.41).

Of course the renunciation of rights need not be *carte blanche* for the 'right of the stronger'. The Christian message does not seek to abolish the legal order. But it does seek to relativize the law for the sake of human beings and peace. That is a demand for politicians in particular instances to refrain from implementing rights with power and violence. Statesmen with a Christian disposition after the Second World War, supported by the churches, did this successfully for reconciliation between France and Germany and later between Germany and Poland and the Czech Republic. Mahatma Gandhi's and Martin Luther King's idea and practice of non-violent resistance that can effectively change the balance of power are also influenced by Jesus.

What is true in world politics also applies in the petty wars of everyday life. Wherever the individual or a group remembers that a legal standpoint need not necessarily be imposed mercilessly in every situation, it makes peace, forgiveness, reconciliation possible. So many disputes in a family, between neighbours, in a business, in a city can be avoided *a priori* or at least settled afterwards where particularly in the legal sphere concrete humanity is exercised between individuals and groups instead of justice 'by the book', enabling a spirit of deeper justice to grow. Happily, for some years mediation and arbitration have been practised once again, and this helps to avoid some legal disputes. At any rate the promise of the Sermon on the Mount that the 'non-violent' will inherit the earth' (Matthew 5.5) applies.

## Using power in favour of others

I am thinking of the problem of economic power, which was often used brutally even before the global economic crisis to reduce costs and rationalize jobs. Employers are constantly in conflict with the trade unions and both blame the government. So more and more frequently in recent years there has been talk of 'predatory capitalism', since power is often used brutally for particular special interests – the opposite of a social market economy.

What can the Christian message do? Here, too, of course I know that moral appeals alone are no use. The Christian message does not tell us how, for example, the magical rectangle – full employment, growth of the economy, price stability and a balance in imports and exports all at the same time – is to be achieved. Supply and demand, exports and domestic trade seem to obey iron laws. 'Social Darwinism' (which does not come from Darwin) teaches that everyone seeks to exploit the competitive struggle for his or her own ends.

But the Christian message makes me think of what cannot be achieved by laws alone: that in the unavoidable conflicts of interest there is no harm in banks, businesses or trade unions not fully exploiting their power against others. Businesses need not foist every increase in production costs on to consumers, trade unions need not press for unrealistic wage increases. In quite specific situations – not as a general rule – the banks can use their power in favour of others, for the common good. Indeed in the individual case one can even give away power, profit, influence: 'And if anyone would sue you and take your coat, let him have your cloak as well,' as Jesus' Sermon on the Mount (Matthew 5.40) has it.

The often reckless capitalism of recent years must be limited by a number of legislative steps. But at the same time it needs a change of disposition. Especially those mainly responsible for the global economic crisis – bankers, central bankers, politicians and journalists – must see that behind the pernicious rank growth of the financial markets, the inflation of the money in circulation and the property decline stand an uncontrolled greed for profit and economic megalomania which must be bridled. The economy must again be subordinated to politics and both the economy and politics to ethics. That means that money may no longer be the supreme value. That 'property brings obligations' already stands in the Basic Law of the Federal Republic of Germany. Economic power must be used at the same time 'for the general good', the good of all those involved in the economic process ('stakeholders') and not just of the shareholders. Such a message is not an opium of comfort but a realistic pointer wherever the powerful threaten to oppress the powerless and use power to overshadow the law.

What is true on a larger scale in business is also true on a smaller scale: wherever an individual or a group remembers that the now unavoidable competitive struggle must not be carried on at the expense of human beings and humanity, they contribute to its humanization and also make mutual respect, heed for others, mediation and consideration possible in the economic competition. And that means a fair balance of the different interests. This becomes stable if in the different spheres so close a web of interests is woven that to cut off one of the lines of communication brings more disadvantages than advantages to each side. In a period of mass unemployment this is particularly important. The promise of the Sermon on the Mount to the 'merciful' is that 'they shall obtain mercy' (Matthew 5.7).

## Being moderate in consumption

I am thinking of the problems of economic growth and the welfare society. On the basis of an economic theory praised on all sides there should be constant production so that there can be constant consumption. More and more must be consumed so that supply expands far above the level of demand, fuelled by advertising, promotions and special offers. The consumption of goods becomes the decisive indicator for a successful life. And this is world-wide – not just in Europe and America but for example also in India and China – with grave consequences for the environment.

What does the Christian message say in this situation? I am aware that it cannot offer any technological solutions to climate change and protection of the environment, to the distribution of water and raw materials, to reducing noise levels and removing waste. Nor are we given any instructions as to whether these or those ideas and reforms are appropriate for abolishing the gulf between poor and rich, between industrialized and developing countries. But the Christian message does teach me freedom from the compulsion to consume. It makes no sense to build up one's happiness solely on pleasure and prosperity; one cannot be guided by the laws of prestige and competition and should not indulge in the cult of superfluity, nor can transitory cravings satisfy the great desire for eternal happiness within men and women.

Those 'maximists' who note the price–worth ratio in all things and always want to find something better are not usually happy people. Those 'contented ones' who do not engage in endless comparisons but can be satisfied with what they have chosen and so inconspicuously practise sufficiency are more likely to be happy. This too is true in things great and small; moderation instead of pernicious greed. What is to be striven for is a basic attitude of inner freedom: a sovereign lack of demands and ultimately carefree relaxation that does not waste itself in anxiety for the morrow but remains focused on the present. In the Sermon on the Mount these 'poor in spirit' are promised that they will inherit the kingdom of God (Matthew 5.3).

## Upbringing in mutual respect

I am thinking of the problems of upbringing: styles of upbringing, methods of upbringing and the persons involved – father, mother, teacher, nurturer, trainer – have entered into a deep-seated crisis since the cultural revolution of 1968. These persons see themselves exposed to massive criticism and impatient taunts from left and right. For some they are too conservative and for others too progressive; for some too political and for others too apolitical; for some too authoritarian and for others too anti-authoritarian. Perplexity and a lack of bearings are widespread.

What does the Christian message tell me in this situation? It gives no pedagogical information as to how children should be brought up, how they should be taught today, how school and vocational education should be organized better and more effectively, what kind of schooling is best for what age, how education for young people must change in puberty and adolescence.

But the Christian message tells me what is decisive about the basic attitude of the nurturer to the child and the child to the nurturer and also gives me the reason for commitment despite disappointments and failures. At any rate children should not be brought up for the sake of one's own prestige, respect and interests, but always for the sake of the children themselves. So upbringing is not to be understood essentially as a subtle form of domination, or repression, but rather in mutual respect for the worth of the other, whether child or adult.

Children should not be naïve-romantic 'partners' but should be truly 'brought up' by adults, a laborious day-by-day process. But children are never there simply for the sake of those who bring them up, just as those who bring them up are not there simply for the sake of the children. Adults should not dominate their children tyrannically or even exploit them; equally, children should not exploit those who bring them up. Adults should not seek to impose their will on children or vice versa. Mutual respect for the dignity of the other in the Christian spirit means for those who bring children up a surplus of trust and kindness that cannot be compelled and is unconditional, and above all love which does not allow itself to be led astray. Children need to show a trusting acceptance of the boundaries laid down in the spirit of co-operation and gratitude.

Such a relationship between adults and children makes a meaningful, fulfilled life possible even in a phase of uncertainty and lack of orientation. To those who understand upbringing in this sense the promise of

Jesus is given: 'Whoever receives one such child in my name receives me' (Mark 9.37).

## Sport in fairness

Sport, too, is part of life, if not necessarily so, and therefore is also part of the art of living. As one who regularly went skiing in the Alps until my 80th birthday I know that skiing, unlike my daily swimming, is – and remains – a high-risk sport, for which the wise take out special insurance. Accidents with fatal consequences can take place in a fraction of a second. Every skier can report adventure and falls, sometimes also carelessness and stupidity. Despite improved equipment, risks have not diminished in recent years; quite the contrary. The most dangerous accidents are collisions with other skiers, and death can result. So it is not surprising that some are calling for more rules on the pistes, more written regulations, in some circumstances even a kind of piste police.

But does that help? I'm thinking not only of the sport of skiing but also of other kinds of sport, especially football. The world of sports, like society generally, is already suffering under a tremendous amount of regulating, provoked by professionalization and commercialization. So laws and legal authorities are not lacking. But what is often lacking is what is 'unwritten', what cannot be prescribed legally: the inner attitude, the basic moral attitude. There is no 'ethic', and without this the written rules can be evaded, ignored, undermined. 'Ethic' means an obligation to binding values, irrevocable criteria and basic personal attitudes.

In 2005 at the Protestant Kirchentag in Hanover I had a constructive public discussion on world sport and the global ethic with officials of the German Football League (President, league trainer, a referee and a national player). All were agreed that the best rules are useless unless people feel inwardly committed to them. Sport is the sphere of our reality in which everything depends on the rules not only being 'known' but also observed. When people speak of the 'spirit' of sports, they mean readiness for fairness, which includes equality of opportunities and truthfulness.

The popular sport of football in particular should be the best, most impressive manifestation of fairness. 'Fair play' means respectable and comradely behaviour, and it is not by chance that 'sporting behaviour' has become a proverbial phrase. However, constant reflection on what fairness in sport means for each individual involved is necessary: rational action in accordance with unwritten moral laws. Those who take advantage of others and especially those who in the process violate a communal consensus are unfair. In recent years according to players and officials even the hitherto blameless professional status of referee has come under the general suspicion of corruption; indeed the whole of football – including fans who are prepared to do violence – is under a cloud. Much trust has been destroyed. An apparently whole football world has collapsed. But handball, cycling and other kinds of sport are also threatened.

How do we achieve fair football, fair sport? More is necessary than 'the observance of rules specific to sport compelled by the threat of sanctions', to quote the Konstanz working party for sporting law in 1998. What is called for is 'an overriding mental attitude committed to ethical principles which also affirms these rules inwardly, does not aim at the success naturally striven for with every effort at any price, does not see the opponent as the enemy who has to be conquered by every means, but rather respects him as a partner in sporting competition, and therefore allows him the right to equality of opportunity, to respect for his physical integrity and his human dignity regardless of nationality, race and origin'.

One can understand all this as a concrete expression of the Golden Rule, 'Do not do to others what you do not want to be done to you', a rule that applies to different teams, fans and nations. In the light of the Sermon on the Mount this can even become a positive rule: 'Whatever you wish that men do to you, so do to them' (Matthew 7.12).

Football can be a serious rival to religion; it can become a substitute religion. People talk of the 'cult' and the 'God of football'. And the ritual in the stadium shows some parallels to the liturgy: when sportsmen kiss a trophy, this recalls the kissing of icons. When the trophy is raised, it is reminiscent of raising the monstrance in Catholic ceremonial. And it can hardly be disputed that the common singing and chanting of thousands evokes quasi-religious community experiences. It is not the individual phenomena as such that are decisive but the whole mood that suggests to the individual that what he is experiencing is the greatest thing in life. However, when football only fills an emptiness of head and heart and there is nothing else there, it is dangerous for people. Beer and whisky are not a medicine but promote a nihilistic delight in the use of violence.

On the right presuppositions the globalization of sport is an opportunity. I am convinced that sport has a unique opportunity to bring together people from many nations, cultures and religions. Sports events that are run well show this. Sport has a significance that transcends nations, cultures and religions. Here despite commercialization and doping lies the power of the 'Olympic idea', which is not wholly spent. That is of great symbolic force for intercultural and interreligious understanding.

People have agreed on a set of rules to control behaviour – regardless of their national, cultural or religious shaping. With the help of sport they practise encounter, collaboration, understanding. This is an excellent example of a global ethic. And since sport is about more than just 'rules', but is about a certain 'spirit', this too is of the utmost cultural, religious and political importance. The spirit of fairness, equality of opportunities, tolerance, human dignity, partnership can be practised by people of all cultures and religions, not because they have to strip off or ignore their religions and cultures in sport, but because they find support for these ideals and values in their cultures and religions. So I would plead for a new credibility for football and sports generally, to which all have to make their contribution: players and athletes, referees, officials and of course the public.

## Health but not a fixation on health

I can understand why people keep saying to me, 'Health – that's the important thing!' Health is indeed the basis of life, and health care is part of the art of living. But is health really the most important thing?

Beyond question many people make themselves ill by an unhealthy life: smoking, alcohol, drugs, lack of moderation, laziness, worrying. Even if they do not ruin life, they harm it and possibly shorten it. But there is no need for me to offer recipes here for healthy eating and sleeping, for slimness and wellness of the kind that are propagated every day in the media.

It has doubtless contributed to my long life that I have had daily exercise through sport, eaten a healthy diet, drunk wine only in moderation and in general lived a disciplined life. But at the same time it has always been clear to me that health is not the supreme good. If everything in life centres on health, that life becomes egocentric. Nothing can guarantee good health, defined by the World Health Organization as physical, mental and social well-being. The constant swallowing of pills does not produce such well-being. And even repeated cosmetic surgery cannot produce a 'forever young' appearance. Who knows, in some cases the tormented soul might be helped more by a visit to a house of God than to a fitness studio.

Modern biology shows that healthy laughter is the best medicine:

instead of 'stress hormones', adrenaline and cortisol, 'happiness hormones', endorphins, are produced which bring relaxation. For me only music, which has been called the sweetest medicine, can compete with laughter. Immanuel Kant tells us that as compensation for the many wearinesses of life heaven has given human beings three things: hope, sleep and laughter. In spite of all my difficulties with the church I have never given up hope. And you often hear laughter in our house: we all have a strenuous but usually also a happy life.

But when I am deeply worried I am not always able to sleep well, and I know that I cannot remain healthy for ever. Many promises by biologists and physicians of an endless prolongation of life are illusory. Health concern must not become a religion of health. So it is to be welcomed that a doctor, Manfred Lutz, pleads 'in opposition to the diet sadists, the craze for health and the fitness cult' for a simple enjoyment of life. But in any case few people today believe that doctors are demigods, fewer and fewer doctors fear the Medical Council as a Holy Inquisition and even in hospitals the Graeco-Latin sacral medical language is avoided as far as possible when talking to patients. But the pharmaceutical industry, the doctors and pharmacists, the hospitals and the politicians, are reluctant to yield to government pressures on the health service to make savings.

In all this the important thing is that the sick person, even the terminally ill human person, remains completely and utterly a human being. And there are people who can live to some degree happily with their sickness, even if this seems to be granted only to a few. Other burdens, for example severe guilt, atoned for or unatoned, can weigh more heavily than sickness itself.

One of my favourite sayings in the Sermon on the Mount is 'Therefore do not be anxious about tomorrow . . . Let the day's own trouble be sufficient for the day.' As I have said, Jesus himself, for all his seriousness about life, was not a gloomy ascetic; he took part in human life and all its festivities, and therefore historically, though in a slanderous way, was subjected to the charge of being 'a glutton and a drunkard' (Matthew 11.18f.). However, the story of the changing of water into wine at the marriage in Cana in Galilee in the Gospel of John (John 2.1–12) is legendary. Sometimes it could be right to follow the advice which the Paul of the Pastoral Letters gives to his pupil Timothy: 'Do not drink just water, but use a little wine for the sake of your stomach and your frequent ailments' (1 Timothy 5.23).

## The art of living

Whether people are believers or not, their plans and efforts are focused on this world. If they want to, they can fulfil their lives much better, fill them with every possible experience to a greater degree than any previous generation. So today the art of living often simply consists in living our lives better, in a more fulfilled way.

But do we have a more fulfilled life simply because we can fill it ever more easily, because we live at an increasingly rapid pace? I feel that the observations made by the sociologist Hartmut Rosa in his book *Beschleunigung: Die Veränderung der Zeitstruktur in der Moderne*, 2005 ('Acceleration: The Change in the Structure of Time in Modernity') also apply to me: technological acceleration (of transport, communication and production) has resulted in an acceleration of social change, for example of aesthetic literary, musical and philosophical modes and styles. Both accelerations have also led to an acceleration of the tempo of life. We attempt to do more things in a day, a week or a life: by more rapid action, by cutting down on breaks, waiting time and empty time and by multi-tasking. In this way we find ourselves in an 'acceleration circle' in which one dimension of speed drives the other. All this is the cause of much stress.

However, I have always been aware that with all this acceleration we cannot realize an eternal life before death, indeed that this life can come to an end at any moment. Sometimes, thinking back, I feel that I have lived seven lives in my extremely varied experiences. But I have never been under the illusion that I have overcome my finitude with a more rapid and thus more fulfilled life and thus made not only my life but also my dying meaningful.

If towards the end of this book I were to sum up what the art of living consists in for me personally, I would refer to all the things that I have tried to explain earlier:

- trust in life, supported through all the different ages and phases of life;
- joy in life, which I have been able to keep despite all the troubles and disappointments;
- a way of life, which I have attempted to follow consistently despite all the demands and opposition;
- a meaning in life, which I have always found and realized in my spiritual and mental activity, orientated on a greater meaning;

- the ground of life, from which I live, that ground of grounds on which my trusting faith rests;
- the power of life, which as Holy Spirit is the origin, centre and goal of the life-process and also gives me strength to go my way to its end;
- the model of life, which I have followed since my youth and which time and again raises me upright;
- the suffering in life, which in accordance with this model of life I hope to fight and at the same time cope with inwardly.

No one can escape growing older – and physically that makes life increasingly more difficult. But so much relieves our generation of the burden of years. We shouldn't be irritated but take it for granted that now we have to wear spectacles, a hearing aid, a set of dentures, or whatever. The achievements of medicine and pharmacy help older people, as do better living conditions and possibilities of travel. But despite all the aids and medications our organs become weaker and our bodies are no longer so much at our service as they were in earlier years. Especially our skeletons, which are put under pressure every day, show weaknesses and sometimes also pain at sore points.

'Give up the things of youth with grace,' advises the Protestant theologian Elisabeth Moltmann-Wendel in the title of her understanding book on growing older (2008). We have practised walking upright for so long. But why not ask for a chair and sit if standing is difficult? Why not lie down when one feels the need to, so that one can relax, 'let oneself go'? And finally, let go of our memories: why not talk about our experiences, about so much that has been suppressed and not really healed? I personally have experienced how liberating and healing it is to work on and write my own memoirs. After *My Struggle for Freedom* and *Disputed Truth*, will I be able to finish the third volume, which I have already begun? I have my doubts, but take things as they come.

## The art of dying

Everything turned out differently from what I expected. With many contemporaries I have been given a new period of life beyond what used to be the normal lifespan as a result of the tremendous progress in hygiene and medicine. So I am already in my ninth decade. How much longer? The older I get, the more deeply concerned I am to have a dignified end to my life. The *ars vivendi*, the 'art of living', also essentially includes the *ars moriendi*, the 'art of dying' – if time is given me for that.

In the 1950s, at the age of 23, my brother had to suffer for many months from a brain tumour until he choked on water in his lungs. I know that I do not want to die like that. The famous Tübingen professor of literature Hans Mayer starved himself to death at the age of 94, and I know that this too will certainly not be the will of God for me. Having watched my dear colleague and friend Walter Jens fading away with dementia – though he had the best possible care, he often wept, cried out and thrashed around – I know that I must not ignore the point in time when I should take responsibility for ending my life into my own hands. So how would I like to die?

*Mors certa, hora incerta* – death is certain but the time of death is uncertain. When and where and how our life will come to an end is unsure. In my younger days, as I have described, I expected an early death. And often, when I had brought a book happily to an end, my gratitude was great; it was good that I had been able to complete it (while actually working I did not feel a compulsion to finish it). My standpoint has always been: if it happens, it happens. I have no nostalgia for former times, do not allow myself any sadness at growing old, do not hold on compulsively to being young. Those who have death before their eyes every day are less afraid of death. When I am sometimes asked in an interview 'How would you like to die?' I usually reply with a smile: 'On the way to an appointment.' And I add, 'At any rate, not in a nursing home.'

I am firmly convinced that my life, given me by God, is my own personal responsibility to the last breath – and not the responsibility of a doctor, priest or judge. So in 1995 in the book that I wrote with Walter Jens, *A Dignified Dying*, I made 'a plea for responsibility for oneself', and in 2009 I reinforced it with twenty theses that I need not sum up here. For me it is part of the art of dying that I needn't prolong temporal life endlessly, because I believe in an eternal life. And when the time comes, if I still can, I myself would want to decide on the time and manner of my death and would want other aspects of my Living Will to be observed. I am confirmed in my view by the fact that in June 2009 the German parliament declared doctors and carers to be bound by Living Wills in every case.

In the course of the decades I have been able to maintain that trust, grounded during the first year of my life, as a well-tested trust, through all burdens and disappointments, trials and tribulations. But will I really be able to maintain this trust to the end? I don't know; no one does. Since the time of Augustine, people have spoken of perseverance, sustaining and maintaining to the end, as a special grace, the *gratia perseverantiae finalis*.

I hope that this special grace will be granted to me, to preserve to the end this special trust on which everything ultimately depends, no matter what my achievements and failure in life may have been. Should it be granted me, I would like to die in full consciousness and to say farewell with human dignity, with all that has to be settled settled, in gratitude, in expectation and in prayer.

But what if I am wrong, and I do not enter God's eternal life, but nothingness? In that case, as I have often said and am convinced, at any rate I will have lived a better life than I would have done without this hope.

'Was that all?' remarked the Jewish Berlin writer Kurt Tucholsky, who in 1935 committed suicide out of despair at the success of the National Socialists. He said, quite simply, 'If I were to die now, would I say "Was that all?" and "I didn't understand things properly" and "It was a bit loud"?'

But I don't think like that. That wasn't all. I want to understand my life properly, finally to see from the front the tapestry of my life with its many threads and colours that had looked so confusing from the back. And so everything no longer 'loud' but peaceful, joyful, fulfilled. This is my hope for an ultimately successful eternal life, in peace and harmony, lasting love and abiding happiness. Before that end my experience is summed up by the remark made by the great Augustine at the beginning of his *Confessions*: '*Inquietum est cor nostrum, donec requiescat in Te, Domine* – Our heart is restless until it rests in you, God' (*Confessions* I.1).

# Chapter 10

## Vision of Life

*Dangers await only those who do not react to life.*
President Mikhail Gorbachev, speech in East Berlin on 7 October 1989 on
the 40th anniversary of the foundation of the German Democratic Republic

A way in life is grounded in trust in life – guided by a vision of life.

We have reached the lofty goal of our spiritual tour of the mountain:
from a secure, firm standpoint a view of the whole world is possible,
which embraces not only the world of religions and cultures but also the
world of science, economics and politics. As a result of my origin and
education – I grew up in a land of freedom and direct democracy, but
surrounded by totalitarian regimes – I have always been keenly aware of
the politics of the time. But I never wanted to be a 'political theologian'.
For 'political theology' was in fact always a politicizing ideology, even for
the one who invented the concept, Eusebius, bishop at the court of Constantine; much later for the German constitutional lawyer Carl Schmitt,
who prepared the way intellectually for National Socialism; and finally
also for the Marxist-thinking Latin American revolutionaries in the
second half of the twentieth century. I never wanted to be at the service
of parties, either political or ecclesiastical, but at the service of all, of
the common good. With this aim, over the years I have worked out a
theology that is critical of society – against the background of world (and
not just Latin American) politics and firmly located not in an ideology
but in reality.

### Farewell to the big pseudo-religious ideologies

I have never had time for utopias. 'Utopia' literally means a 'nowhere'.
With their promises of a beautiful, fine world to come, whether socialist

or capitalist, in past decades utopias have led many people astray. My spirituality was meant to remain realistic; no ideas that were not earthed, no shrewdly devised plans that could not be implemented, no fanatical ideas of the future without any real reference to the present. However, a realistic vision looking towards the future seems to me to be helpful for the present. By that of course I do not mean an optical illusion or a supernatural manifestation, but a well-founded overall view of the life of the individual and the life of society. However, such a view presupposes disillusionment, sobering up.

I had two early warnings. One was George Orwell's anti-utopian *1984*, published in January 1949, aimed at Socialist totalitarianism, which soon afterwards I found cruelly confirmed in Alexandr Solzhenitsyn's books. The other was Aldous Huxley's horror vision of a *Brave New World*, published in 1932, which depicts a capitalism brought about by scientific and technological development in the year 632 AF (= after Ford), in which mass production and mass consumption have taken the place of God and religion.

I am not one of those who in Western Europe or Latin America all too uncritically fell in with the revolutionary socialist ideology of progress. The peaceful revolution of 1989 in Eastern Europe and the collapse of the real socialist system had literally rendered these sympathizers in the West speechless. The miserable state of the Eastern bloc countries – economically, socially, politically and culturally – had driven the masses there to protest on the streets, provoked them to a vote of no confidence with their feet and swept away the totalitarian regimes. But the Western intellectuals who formed a vociferous opposition in the 1960s and 1970s remained amazingly dumb in the face of the new urgent questions. The great ideologies or the 'scientific' total explanations, which had long functioned as pseudo-religions and in which people believed, were bidden farewell without great speeches at their funerals. What Max Weber called the 'demystification of the world' did not succeed, and a 'return of the religions', which had never really taken their leave, was unmistakable.

Nor, however, did I want to join those who believed in an evolutionary technological capitalist ideology of progress. The failure of faith in science is also unmistakable; the atom bomb, poison gases and genetic manipulation are also products of science. And the unmistakable technological progress has at the same time confronted humanity with ecological, economic and social collapses that have resulted in a global economic crisis in the face of which the 'real politicians' and great movers and shakers in economics and the financial world have largely stood perplexed. Climate change, preservation of the environment, the distribution of water and raw materials, combating noise and removing pollution, but also a growing gulf between rich and poor, between modern industrialized countries and developing countries – how are all these to be coped with?

So we must also bid farewell to the belief in reason and science and technological pseudo-religion that promised to solve all problems with technology, misled millions and finally frustrated them. We do not live in a 'second modernity', as those people think who were unwilling to perceive the epoch-making paradigm shift after the Second World War, but in a post-modernity which sets completely different emphases from reason, progress, nation, and in which the religions too are important for people world-wide. However, we have likewise not been helped by black counter-utopias, programmes for church restoration and fearful pictures of the future inspired by religion. We need a constructive vision.

So for a long time I have been concerned to discover and revaluate the humane ethic that has been neglected in these ideologies. This is not because I venerate a moralism that overvalues and overloads morality, sexual morality in particular, and wants to make morality the sole criterion of action. I respect the relative independence of the different spheres of human life such as economics, science, law and politics, and do not allow myself to be exploited by the interests of any institution, state, party, church or association of interests. But as a free man I would want to argue that people should remain open to reform in all these spheres of life and institutions, and in business, politics and society remain within an overall ethical framework, not only in a narrow national framework but against a cosmopolitan horizon.

## A realistic vision of hope

In the present epoch-making paradigm shift in which the world, its politics, economy and culture are caught up, we urgently need a 'vision' that attempts to survey the outlines of a more peaceful, more just, more humane world. This needs to be an overall vision, a holistic basic orientation for the present with an eye to the future. Looking towards the future I do not want to utter oracles or riddles, read the runes or prophesy, speaking in the dark about conjectures and illusions. On the other hand I do not want simply to extrapolate particular pieces of data and tendencies statistically, claiming to be able to forecast the future precisely. By 2008 at the latest the economic crisis which then broke out showed the basic weakness of these mathematical constructions and models based on optimistic assumptions.

In my view there is a fundamental need for a vision developed by argument of a better world order in the light of which strategy and tactics can be decided. I used my first three decades as a theologian to occupy myself with the many levels of the problem in the church and Christianity, and the next three to work my way above all into the extremely complex problems of the world religions, world politics, world ethics and a global ethic.

Such a vision must combine diachronic and synchronic thought; it must both have in view the great world eras and the different regions of the world, and thus discover the wider connections. I have documented this particularly in my trilogy on *Judaism*, *Christianity* and *Islam* and in publications on the Indian and Chinese religions. In addition there is need everywhere for an unprejudiced critique of the conditions that really exist and at the same time a rational demonstration of viable constructive alternatives that could offer concrete impulses for reform.

But a viable sketch of the future which starts from the present social reality and at the same time transcends it with a view to a better world order is difficult to realize. The Europe of the post-war period had statesmen of stature, tested by suffering and ethically motivated, who led their people to reconciliation, peace and a new state order. But the world after 1989 often seems to have at its disposal only power and party politicians with a pragmatic attitude, who share the responsibility for the present financial, economic and social crisis, a crisis of trust.

Heads of states and politicians are not, of course, solely to blame for everything, but those who elected them. Resistance to reforms are widespread among the people everywhere. Already at the beginning of the 1950s Martita Jöhr, who later founded the Swiss Global Ethic Foundation, motivated her husband, the important economist Adolf Jöhr, to investigate more closely the psychological factors in fluctuations in the level of economic activity. In the meantime a special branch of science, behavioural economics, has come into being which investigates the special psychological features in human and especially economic modes of behaviour which are often in contradiction to the assumed model of a *homo economicus*, who allegedly always tried to maximize utility solely by reason. So today the opponents of reforms are also being analysed. Nevertheless, I do have some hopes.

## A plea before the United Nations

What is at issue today is no less than a 'new paradigm of global relations' which I sketched out in books such as *Global Responsibility* (1990, ET 1991) and *A Global Ethic for Global Politics and Global Economics* (1997) and spelt out in *Globale Unternehmen – globalen Ethos: Der globale Markt erfordert neue Standards und eine globale Rahmenordnung* ('Global Enterprise – Global Ethic: The global market calls for new standards and a global framework', 2001). Many ideas that I put forward there found their way into the manifesto for the United Nations, *Bridges into the Future* (2001). I belonged to a twenty-member 'group of eminent persons' who had been called on by Secretary General Kofi Annan to work out a report on the dialogue of civilizations through a new paradigm of international relations; at the same time I was able to learn much from others. We presented our manifesto on 9 November 2001 (not long after the fatal 9/11) to the Secretary General and the UN General Assembly in New York under the title *Crossing the Divide*. On this occasion I was able to present the following statement to the General Assembly:

> Many people in today's problems and troubles are asking themselves: will the twenty-first century really be better than the twentieth century of violence and wars? Will we really get a new world order, a better world order? In the twentieth century we missed three opportunities for a new world order:
>
> - 1918 after World War I because of European 'Realpolitik',
> - 1945 after World War II because of Stalinism,
> - 1989 after the reunification of Germany and the Gulf war because of a lack of vision.
>
> Our group proposes such a vision of a new paradigm of international relations that takes into consideration new actors on the global scene.
>
> In our days the world religions have reappeared as actors in world politics. To be sure, throughout history religions have far too often shown their destructive face. They have inspired and legitimized hatred, enmity, violence, even wars. But in many cases they have inspired and legitimized understanding, reconciliation, co-operation and peace. Over the last decades initiatives of inter-religious dialogue and co-operation have grown all over the world.
>
> In this dialogue the world's religions have rediscovered that their own fundamental ethical teachings support and deepen those secular ethical values that are enshrined in the Universal Declaration of Human Rights. At the 1993

Parliament of the World's Religions in Chicago more than 200 representatives of all world religions for the first time in history expressed their consensus on a set of shared ethical values, standards and attitudes, the basis for a global ethic, which have been taken up in the Report of our group to the UN Secretary-General and this General Assembly. What then is the basis for a global ethic, shared by people of all great religions and ethical traditions?

First, the principle of humanity: 'Every human being – man or woman, white or coloured, rich or poor, young or old – must be treated humanely', more explicitly expressed in the 'Golden Rule' of reciprocity: 'What you do not wish done to yourself, do not do to others.' These principles are unfolded in four central areas of life and call every person, institution and nation to take their responsibility:

• for a culture of non-violence and reverence for all life,
• for a culture of solidarity and a just economic order,
• for a culture of tolerance and a life in truthfulness,
• for a culture of equal rights and partnership between men and women.

Particularly in an age of globalization such a global ethic is absolutely necessary. For a globalization of economy, technology and communication also results in a globalization of problems which threaten to overwhelm us all over the world: problems of ecology, nuclear technology, and genetic engineering but also of globalized crime, and globalized terrorism. At such a time it is a matter of urgency that the globalization of economy, technology and communication be supported by a globalization of ethics. In other words: Globalization requires a global ethic, not as an additional burden but as a base and support for human beings, for civil society.

There are some political analysts who predict a 'clash of civilizations' for the twenty-first century. This is, however, our alternative vision for the future, not just an optimistic idea but a realistic vision of hope: The religions and civilizations of the world in coalition with all people of goodwill can contribute to avoiding such a clash, provided they realize the following insights:

• No peace among the nations without peace among the religions.
• No peace among the religions without dialogue between the religions.
• No dialogue between the religions without global ethical standards.
• No survival of our globe in peace and justice without a new paradigm of international relations based on global ethical standards.

That is what I said at that time. But if this vision was not to remain general and abstract, I had to go more closely into the theoretical and practical questions of politics and business, and this required a good deal of work from me. But in this way I could substantiate and spell out ideas, set down in my own studies, which I had long cherished.

## The new paradigm of a more peaceful world politics

Since the time when, as a fifth-former in 1940, I wrote a 32-page essay on the outbreak of the Second World War, I have followed current events day by day with passionate interest. The political paradigm of European modernity that dominated until the end of the Second World War was clearly focused on violence and war and not on peaceful co-operation – combined with a Machiavellian contempt for political morality.

The new paradigm which has been establishing itself since 1945 in Europe and the world in principle indicates a politics of regional understanding, convergence and reconciliation instead of the modern politics of national interests, power and prestige (as still in Versailles or in the second Bush administration). This has been pursued in an exemplary way by France and Germany and has spread from the EU to the whole continent. In concrete political action – also in the Middle East, Afghanistan, Kashmir and Sri Lanka – instead of the former confrontation, aggression and revenge it requires mutual co-operation, compromise and integration.

This new political overall constellation evidently presupposes a change of mentality that extends far beyond the politics of the day:

- New organizations are not enough; a new mindset is also needed.
- National, ethnic and religious differences must no longer be understood in principle as a threat, but must be seen at least as possible enrichment.
- Whereas the old paradigm always presupposed an enemy, indeed an arch-enemy, the new politics no longer needs an enemy but partners, rivals and often also opponents.
- Instead of military confrontation at all levels, there is economic and social competition. It is no longer war that brings salvation but international law and international understanding.
- It has become evident that national prosperity is promoted in the long run not by war but only by peace, not by standing against or alongside one another but by working together.
- And because the different interests which now exist are satisfied by co-operation and the interweaving of interests, a politics is possible

which is no longer a zero-sum game in which one wins at the expense of the other, but a positive-sum game in which everyone wins.

Of course in the new paradigm, politics has not only become easier but remains the 'art of the possible' – now of course non-violent. If it is to function, it cannot be based on a 'post-modern' random pluralism in which anything goes. Rather, it presupposes a social consensus on certain basic values, basic rights and basic obligations. This basic consensus must be supported by all social groups, by believers and non-believers, by the members of the different religions, philosophies or ideologies. So not only a new politics and a new diplomacy are called for here, but a conversion of hearts, a true mutual acceptance, a new ethic.

Global politics, global economics and the global financial system in essentials determine our own national and regional destiny. People everywhere are gradually beginning to see that there are no longer national or regional islands of stability. And despite the strong national and regional splitting of interests the world is already so closely interwoven politically, economically and financially that economists speak of a global society and sociologists of a global civilization as an interconnected field of action in which we are all involved, directly or indirectly. The global economic crisis shows how much that is the case.

## The new paradigm of a more just world economy

I am one of those rare theologians who regularly also take a look at the financial pages of the newspapers; even as a student I was intensely concerned with questions of social philosophy and social politics. In my book *A Global Ethic for Global Politics and Global Economics* (1997) I subjected the model of the welfare state (Sweden) and the model of neo-capitalism (United States) to thorough criticism. I then made a thorough investigation of the new global concepts in economics and politics: on the one hand a pure market economy as in the economic ultra-liberalism of say, Milton Friedman, on the other the social market economy following the ideas of Ludwig Erhard, but which in our time has to include ecology and must be extended to global dimensions. With many others, as early as 1990 I argued for a global eco-social market economy which, if it is to function, needs a global ethic. My fundamental position is based on two demarcations.

My first demarcation is against a convictional ethic that lacks any economic dimension, of the kind that is sometimes argued for by church people or trade unionists. Those who set the universality of moral demands above all economic rationality, i.e. without noting the laws of economics, are not advocating a morality but a moralism.

My second demarcation is against an ethics of success that lacks any conviction, of the kind that is advocated especially by managers obsessed with success, and economists and journalists without a conscience. Those who propagate economic views without any ethical norms do not advocate the interests of the economy but those of an economic reductionism, an economism. Success can by no means be accorded the primacy that belongs to ethics. I may not pursue my own interests, but must justify any entrepreneurial action ethically, even if this may be asking too much in specific cases under the pressure of competition.

My conclusion, then as now, is that economic strategies and ethical judgements must be combined convincingly. But evidently, as the global economy has unavoidably and with justification become globalized, a new model of capitalism has slipped in. Even those who have a positive attitude to the commercial world will have to criticize this 'neo-capitalist model'. It is unacceptable because of its anti-social consequences for countless people and its lack of an ethical standard, and is mainly responsible for the current economic crisis.

It is asserted time and again that the global financial crisis of 2008 could not have been predicted. But as early as 1997, in the face of the rapidly increasing turbulence in the global financial system, I had warned against a repeat of the stock market crash and the collapse of the economic order that happened between 1929 and 1933. In *A Global Ethic for Global Politics and Global Economics* I had written: 'The slightest remark, for example, by the President of the American Federal Bank, Allan Greenspan, at the beginning of December 1996, that an "irrational exuberance" had led to an overvaluation of the financial markets was enough to drive the nervous investors of the high-flying stock markets of Asia, Europe and America into a spin, and panic selling. This also shows that crises in globalization do not *a priori* balance out, but perhaps get progressively worse' (p.219). Already at that time I ventured the supposition, heretical to economists, that chaos theory could also be applied to the economy: the smallest causes could have devastating effects. At any rate one could by no means rule out 'the return of the global economic crisis and the collapse of the global economic order of 1929–1933'.

In the meantime what Hans-Martin Schönherr-Mann has called the 'credit capitalism' of businesses, private and public institutions, in which everything is paid for with credits, has led to the collapse of the banking system. In my lecture tour across the United States in 2008 I could see how in the meantime people even there had started complaining about the greed for profit in business and the megalomania in politics. I felt my views confirmed by US President Obama, who in his inaugural speech in January 2009 said:

> That we are now in the midst of crisis is well understood. Our nation is at war, against a far-reaching network of violence and hatred. Our economy is badly weakened, a consequence of greed and irresponsibility on the part of some, but also our collective failure to make hard choices and prepare the nation for a new age. Homes have been lost; jobs shed; businesses shuttered. Our healthcare is too costly; our schools fail too many; and each day brings further evidence that the ways we use energy strengthen our adversaries and threaten our planet. These are the indicators of crisis, subject to data and statistics. Less measurable but no less profound is a sapping of confidence across our land.

A failure first of the markets, secondly of the institutions and thirdly also of morality calls for ethical rules for the pursuit of profit, which in principle is justified. But ethics is not just the icing on the cake, it is not just an additional gift to the global market economy. The new financial architecture that is urgently needed must be supported by an ethical order. Only with some elementary ethical norms, as these have developed since the human race came into being, can fatal human greed and hubris be tamed. Here I hope for a strong contribution from the churches, the religions and the international community.

## Hope for a unity of the churches

I am and remain a loyal member of my church. I believe in God and his Christ, but I do not believe 'in' the church. In the church I reject any identification with God, any self-seeking confessionalism and remain open to the whole Christian community of faith, all the churches.

My own vision has constantly expanded over the decades: from the unity of the churches to peace between the religions and finally to a true community of nations. But now that after eight decades of life I have presumably reached my last decade, I cannot predict which expectations will be fulfilled, any more than I could do earlier. Therefore in this last chapter I express my great concern as a *spero*, what I hope for.

This hope, my threefold hope, held by many others, will outlast my lifetime.

For all my life as a theologian I have committed myself to the renewal of the Catholic Church and theology and an ecumenical understanding between the Christian churches. I have been able to see some success, above all under Pope John XXIII and during the Second Vatican Council.

But I have also had to accept setbacks, particularly under the Popes after the Council; they and the Curia, their power apparatus, betrayed the Reform Council and used the Roman system – opposed to the Reformation, opposed to modernity, rooted in the Middle Ages – to block all reforms with a now completely domesticated episcopate.

But the warning 'Dangers await only those who do not react to life' is relevant. Behind the splendid façade of the papal church as presented in the media the collapse of the structure of pastoral care is becoming ever more evident: the supply of celibate clergy is drying up and there are countless paedophilia scandals; thousands of communities are without clergy and churches are being sold off by the dozen; parishes are being forcibly fused into giant 'pastoral care units' and there are fewer and fewer baptisms and marriages, fewer and fewer churchgoers. Emancipated women are leaving the church and young people are uninterested. Won't growing need and declining church taxes, where they are levied, compel reform?

My hope is not for a uniform unitary church; the confessional, regional and indeed national profile of the Christian churches should not be blurred. What I hope for is an ecumenical unity between the Christian churches in reconciled difference. But isn't that a foolish hope? No, it is a realistic vision, and the first steps to implement it were taken at the grass roots long ago.

So I am not giving up my hope: an ecumenism between the Christian confessions is possible, indeed necessary. It has to grow from below in the face of reluctant church authorities. This is my vision:

- Man-made dogmas that divide the churches will retreat behind the truth of God and the message of Jesus. Mediaeval pre-modern structures that deny people, above all women, their privileges, will dissolve. Arrogant church authorities that have been grabbing more and more power for themselves over the centuries will be reduced to a more humane dimension.
- One day all the mediaeval and early modern privileges and claims of the Catholic Church over and against the other Christian churches,

their ministries and worship will be overcome. 'Infallible' papalism and pseudo-Christian idolatry of the Pope will give way to a Petrine office which stands at the service of the whole of Christianity and functions in the framework of synodical and conciliar structures.

- Biblicist fundamentalism and the tendencies towards division and regional provincialism of Protestant origin will also be repressed in favour of a church which is responsible to the world and to the enlightened 'freedom of a Christian' which shows neither moralizing self-righteousness nor dogmatic intolerance.
- An Eastern Orthodox traditionalism and liturgism will also be superseded. They will be transformed into a Christianity which is more related to its origins and at the same time to the contemporary world, which can work like yeast in the reshaping of politics and society, also in the Eastern European countries.

All in all this will be no restored church world but will mean churches that are more orientated on the gospel and open to the needs of contemporaries.

## Hope for peace between the religions

I am and remain a religious person. But that does not mean that I find myself in conflict with the non-religious, with secularists, with laicists. I feel that I am a completely secular person, but I think that with good reason I must reject ideological secularism and programmatic godlessness.

As a Christian theologian I have increasingly fought for a change in the attitude of Christian churches to the other world religions. I have seen some successes: in the decrees of the Second Vatican Council about freedom of the conscience and religious freedom, about Judaism, Islam and the other world religions, and in countless inter-religious dialogues, conferences and encounters all over the world.

But here too there have been setbacks. Religions still play a part in supporting or legitimating wars on our globe. The lasting occupation of the Palestinian territories by the state of Israel with the support of the United States has been a central hotbed of conflict for forty years. Scorning numerous UN resolutions and international law, instead of withdrawing Israel has built up settlements. Israel thought that it could break the Arab resistance through inhuman laws in Lebanon and Gaza. Here too the warning 'Dangers await only those who do not react to life ' is relevant. There can be no peaceful life for a state behind a wall (such as the wall in the German Democratic Republic) in a hostile environment, and all the wars that have been won are useless if each time the peace is lost. Every friend of Israel is particularly pained by the fact that little is left of the tolerance for members of all faiths grounded in its basic laws, and the moral credibility of this state has almost completely been lost in the decades of obstructionist politics.

I do not hope for a unity of religions or any syncretism. I hope for an ecumenical peace among the world religions. That means peaceful co-existence, growing convergence and creative pro-existence of the religions – in the common quest for a greater truth and the mystery of the one and true God that will only be revealed fully at the end-time. Is this an empty utopia? No, it is a realistic vision, the realization of which has already begun at the grass roots of the great religions, which often have a more cosmopolitan orientation than the national states and their politics.

Despite all the problems I am not giving up hope; peace between the religions is possible, indeed necessary. That is my vision: no peace among the nations without peace among the religions, but no peace among the religions without dialogue between the religions. There need be no contradiction between truth and peace, as uninformed sociologists think. Any religion can maintain its claim to truth – as long as it respects the truth of others, is tolerant in its practice and ready with them to arouse and mobilize the moral energies of humankind. My vision of hope is:

- More and more people will realize that the three great prophetic religions – Judaism, Christianity and Islam – form a first interconnected river system with a Near Eastern Semitic source, in which people all confess the one God of Abraham, the God who creates and consummates this world, a course of history directed towards the future, and a fundamental ethic of elementary humanity (the Ten Commandments).
- But more and more people will learn in the ecumenical spirit of reconciliation to allow themselves to be enriched by the second great river system of Indian mystic origin (above all Hinduism and Buddhism) and by the third which has a Chinese, wisdom-type character (Confucianism, Daoism) – by their spiritual values, their mystical depth and their view of the world and human beings handed down over centuries.
- Conversely, the three prophetic religions will give of their own inex-

haustible spiritual and cultural heritage in a way far removed from any religious colonialism, far removed from any triumphalistic arrogance, far removed from any spiritual disparagement or monopoly.

All in all, this is not an ideal world of religions but a vision of religions that live together in peace without giving up their truth.

## Hope for a community of nations

I still have only a Swiss passport but I also tell my countrymen that I am a German history professor – admirably treated over five decades. I have no identity problems. Today my national identity includes a European identity. I am a patriot and a cosmopolitan at the same time.

Since my student years in Rome and Paris I have had experience in international theology. On numerous trips round the world, in inter-religious conferences, as guest professor in the United States, and in long hours of conversation, I have learned that theology along with the churches and religions must make its contribution to an understanding among the nations. Successes in such understanding are visible: centuries-old traditional enemies (such as Germany and France) have been reconciled; the process of forming a community of states in Europe is progressing despite all the bottlenecks and obstacles. A dramatic improvement in relations between East and West has begun since the fall of the Berlin wall.

But there are also setbacks. Over and against the process of integration in Europe and understanding between East and West there is increasing tension between North and South. The bitterest disappointment for the whole world was the lapse of the dominant democracy, the United States, under President Bush Jr between 2001 and 2008, into the paradigm of a confrontational unilateral power politics that had long been thought a thing of the past. Instead of reciprocal understanding, reconciliation and integration, as in the European Union (previously encouraged by America), there was an arrogant, megalomaniac, unilateral American imperialism and militarism.

Here too the warning 'Dangers await only those who do not react to life' is relevant. Both Bush's foreign policy, which was costly in every respect (Afghanistan, Iraq, Palestine, Iran), and his domestic policy (collapse of the property market, the banking system and the failure of systems of supervision) led to the global economic crisis and at the end of his office the lowest level of credibility of any American President. How will things continue under the new President?

I do not hope for a unitary world government or world bureaucracy. Nor for rule in the name of a culture or religion, nor for old or new psychological and spiritual compulsion under the aegis of religious legalism, dogmatism or moralism. On the contrary, I hope for freedom for, and solidarity with, unbelievers too and the many doubters poised between belief and unbelief. I hope for an ecumenical community among the peoples, truly 'united nations', and at their service religions the deepest fundamental intentions of which – the salvation of the whole person and all people – will be recognized and realized by human beings themselves. Is this all perhaps a naïve mirage? No, it is a realistic vision, the fulfilment of which has already begun in many places.

So despite all the difficulties I do not give up hope: a community of nations is possible, indeed necessary. This is my vision:

> In a comprehensive ecumenical way the religions – in North and South, East and West – will again be able to take up in quite a new way their moral responsibility
> - for the peace and thus the external pacification of the earth;
> - for justice and thus for the removal of unjust social, political and economic structures;
> - for the preservation of creation and thus the inhabitation of the earth in the framework of an environment worth living in.

But what will the future be?

## History cannot be calculated

Finally, I must ask whether such a vision is not perhaps in the end also a utopia – to be found nowhere. If one looks at the present, not least at the present state of my own Catholic Church, one could have increasing doubts. But I shall look back briefly in order to look forward:

As a student I was strongly impressed by the historical dialectic of Hegel (*Philosophy of World History*) and Karl Marx (*Communist Manifesto*). But I soon noted that these were idealistic or material constructions. There are no laws resembling natural laws in history. The course of history is not determined by rules from which one could derive maxims for future action.

In the Rome of the 1950s, given the backlog of reforms brought about by the absolutist regime of Pius XII Pacelli and his theological purges, one could have become defeatist. The election of a Pius XIII would have made the situation even worse and exposed the Catholic Church to the revolution of 1968 totally unprepared. But in 1958 Pope John XXIII Roncalli was elected and with the Second Vatican Council (1962–5) he introduced a renewal and ecumenical openness that was at least partially successful.

In the 1970s, when I was saying goodbye in Dresden after a short lecture trip to the German Democratic Republic, those who had invited me said that they probably wouldn't see me again until after their retirement, when they would be allowed to travel to the West. The situation in the Eastern bloc was desperate, given the fossilization of the Soviet system under Brezhnev. The election of another apparatchik as General Secretary of the USSR would have allowed the Soviet system to go on existing for a few more years, as happened under Andropov and Chernenko. But in 1985 Mikhail Gorbachev was elected General Secretary. He accelerated the modernization of the Soviet Union and thus in fact also introduced the implosion of the Soviet system, which had long been on the cards, the fall of the Berlin wall and the dissolution of the Soviet empire.

At the end of the twentieth and beginning of the twenty-first century in the United States I often felt that I was a voice in the wilderness. With the lapse of the United States under George W. Bush into the old paradigm of military confrontation and aggression, one seemed to be pleading for a lost cause in arguing for the new paradigm of understanding, co-operation and integration. The election of another Republican President would not have led to fundamental change and would have prolonged the paralysis of the United States. But in November 2008 Barack Obama was elected President, and he is resolutely attempting to change direction in both foreign and domestic policy.

History does not run its course according to logical rules and economic developments – and we are surprised at this, sometimes painfully, sometimes happily. Determined courses and regularities are not to be found in history as they are in nature. History cannot be calculated – and that corresponds to my experience over all the decades. And important personalities, of course in interaction with others, can exercise a decisive influence on the course of history. From a desperate situation – here I am thinking back to Churchill and de Gaulle – they can lose battles but win the war. But they can also – and here I am thinking of Anwar Sadat and Itzhak Rabin, murdered by fanatics from their own ranks – win battles but lose the war. Didn't they deserve more support in their lifetimes?

Their hour will come. Or are these only dreams?

## My last vision

'Dreams are likes bubbles.' The old German proverb means that what I have dreamed need not necessarily become true.

There are dreams that are better not fulfilled.

There are dreams that unfortunately are not fulfilled.

There are dreams that are only fulfilled later.

On 28 August 1963 the black American civil rights champion and Baptist pastor Martin Luther King gave his prophetic 'I have a dream' speech in front of the Lincoln Memorial in Washington DC. In it he presented his vision of equal rights and equal status for the American blacks: 'And even though we face the difficulties of today and tomorrow, I still have a dream.' On 4 April 1968 he was murdered in Memphis, Tennessee, and that same evening I had to announce this terrible news to a dismayed audience in Riverside Church, New York. But Martin Luther King's vision of non-violent resistance and civil disobedience and of the victory of the blacks had its effect. On 4 November 2008, forty-five years after that Washington speech, Barack Obama was the first black man to be elected President of the United States. Martin Luther King's dream was not a bubble.

Why? 'If one person dreams alone it remains a dream. But if we all dream together, it becomes reality.' These are the words of Archbishop Helder Camara of Recife, one of the most important bishops at the Second Vatican Council, at whose invitation I spoke several times at the Brazilian Council of Bishops. My dream too is dreamed by many, my vision of a reconciled Christianity, of a peace between religions and of an authentic community of nations, is shared by many. I will not see the fulfilment of my dream any more than Martin Luther King did. But I shall not take it with me to the grave. It will be handed on by the longing of whole generations for a more peaceful, more just, more humane world. I believe in that, I hope for that.

And what will happen to me? I hope that for me one day there will be a resolution of all contradictions and an existence in harmony, peace and happiness, and that at my end there will be granted me what throughout the Christian tradition is called the vision, the beatific vision. The apostle Paul described it as follows in the letter to Corinth that I have mentioned in connection with the passage on love:

> Love never ends; as for prophecies, they will pass away; as for tongues, they will cease; as for knowledge, it will pass away. For our knowledge is imperfect and our prophecy is imperfect; but when the perfect comes, the imperfect will pass away.
>
> When I was a child, I spoke as a child, I thought as a child, I reasoned as a child; when I became a man, I gave up childish ways. For now we see in a mirror dimly, but then face to face. Now I know in part; then I shall understand fully, even as I have been fully understood. So faith, hope, love abide, these three; but the greatest of these is love.
>
> (1 Corinthians 13.8–13)

In this I hope that what I believe will be fulfilled.

# For Further Reading: A Selection of Books by Hans Küng in English

*The date of the German publication is given in brackets*

### Christian life

*Justification: The Doctrine of Karl Barth and a Catholic Reflection* (1957), New York: Thomas Nelson and Sons 1964 and London: Burns and Oates 1965

*Credo: The Apostles' Creed Explained for Today* (1992), London: SCM Press and New York: Doubleday 1993

*A Dignified Dying* (1995, with Walter Jens), London: SCM Press 1995

### The church and Christian ecumenism

*The Council and Reunion* (1960), London: Sheed and Ward 1961; American title *The Council, Reform and Reunion*, New York: Sheed and Ward 1961

*Structures of the Church* (1962), New York: Thomas Nelson and Sons 1964 and London: Burns and Oates 1965

*The Church* (1967), London: Burns and Oates and New York: Sheed and Ward 1967

*Truthfulness: The Future of the Church* (1968), London and New York: Sheed and Ward 1968

*Infallible? An Enquiry* (1970), London: Collins and New York: Doubleday 1971

*Reforming the Church Today: Keeping Hope Alive* (1990), Edinburgh: T&T Clark and New York: Crossroad 1990

### Theology and Christian foundations

*The Incarnation of God: An Introduction to Hegel's Theological Thought as Prolegomena to a Future Christology* (1970), Edinburgh: T&T Clark 1987

*On Being a Christian* (1974), London: Collins and New York: Doubleday 1977

*Does God Exist? An Answer for Today* (1978), London: Collins and New York: Doubleday 1980

*Eternal Life?* (1982), London: Collins and New York: Doubleday 1984

*Freud and the Problem of God*, New Haven: Yale University Press 1979

*Great Christian Thinkers* (1994), London: SCM Press 1994

*The Beginning of All Things: Science and Religion* (2005), Grand Rapids, MI: Eerdmans 2007

### World ecumenism

*Brother or Lord? A Jew and a Christian Talk Together About Jesus* (1976, with Pinchas Lapide), London: Collins 1977

*Christianity and the World Religions* (1984, with J. von Ess, H. von Stietencron and H. Bechert), New York: Doubleday 1976 and London: Collins 1987

*Christianity and Chinese Religions* (1988, with Julia Ching), New York: Doubleday 1989 and London: SCM Press 1993

*Tracing the Way: Spiritual Dimensions of the World Religions* (1999), London: SCM Press and New York: Continuum 2002

### Art and music

*Art and the Question of Meaning* (1980), London: SCM Press and New York: Crossroad 1981

*Mozart: Traces of Transcendence* (1991), London: SCM Press 1992 and Grand Rapids, MI: Eerdmans 1993

### The religious situation of our time

*Paradigm Change in Theology* (1984, with David Tracy), Edinburgh: T&T Clark and New York: Crossroad 1989

*Theology for the Third Millennium* (1987), New York: Doubleday 1988 and Edinburgh: T&T Clark 1991

*Judaism* (1991), London: SCM Press and New York: Crossroad 1992

*Christianity: Its Essence and History* (1994), London: SCM Press and New York: Crossroad 1995

*The Catholic Church: A Short History* (2001), London: Weidenfeld & Nicolson and New York: Random House 2001

*Women in Christianity* (2001), London and New York: Continuum 2002

*Islam: Past, Present & Future* (2004), Oxford: Oneworld Publications 2007

## A global ethic
*Global Responsibility* (1990), London: SCM Press and New York: Crossroad 1991

*A Global Ethic: The Declaration of the Parliament of the World's Religions* (ed. with Karl-Josef Kuschel), London: SCM Press 1993

*A Global Ethic for Global Politics and Economics* (1997), London: SCM Press 1997 and New York: Oxford University Press 1998

*How to do Good and Avoid Evil* (2008, with Walter Homolka), Woodstock, VT: Skylight Paths Publishing 2009

## Memoirs
*My Struggle for Freedom* (2002), London: Continuum and Grand Rapids, MI: Eerdmans 2003

*Disputed Truth* (2007), London and New York: Continuum 2008

# A Word of Thanks

Sixty years of doing theology have gone into this book. I have met countless people on the way; I have learned from many and I have been shaped by some. To thank them all by name at the end of a book like this would need a vast number of pages.

I would like above all to thank those who have read my books and listened to my lectures, addresses and sermons. For years, indeed decades, they have encouraged and supported me and asked critical questions. As a theologian I see myself not only as a scholar but also as a pastor, seeking to give people orientation and help in their lives with my theology. I have always drawn much strength and courage to continue on my way from the countless reactions I have constantly received. Thank you with all my heart.

I want to express special thanks to the audience of almost a thousand who attended my nine lectures 'What I believe' at the University of Tübingen in the summer semester of 2009. To have such a large and loyal audience at the age of 81 has filled me with joy and deep gratitude.

I want to thank those who were directly involved in the production of the lectures and this book: my loyal colleagues here at home and in the Global Ethic Foundation team, and the staff of Piper Verlag who have made their contribution towards publishing the book in their usual pleasant and professional way.

I am delighted that the English edition is being published by Continuum International, London and New York, and for this I am particularly grateful to the publisher, Robin Baird-Smith. The English translation is once again by Dr John Bowden, for decades my masterly translator, who together with his long-standing colleague Margaret Lydamore has done an excellent piece of work. My deeply felt thanks go to him at the end of this book.

*Hans Küng*
*Tübingen, November 2009*